ACCESS TO
SOCIAL JUSTICE

Bristol Studies in Law and Social Justice

Series Editors: **Alan Bogg**, University of Bristol, UK and
Virginia Mantouvalou, University College London, UK

This series explores the role of law in securing social justice in society and the economy. The focus is on 'social justice' as a normative ideal, and the law as a critical tool in influencing (for good or for ill) the social structures that shape people's lives.

Also available in the series:

- *Labour Law and the Person* by Lisa Rodgers
- *Low-Paid EU Migrant Workers* by Catherine Barnard, Fiona Costello and Sarah Fraser Butlin
- *Climate Litigation and Justice in Africa* edited by Kim Bouwer, Uzuazo Etemire, Tracy-Lynn Field and Ademola Oluborode Jegede
- *Class and Social Background Discrimination in the Modern Workplace* by Angelo Capuano
- *Beyond the Virus* edited by Sabrina Germain and Adrienne Yong

International Advisory Board

Philip Alston, New York University, US
Bridget Anderson, University of Bristol, UK
Alysia Blackham, University of Melbourne, Australia
Hugh Collins, London School of Economics and Political Science, UK
Sandra Fredman, University of Oxford, UK
Roberto Gargarella, University of Buenos Aires and University Torcuato Di Tella, Argentina
Martijn Hesselink, European University Institute, Italy
Tarunabh Khaitan, University of Oxford, UK and University of Melbourne, Australia
Jeff King, University College London, UK
Prabha Kotiswaran, Kings College London, UK
Nicola Lacey, London School of Economics and Political Science, UK
Sandra Liebenberg, Stellenbosch University, South Africa
Guy Mundlak, Tel Aviv University, Israel
Tonia Novitz, University of Bristol, UK
Colm O'Cinneide, University College London, UK
Kerry Rittich, University of Toronto, Canada
Robin West, Georgetown University, US

Find out more at:

https://bristoluniversitypress.co.uk/
bristol-studies-in-law-and-social-justice

ACCESS TO SOCIAL JUSTICE

Effective Remedies for Social Rights

Katie Boyle, Diana Camps,
Kirstie Ken English, Jo Edson Ferrie,
Aidan Flegg and Gaurav Mukherjee

First published in Great Britain in 2025 by

Bristol University Press
University of Bristol
1–9 Old Park Hill
Bristol
BS2 8BB
UK
t: +44 (0)117 374 6645
e: bup-info@bristol.ac.uk

Details of international sales and distribution partners are available at bristoluniversitypress.co.uk

© Boyle 2025, © Camps 2025, © English 2025, © Ferrie 2025,
© Flegg 2025, © Mukherjee 2025

The digital PDF and ePub versions of this title are available open access and distributed under the terms of the Creative Commons Attribution-NonCommercial-NoDerivatives 4.0 International licence (https://creativecommons.org/licenses/by-nc-nd/4.0/) which permits reproduction and distribution for non-commercial use without further permission provided the original work is attributed.

British Library Cataloguing in Publication Data
A catalogue record for this book is available from the British Library

ISBN 978-1-5292-3791-7 paperback
ISBN 978-1-5292-3793-1 ePub
ISBN 978-1-5292-3792-4 OA PDF

The right of Katie Boyle, Diana Camps, Kirstie Ken English, Jo Edson Ferrie, Aidan Flegg and Gaurav Mukherjee to be identified as authors of this work has been asserted by them in accordance with the Copyright, Designs and Patents Act 1988.

All rights reserved: no part of this publication may be reproduced, stored in a retrieval system, or transmitted in any form or by any means, electronic, mechanical, photocopying, recording, or otherwise without the prior permission of Bristol University Press.

Every reasonable effort has been made to obtain permission to reproduce copyrighted material. If, however, anyone knows of an oversight, please contact the publisher.

The statements and opinions contained within this publication are solely those of the authors and not of the University of Bristol or Bristol University Press. The University of Bristol and Bristol University Press disclaim responsibility for any injury to persons or property resulting from any material published in this publication.

Bristol University Press works to counter discrimination on grounds of gender, race, disability, age and sexuality.

Cover design: Blu inc
Front cover image: Stocksy/Hellen Cooke

For Lorraine Cox, Shakar Omar Ali and
Sharon Pantellerisco

Contents

Series Editors' Preface		ix
List of Figures and Tables		x
About the Authors		xi
Acknowledgements		xiii

1	**Access to Social Justice**	**1**
	The social rights accountability gap in context	5
	Our theoretical framework: deliberative democracy theory and critical discourse theory	13
	Critiques of social rights adjudication	14
	Principles of adjudication	17
	A three-dimensional theory of justice: distribution, recognition and representation	19
	Why discourse?	20
	Our normative framework: access to social justice and the right to an effective remedy	27
	Our approach to methods, analysis and theory	32
	Structure of the book	41

2	**The International Human Rights Framework for Economic, Social and Cultural Rights**	**42**
	Progressive realization	43
	The right to food	52
	The right to adequate housing	57
	The right to social security	62
	The right to fuel: an emerging economic, social and cultural right	67
	Conclusions	84

3	**What Our Case Studies Told Us about Social Rights in Each Part of the UK**	**86**
	Scotland: lock-change evictions of those seeking asylum in Glasgow	87

	England: digitization, algorithms and the direct impact on social security provisions	100
	Wales: closer to government, but with variable impact	111
	Northern Ireland: terminal illness criteria impede access to benefits	128
	Conclusions	139
4	**The Access to Justice Journey: From Violation to Remedy**	**142**
	Awareness and legal consciousness	142
	Emotional, financial and legal resources	144
	Complexity of the journey: getting 'stuck in administrative mud'	150
	Adequate and effective access to justice	153
	Reaching an effective remedy is not guaranteed	158
	Justice equals access to an effective remedy	159
	The legal right to an effective remedy	160
	Practitioner perspectives on what constitutes an effective remedy	162
	Tribunal data	169
	Systemic injustice and structural responses: a missing component	174
	Comparative practice in structural relief	176
	Conclusions	185
5	**Challenging Discourses That Marginalize: Reclaiming the Narrative**	**186**
	Competing discourses: immigration and Scottish housing	189
	Accountability gaps: outsourcing government functions	195
	Prejudicial practices: privatized housing	198
	Assessments, automation and algorithms	201
	Resource distribution: discourses of entitlement	208
	Valuation discourses: constructing 'worthiness'	211
	Complexity and fragmentation	216
	Conclusions	218
	Recommendations	224
Index		229

Series Editors' Preface

Bristol Studies in Law and Social Justice explores the role of law in securing social justice in society and the economy. The focus is on 'social justice' as a normative ideal, and the law as a critical tool in influencing (for good or for ill) the social structures that shape people's lives. This international series is designed to be inclusive of a wide range of methodologies and disciplinary approaches. Contributions examine these issues from multiple legal perspectives, including constitutional law, discrimination law, human rights, contract law, criminal law, migration law, labour law, social welfare law, property law, international and supranational law. The Series has broad jurisdictional coverage, including single-country, comparative, international and regional legal orders, and encourages a critical and interdisciplinary approach to legal analysis.

List of Figures and Tables

Figures

4.1	First-tier social security appeals (number of cases)	170
4.2	First-tier social security appeals (%)	171
4.3	Personal Independence Payment (number of cases)	172
4.4	Personal Independence Payment (%)	173
4.5	First-tier Tribunals (immigration and asylum): number of appeals determined at hearing or on paper (%)	174

Tables

1.1	Defining principles of adjudication	18
1.2	Thematic analysis	37
3.1	Scotland case study participants	87
3.2	England case study participants	101
3.3	Wales case study participants	112
3.4	Northern Ireland case study participants	129
4.1	Social security and child support (number of cases)	170
4.2	Percentage of cases cleared at hearing upholding decision or finding in favour of the claimant	170
4.3	Personal Independence Payment (number of cases)	171
4.4	Personal Independence Payment (%)	172
4.5	First-tier immigration decisions allowed and dismissed (%)	173

About the Authors

The authors of this book were all engaged in leading different strands of research under the Nuffield Foundation-funded project on 'Access to Justice for Social Rights: Addressing the Accountability Gap'. Boyle conceived of the idea for the project and secured the funding, thereafter Boyle, Camps, English, Ferrie, Flegg and Mukherjee (listed in alphabetical order) each performed an invaluable role in the development of the methods, data acquisition, analysis, interpretation, doctrinal research and drafting of this manuscript. Specific individual contributions are noted below alongside institutional affiliations. The authorship of this book acknowledges and celebrates the work of Research Fellows as co-authors, some of whom were students during the project duration. We recognize the invaluable role that researchers at different career levels play in delivering projects of this scale and encourage others to do the same in ensuring work is made visible, particularly when power dynamics can render students and postdoctoral researchers in precarious positions. Our approach to research integrity is informed by the Committee for Publication Ethics (COPE) and the UK Research Integrity Office (UKRIO).

Katie Boyle is Professor of Human Rights Law and Social Justice at the University of Strathclyde, Glasgow. Her research examines the legalization of human rights, specifically economic and social rights, in different constitutional settings. She was the Principal Investigator of the Nuffield Foundation project. She identified the research gap that underpins the book, led the interdisciplinary research, managed the project to completion and completed the book manuscript.

Diana Camps is Lecturer in Education at the University of Glasgow. She was a Research Fellow in Social Rights and was responsible for managing the qualitative strand of the project. Her expertise is in critical sociolinguistics and discourse analysis, focusing on the role of language in (re)producing injustice. She was responsible for developing the research instruments and empirical data collection and has contributed significantly to data analysis and writing.

Kirstie Ken English is a mixed-methods researcher and quantitative methods tutor at the University of Glasgow. Their areas of expertise are gender, sexuality, human rights and the production and use of equality, diversity, and inclusion data. They assisted with the qualitative analysis of the practitioner interviews, conducting the thematic analysis featured in this project.

Jo Edson Ferrie is Professor of Sociology at the University of Glasgow. She is known for her expertise in human rights realization and her development and application of advanced methodologies. She was appointed to the project's advisory group. Her contributions were instrumental to the methodological framework, analysis and theorizing of findings.

Aidan Flegg is a PhD student undertaking sociolegal research in economic, social and cultural rights. His PhD research is based at the Universities of Glasgow and Strathclyde in collaboration with the Scottish Human Rights Commission. His contributions to the book included researching and writing about the legal obligations for economic, social and cultural rights, and carrying out data analysis on tribunal cases.

Gaurav Mukherjee is Hauser Postdoctoral Global Fellow at the New York University (NYU) School of Law. He has published widely in the field of social and economic rights, and currently researches the links between social welfare and democratic decline at NYU. He worked on the parts of the project that involved comparative law and social rights remedies.

Acknowledgements

We would like to thank our funder, the Nuffield Foundation, and in particular Ash Patel, Rob Street, Imogen Parker and Ellen Wright, for supporting the research that underpins this book. Thanks are also due to the anonymous peer reviewers of the funding bid and of our book proposal, both of whom provided invaluable feedback. We are indebted to the members of our Expert Advisory Groups (EAGs) on the Nuffield-funded project, each of whom supported the development and delivery of the research at various stages in immeasurable ways – all views expressed are the authors' own and should not be affiliated with our EAG members or other associate partners. We are grateful to a number of key contributors to the delivery of this book, including Sarah McGoogan, Aidan Fisher, Nuala McBride and Molly McCall, each of whom played a critical role in bringing the manuscript to realization as Research Fellows based at the University of Strathclyde. We would like to thank the editorial support team at Bristol University Press for their guidance, encouragement and patience in the preparation of the publication of the book. Finally, we must thank our research participants who gave their time and expertise so generously in order for this study to materialize. We are forever grateful to them for telling us their stories and for the invaluable work they do every day to support rights holders seeking access to justice for social rights.

The Expert Advisory Group on Social Rights consisted of the following members: Paul Hunt, Jeff King, Aoife Nolan, Colm O'Cinneide, Rory O'Connell, Anashri Pillay and Bruce Porter.

The Expert Advisory Group on Research Methods consisted of the following members: Michael Adler, Alfonso del Percio, Michelle Donnelly and Jo Edson Ferrie.

The Expert Advisory Practitioner Panel consisted of the following members: Meghan Abraham, Les Allamby, Matthey Blow, Jamie Burton, Kavita Chetty, Carla Clarke, Grey Collier, Eleanor Deeming, Ciara Fitzpatrick, Kevin Hanratty, Ali Harris, Simon Hoffman, Alan Miller, Ursula O'Hare, Katie Palmer, Ash Patel, Katherine Perks, Imogen Richmond-Bishop and Mhairi Snowden.

The Nuffield Foundation is an endowed charitable trust that aims to improve social wellbeing in the widest sense. It funds research and innovation in education and social policy and also works to build capacity in education, science and social science research. The Nuffield Foundation has funded this project, but the views expressed are those of the authors and not necessarily those of the Foundation. More information is available at: www.nuffieldfoundation.org.

1

Access to Social Justice

This book proposes a conception of social justice in the UK which corresponds with the state's international obligations in relation to social rights (SR). SR comprise the essentials to a life with dignity, including the rights to housing, food, fuel and social security.[1] The book addresses both the substantive violations of these rights and how they manifest, as well as the gaps that impede access to social justice. The chapters in this book are situated at the intersection of various related yet separate bodies of literature, including administrative law, access to justice, social justice and human rights discourses. In addition, we apply theoretical lenses which situate the contributions of these disciplinary perspectives against the backdrop of structural injustice, valuation discourses, hegemony and power narratives, critical sociolinguistic theory, deliberative democracy theory and critical discourse theory. We are interested in accountability for violations of SR and making social injustice visible. As a result, our interdisciplinary discussions pivot around these

---

[1] Social rights form part of the international human rights framework and in particular are derived from the International Covenant on Economic, Social and Cultural Rights: UN (General Assembly), *International Covenant on Economic, Social and Cultural Rights (ICESCR)*, Resolution 2200A (XXI) of 16 December 1966. Economic, social, cultural, civil and political rights are indivisible in nature according to the international human rights framework. In this book, our focus on social rights was prompted by the recurrence of social rights issues identified in Ramona Franklyn et al, *The Legal Problem and Resolution Survey for England and Wales (LRPS)* (Ministry of Justice Analytical Series, 2017), together with the prevalence of issues in the recommendations of the UN Committee on Economic, Social and Cultural Rights (CESCR), 'Concluding Observations on the Sixth Periodic Report of the United Kingdom of Great Britain and Northern Ireland' (2016) E/C.12/GBR/CO/6. We secured funding from the Nuffield Foundation to research further into access to justice gaps for the social rights to housing, social security, food and fuel across the UK. It is this research which forms the substance of this book. It may be helpful to note that the language used when engaging with social rights sometimes refers to 'economic, social and cultural rights', 'socio-economic rights', 'economic and social rights' or 'international human rights'. Sometimes this terminology can be used interchangeably.

different axes of enquiry and engage across disciplines in a way that requires multiple contextualizations and challenges multiple conceptions of justice, and what it means to access it. Our empirical street-level insights provided by practitioners across the advice sector in each jurisdiction of the UK helps us to do this in a way that sets aside long-held disciplinary framings with the aim of discovering new knowledge. In other words, we sought to immerse ourselves in the everyday reality of the advisors who seek to support people overcoming social injustice, allowing us to discover phenomena that would otherwise remain invisible and the acquisition of new perspectives on things we thought we already understood.[2] Our challenge to our readership is to join us on this journey.

Access to justice as a discipline is vague, indeterminate and disparate. In other words, it means different things to different epistemic communities (practitioners, rights holders, frontline services, decision makers and so on) and comprises different meanings in a number of different disciplines (immigration, criminal law, social security, administrative justice, public law and so on). Garth and Cappelletti (pioneers of the access to justice discipline) argued, at the conception of the access to justice movement, that '[f]irst, the system must be equally accessible to all; second, it must lead to results that are *individually and socially just*'.[3] The literature and practice have made significant progress in terms of seeking to advance effective access to legal processes, including issues relating to advice, information, awareness raising, legal consciousness, legal capability, legal empowerment, advocacy, removing discriminatory barriers, identifying unmet legal needs, co-locating services, and demonstrating the social determinants of legal problems and the social impact when they go unaddressed.[4] These advances are critical to ensuring

---

[2] Jean Lave, *Apprenticeship in Critical Ethnographic Practice* (Chicago: University of Chicago Press, 2011), pp 36–37.

[3] Bryant Garth and Mauro Cappelletti, 'Access to Justice: The Newest Wave in the Worldwide Movement to Make Rights Effective', (1978) 27(2) *Buffalo Law Review*, pp 181–292, p 188 (emphasis added).

[4] See, for example, the groundbreaking work of Hazel Genn, Pascoe Pleasance, Nigel Balmer, Lisa van Halla, Jacqui Kinghan, Alan Paterson and others who have been instrumental in building and progressing the access to justice literature, albeit without addressing the substantive and normative social rights dimension of social justice. The vast literature on issues on effective access to (procedural) justice includes Hazel Genn, *Paths to Justice* (Hart Publishing, 1999); Hazel Genn and Alan Paterson, *Paths to Justice Scotland: What People in Scotland Do and Think about Going to Law* (Oxford: Hart Publishing, 2001); Hazel Genn et al, *Understanding Advice Seeking Behaviour: Further Findings from the LSRC Survey of Justiciable Problems* (London: Legal Services Research Centre, 2004); Lisa Vanhala and Jacqui Kinghan, 'The "Madness" of Accessing Justice: Legal Mobilisation, Welfare Benefits and Empowerment' (2022) 44(1) *Journal of Social Welfare and Family Law*, pp 22–41; Hazel Genn, 'When Law Is Good for Your Health: Mitigating the Social Determinants of Health through Access to Justice' (2019) 72(1) *Current Legal Problems*,

unhindered and effective access to appropriate non-judicial and judicial processes, that is, access to legal processes that may lead to justice. However, a gap has emerged: access to justice requires a 'thicker' conception of justice itself to include a substantive and normative component (in our case, drawing on international human rights law), meaning that the discipline must look beyond enabling access to fair legal proceedings, moving towards how to facilitate effective remedies, or 'socially just' outcomes, of those processes.[5] In other words, a thicker conception of access to justice embodies a concern with the 'ability of people to defend and enforce their rights and obtain just resolution of legal problems in compliance with human rights standards [including SR] through impartial, formal or informal institutions of justice and with appropriate legal support'.[6] This book aligns with this broader conception of access to justice and legal needs using a multidimensional approach that extends 'to social justice and the distribution of welfare, resources and opportunity'.[7]

Barriers in accessing justice is a global phenomenon and social injustice is pervasive. The practical implications of the lack of SR enforcement manifest in a litany of SR violations across multiple areas that engage with our everyday lives. This book engages with those areas where SR violations are most keenly felt, and how the absence of access to justice and effective remedies exacerbates this. Those who experience violations of SR are those who are mostly likely to be excluded from hegemonic structures of power. They face intersectional structural injustice and barriers on the basis of immigration status, disability, gender, age, ethnicity and socioeconomic disadvantage, among other things. They may be at risk of homelessness, face significant debt, experience in-work poverty, be fleeing domestic abuse and so on. Clustered injustice recognizes that people in such positions often experience multiple synchronous clusters of legal problems for which the

---

pp 159–202; Lisa Vanhala and Jaqui Kinghan, *Using the Law to Address Unfair Systems: A Case Study of the Personal Independence Payments Legal Challenge* (The Baring Foundation, 2019); Lisa Vanhala and Jaqui Kinghan, *Literature Review on the Use and Impact of Litigation* (Public Law Project, 2018); Lisa Vanhala and Jaqui Kinghan, *Using the Law for Social Change: A Landscape Review* (The Baring Foundation, 2018); Marjorie Mayo et al, *Access to Justice for Disadvantaged Communities* (Bristol: Policy Press, 2015); Ellie Palmer et al, *Access to Justice: Beyond the Policies and Politics of Austerity* (Oxford: Hart Publishing, 2016); Organisation for Economic Co-operation and Development (OECD), *Legal Needs Surveys and Access to Justice* (New York: Open Society Foundation, 2019).

[5] Future research on access to justice requires 'revisiting our substantive conception of justice as well as the means of accessing and achieving it': Katie Boyle, *Economic and Social Rights, Incorporation, Justiciability and Principles of Adjudication* (Abingdon: Routledge, 2020).

[6] Pascoe Pleasence et al, 'Access to and Quality of Justice' in Praia City Group, *Handbook on Governance Statistics* (London: Governance Statistics, 2020).

[7] OECD (n 4), p 24.

traditional 'single issue' lawyering approach is ill-equipped.[8] Their situation is therefore compounded by the fact that SR violations are often systemic in nature, but the legal system is individualized and siloed into distinct 'legal problems'.[9] They may live below absolute and relative poverty measures and do not have access to appropriate legal, emotional or financial resources to challenge the SR violations they encounter (social welfare by way of an example is excluded from legal aid provision).

We interviewed 26 practitioners across the UK, using a case-based approach that focused on real legal cases across the UK's jurisdictions. The practitioners we interviewed ranged from street-level advisors (such as at food banks) to barristers representing rights holders in the Supreme Court. This cross-tier advice sampling methodology meant that we were able to understand more about the types of SR violations that end up reaching the courtroom as well as the ones that do not. The book's theoretical approach (discussed later on) addresses critiques of SR adjudication drawing from principles of deliberative democracy theory.[10] The approach to the qualitative data was framed using these principles to guide our semi-structured interviews. We then analysed and theorized our findings using a critical discourse lens. It became clear that there are insufficient routes to remedy for violations of the rights (as discussed in Chapter 4, the legal system is inept with a significant accountability gap, meaning that the UK is not meeting its international obligations). In addition, the empirical research demonstrated that exclusionary discourses further disenfranchise and marginalize those who experience SR violations. The research demonstrates the importance of reclaiming the narrative of SR as legal rights.

We propose framing access to social justice as a journey. This journey addresses some of the procedural barriers in accessing justice as well as the more substantive components and how to overcome them. First, rights holders must be aware of their rights in order to claim them (legal consciousness). Second, they must have sufficient legal, financial and emotional resources to navigate the system (legal capability). Third, the complexity of the system must be acknowledged and addressed – often people get stuck in 'administrative mud', meaning they cannot reach an effective and timely remedy. Fourth, the legal framework relies on single-issue lawyering rather than recognizing the nature of systemic and clustered injustice – this requires reconfiguring the system to enable judicial and nonjudicial routes to

---

[8] Luke Clements, *Clustered Injustice and the Level Green* (Legal Action Group, 2020); Pasco Pleasence, *Causes of Action: Civil Law and Social Justice*, 2nd edn (London: The Stationery Office, 2006).

[9] Clements (n 8), p 2.

[10] Boyle (n 5) develops principles derived from deliberative democracy to address the critiques of SR adjudication.

collective justice for systemic violations and preventative justice for clustered violations. The UK legal framework does not adequately protect SR – there is insufficient intensity of review and an insufficient understanding of what constitutes both an individual and collective 'effective remedy'. This means that the justice system is not currently fit for purpose in terms of addressing SR violations. Finally, the system requires to be recalibrated in order to self-correct when failures are identified – this was described as a missing 'feedback loop', meaning that where systemic and collective failures are identified, a feedback loop should prevent further violations from recurring. Ultimately, we propose that the concept of an effective remedy should align with international human rights law, enabling access to effective processes and effective outcomes that actually address the violation in practice, both for the individual and for the wider community impacted by the violation. We call for the development of collective and structural remedies to achieve this.

These contributions sit alongside a deep critical theoretical lens that further deepens the review of the access to SR justice gap by identifying and addressing discourse that marginalizes and disempowers both rights holders and the practitioners that support them. The book comprises both practical and theoretical reframings that change the way we think about SR, administrative justice, access to justice and social justice, and what to do to address the gaps identified. These lessons apply to our UK case study and beyond – providing lessons for access to justice interventions globally.

The social rights accountability gap in context

The book situates traditional understandings of bureaucratic justice and administrative justice[11] within the human rights sphere. In other words,

---

[11] Jerry Mashaw, *Bureaucratic Justice: Managing Social Security Disability Claims* (Yale University Press, 1983). See also Michael Adler, 'Understanding and Analysing Administrative Justice' in Michael Adler (ed.), *Administrative Justice in Context* (Oxford: Hart Publishing, 2010); Robert Kagan, 'Varieties of Bureaucratic Justice' in Nicolas Parrillo (ed.), *Administrative Law from the Inside Out: Essays on the Themes in the Work of Jerry Mashaw* (Cambridge: Cambridge University Press, 2016); Marc Hertogh, 'Through the Eyes of Bureaucrats: How Front-Line Officials Understand Administrative Justice' in Michael Adler (ed.), *Administrative Justice in Context* (Oxford: Hart Publishing, 2010); Simon Halliday and Colin Scott, 'A Cultural Analysis of Administrative Justice' in Michael Adler (ed.), *Administrative Justice in Context* (Oxford: Hart Publishing, 2010); Joe Tomlinson and Robert Thomas, 'Administrative Justice: A Primer for Policymakers and Those Working in the System', *UK Administrative Justice Institute*, 2016, https://essexcaji.org/2016/09/09/administrative-justice-a-primer-for-policymakers-and-those-working-in-the-system. For a brief discussion of these approaches, see Paul Daly, 'Thinking about Administrative Justice: The Power of Mashaw's Models', *Administrative Law Matters*, 2019, https://www.administrativelawmatters.com/blog/2019/11/01/thinking-about-administrative-justice-the-power-of-mashaws-models

our aim is not to review the system in the context of its bureaucratic or administrative operation, or whatever model it pertains to (whether that be bureaucratic rationality, professional treatment, moral judgement, managerial, consumerist, market-based or otherwise),[12] but to apply a critical lens that assesses whether the model employed is fit for purpose in terms of ensuring justice for violations of SR. The focus is therefore more closely tied to the second and third of Buck, Kirkham and Thompson's three strands of administrative justice: getting it right; putting it right; and setting it right.[13] By focusing on access to justice, we are concerned with how public and administrative law addresses violations of SR in terms of putting it right (addressing the violation) and setting it right (ensuring it does not happen again). This requires an analysis that reaches beyond administrative decision making and turns towards the remedial space, that is, appeals, complaints, ombuds procedures, tribunals and, ultimately, the role of the court.[14]

This contextualization is important because administrative justice continues to go through processes of reform (moving through the different typologies). It does so without necessarily applying a critical human rights lens – in other words, with some notable exceptions,[15] there is a substantial absence of SR discourse in much of the vast literature that engages with administrative

---

[12] For a discussion on the different models of administrative justice, including Mashaw's bureaucratic justice and subsequent typologies developed by Adler, Kagan, Scott and Halliday, Sabel and Simon, see Jerry Masha, 'Models of Administrative Justice' in Marc Hertogh et al (eds), *The Oxford Handbook of Administrative Justice* (Oxford: Oxford University Press, 2022).

[13] Trevor Buck, Richard Kirkham and Brian Thompson, *The Ombudsman Enterprise and Administrative Justice* (Abingdon: Routledge, 2010).

[14] International human rights law recognizes that effective remedies may be secured through administrative mechanisms and need not always require a judicial remedy. Indeed, administrative remedies can provide adequate and appropriate effective remedies if configured to do so. Nonetheless, and particularly in the absence of SR standards informing administrative law, the CESCR confirms that if a right cannot be made fully effective without some role for the judiciary, judicial remedies are necessary. See CESCR, 'General Comment No. 9: The Domestic Application of the Covenant' (1998) E/C.12/1998/24, [9].

[15] For example, Jeff King, *Judging Social Rights* (Cambridge University Press, 2012); Stefano Civitarese Matteucci and Simon Halliday (eds), *Social Rights in Europe in the Age of Austerity* (Routledge, 2017) – see in particular Jed Meers' chapter on the UK; Michael Adler (ed.), *A Research Agenda for Social Welfare Law, Policy and Practice* (Edward Elgar, 2022); Katie Boyle, *Economic and Social Rights Law: Incorporation, Justiciability and Principles of Adjudication* (Routledge, 2020); Mark Simpson et al, 'Legal Protection Against Destitution in the UK: the Case for a Right to a Subsistence Minimum' (2023) 86(2) *Modern Law Review*, pp 465–497; Mark Simpson, *Social Citizenship in an Age of Welfare Regionalism: The State of the Social Union* (Bloomsbury, 2022); Koldo Casla, 'Economic and Social Rights in the UK: Between Pessimism of the Intellect and Optimism of the Will' (2024)(1) *European Human Rights Law Review*, pp 23–30.

law and welfare law in the UK. We can see calls in the literature to address the legacy of austerity, and its impact on poor decision making and quality control,[16] but not from the perspective of a rights holder whose SR have been violated. Likewise, reform such as that emanating from the UK government-led Independent Review of Administrative Law analysed the efficacy of judicial review while completely omitting human rights from its scope.[17] Creutzfeldt and Kirkham forewarn that further reform in administrative law is inevitable, particularly as part of the aftermath and legacy of COVID-19; however, human rights do not feature as part of the incremental or radical theories of change proposed.[18] Gulland makes an invaluable contribution in terms of aligning the discourses of administrative justice and social justice, accounting for the historical development of social justice and the absence of outcome-oriented research in the administrative justice discipline.[19] However, the contribution sidelines the potential of human rights to the margins; indeed, it omits SR from the discussion entirely.[20] This line of argumentation falls prey to the displacement thesis that ignores the emancipatory nature of rights language and its mobilization in social change.[21] Gulland therefore identifies the role that a social justice lens can play in addressing structural inequality, but fails to engage with any of the vast literature on SR as substantive legal rights. Doyle and O'Brien address the administrative SR gap to some extent in proposing a demosprudential rather than a jurisprudential role for the ombudsman to addresses social rights in the spaces close to home.[22] However, the proposals are not without criticism[23] and again do not address SR as legal rights, as we do in this book.

---

[16] Robert Thomas and Joe Tomlinson, 'Mapping Current Issues in Administrative Justice: Austerity and the "More Bureaucratic Rationality" Approach' (2017) 39(3) *Journal of Social Welfare and Family Law*, pp 380–399.

[17] Katie Boyle and Diana Camps, *Response to IRAL Call for Evidence* (University of Stirling, 2020).

[18] Naomi Creutzfeldt and Richard Kirkham, 'Understanding How and When Change Occurs in the Administrative Justice System: The Ombudsman/Tribunal Partnership as a Catalyst for Reform?' (2020) 42(2) *Journal of Social Welfare and Family Law*, pp 253–273.

[19] Jackie Gulland, 'Social Justice and Administrative Justice' in Marc Hertogh et al (eds), *The Oxford Handbook of Administrative Justice* (Oxford: Oxford University Press, 2022).

[20] Gulland (n 19).

[21] Paul O'Connell, 'Human Rights: Contesting the Displacement Thesis' (2018) 69(1) *Northern Ireland Legal Quarterly*, pp 19–35.

[22] Margaret Doyle and Nick O'Brien, *Reimagining Administrative Justice: Human Rights in Small Places* (London: Palgrave Pivot, 2020).

[23] Michael Adler, 'Book Review: Reimagining Administrative Justice: Human Rights in Small Places' (2021) 30(4) *Social & Legal Studies*, pp 669–681; Simon Halliday, '[Book Review]: *Reimagining Administrative Justice: Human Rights in Small Places* by Margaret Doyle & Nick O'Brien (Palgrave Pivot, 2020)' (2021) 28(1) *Journal of Social Security Law*, pp 71–76.

It is important to situate the book's contribution in relation to these overarching epistemic framings of justice and the processes of accessing it. As Doyle and O'Brien note, human rights and administrative justice are unfamiliar partners and, yet, the realization of all human rights are entirely dependent on administrative justice processes and accountability for violations of human rights are entirely dependent on administrative justice accountability. There is an acknowledgement in the administrative justice discourse that justice is often elusive. According to Hodges, there has been too much 'reliance on the mantra of 'access to justice" in administrative justice discourse. That slogan, he argues, 'can hide the fact that justice is often not delivered to individuals and organisations when it is needed. The real question is whether justice is delivered'.[24] This book revisits Garth and Cappelletti's call for 'socially just outcomes' as part of access to justice processes, and we do so by reframing administrative justice alongside the UK's international obligations to realize SR as legal rights. Our empirical data demonstrates that hegemonic exercises of power continue to construct and reproduce discourses that undermine and neglect SR as legal rights, which ultimately hinders progress in creating an effective accountability framework.

Our project therefore requires addressing one of the key gaps in the literature and practice in the UK by providing alternative perspectives on an often neglected area of law domestically, where the national discourse is aligned with a narrative that assumes SR are nonjusticiable, cannot legitimately be enforced by the court, contravene parliamentary supremacy and are aspirational in nature.[25] It may be helpful to note that from the outset, this position is outdated domestically, comparatively and internationally.[26] SR law is often misunderstood and underutilized across the UK's legal jurisdictions,[27] something which the data demonstrates as evident in first-tier advice services all the way through to legal framings applied at times by solicitors and barristers working across SR issues. While public and administrative law, and in particular social welfare law, engage with SR across areas such as health, social care, education, social security, housing and social services, they do not traditionally embrace broader conceptual frameworks that encompass the full international human rights framework. When economic and social rights are addressed in the public and administrative law sphere, they tend to feature under the aegis of

---

[24] Chris Hodges, 'Delivering Justice' (2019) 1 *International Journal of Procedural Law*, pp 149–177.
[25] Boyle (n 5), p 2.
[26] Boyle (n 5); Katie Boyle, 'Models of Incorporation and Justiciability of Economic, Social and Cultural Rights', Scottish Human Rights Commission, 2018, https://www.scottish humanrights.com/media/1809/models_of_incorporation_escr_vfinal_nov18.pdf.
[27] Paul Hunt, *Social Rights Are Human Rights – But the UK System Is Rigged* (Sheffield: Centre for Welfare Reform, 2017).

something else.²⁸ In other words, our discourse around SR is dominated by existing domestic human rights structures which marginalize SR as forming administrative entitlements under limited statutory frameworks (with no normative dimension or minimum core threshold), as aspects of civil and political rights or of formal equality.²⁹

While it may be unlikely that there is impetus for a paradigmatic shift in the constitutional framing of enforcing rights in areas of economic and social policy at the national level,³⁰ it is not an impossibility. Indeed, while the Supreme Court has shown its reluctance to engage in merits-based review of SR enforcement, it has also accepted the legalization of international human rights law by way of incorporation,³¹ something that is already underway at the devolved level and that could ultimately rebalance the UK's positioning on SR enforcement. The state's reluctance to address the SR gap has meant that shifting sands beneath the surface are reorientating constituent parts of the UK towards a substantive rights-based model of the rule of law, while the national political discourse has been focused on the regression and diminution of existing protection. This includes the 'to and fro' discourse on retreating from the European Convention on Human Rights (ECHR) and repeal of the Human Rights Act (HRA) 1998, the last attempt at which was scrapped in 2023.³² Boyle has argued elsewhere that the regressive rights discourse and the threat of repealing the HRA 'exhausts civil society in debates on retention of the status quo rather than progressive reform', creating a chilling effect on the enjoyment of human rights across the UK.³³ The devolved trajectories may ultimately compel the UK to address this normative gap or, alternatively, lead to greater state fragmentation in a fragile unitary state.³⁴ The dominant narrative of rejecting SR as legal rights is subject to challenge at both the devolved level and emerging discourses

---

²⁸ Katie Boyle and Edel Hughes, 'Identifying Routes to Remedy for Violations of Economic, Social and Cultural Rights' (2018) 22 *International Journal of Human Rights*, pp 43–69.
²⁹ Ibid.
³⁰ See the recent decisions from the Supreme Court raising a red flag that the court should not intervene in such areas such as *R (SC) v Secretary of State for Work and Pensions* [2021] UKSC 26, where Lord Reed at [162] draws a line on the role of the court intervening in what is perceived as failed political campaigns.
³¹ *REFERENCES (Bills) by the Attorney General and the Advocate General for Scotland – United Nations Convention on the Rights of the Child and European Charter of Local Self-Government (Incorporation) (Scotland)* [2021] UKSC 42.
³² Following the Independent Human Rights Act Review Report, available at https://www.gov.uk/guidance/independent-human-rights-act-review#the-panels-report, the UK government introduced the Bill of Rights Bill to repeal and replace the Human Rights Act and subsequently scrapped the Bill after first reading.
³³ Boyle (n 5), pp 102–103.
³⁴ Ibid, p 136.

from civil society and oppositional parties at the national level,[35] providing an opportunity to ensure evidence-led research informs potential reform to address this accountability gap.

The practical implications of the lack of SR enforcement manifest in a litany of SR violations across multiple areas, as demonstrated in the qualitative data in what has become colloquially known as the 'Daniel Blake phenomenon'.[36] The project is primarily concerned with addressing gaps in access to justice for SR violations. When engaging with practitioners, there is often little distinction drawn between access to justice as constituting access to a legal process to address that violation and access to the social right provision itself. It may therefore help to reflect on the areas where SR violations are most keenly felt, and how the absence of access to justice and effective remedies exacerbates this.

The 'Daniel Blake phenomenon' has given rise to greater attention to the litany of issues in SR violations, some of which have been subject to judicial review and others which have featured as part of wider public discourse. The devolved jurisdictions regularly deploy 'mitigation measures' to counteract some of the most severe austerity cuts,[37] but this has not bucked the poverty trend, with poverty in Scotland, Wales and England increasing year on year since 2016 (Northern Ireland has seen a slight decrease overall).[38] Research indicates that there is a growing chasm in life expectancy for those from poorer socioeconomic demographics.[39] In January 2024, research on the

---

[35] At the national, level examples of counterdiscourses that are emerging are indicative of movements claiming SR as legal rights. See, for example, recent statements by David Lammy (Labour) on incorporation of SR and the link with accountability for SR violations, such as Grenfell and Windrush: David Lammy, 'Human Rights Are an Integral Part of Labour's Mission', Institute for Public Policy, 7 July 2021, https://labourlist.org/2021/07/human-rights-are-an-integral-part-of-labours-mission-lammys-speech/

[36] Nick O'Brien, 'Administrative Justice in the Wake of *I, Daniel Blake*' (2017) 89(1) *Political Quarterly*, pp 82–91.

[37] For example, while those who have had their claim for asylum refused in England are no longer eligible for support (no recourse to public funds), in Scotland additional mitigation measures are taken to ensure that everyone, including those whose immigration status is precarious, can access healthcare on the same basis. The Scottish government has stepped in to ensure that the bedroom tax is not applicable in Scotland through the deployment of discretionary housing payments and that the benefit cap is mitigated through measures such as the Scottish Child Payment. Likewise, in Northern Ireland, additional mitigation social security packages have been introduced to mitigate the severity of UK austerity policies, such as the bedroom tax and the benefit cap. Similar calls for devolved social security in Wales are now taking place.

[38] Joseph Rowntree Foundation, *UK Poverty 2023: The Essential Guide to Understanding Poverty in the UK* (York: Joseph Rowntree Foundation, 2023), https://www.jrf.org.uk/events/uk-poverty-2023-the-essential-guide-to-understanding-poverty-in-the-uk

[39] Denis Campbell, 'Life Expectancy Gap in England "A Growing Chasm" Exacerbated by Covid' *The Guardian* (London, 10 October 2021).

social determinants of health found that over one million people in England died prematurely over a ten-year period due to a combination of poverty, austerity policies and COVID-19.[40]

This project therefore seeks to ask whether and how the access to justice gap for SR in the UK can be addressed. SR are underprotected in the UK legal system. There is no constitutional setting for rights, not least SR. Of course, SR are not beyond the reach of courtrooms, tribunals, ombudsmen or complaints mechanisms, but for the moment, their enforcement is entirely dependent on being made possible under the rubric of something else. The role of the court plays an important part in our reflections as an important accountability forum for resolving disputes around the provision of SR. This is not to say that the role of the court is necessarily the most appropriate forum. Alternative routes through the legislative and executive branches may be more appropriate – perhaps even leading to political impetus to better protect SR, as is evident in the UK's devolved jurisdictions.[41] And when accountability is required, the project considers whether this might happen through more immediate complaints mechanisms, tribunals, ombudsmen, alternative dispute resolutions or through the roles played by inspectorates and regulators as part of a wider accountability sphere.[42] We recommend a more prominent role for each of these alternative routes to justice in resolving SR disputes drawing on both procedural and substantive standards, but we recognize this requires a clear statutory remit to do so.

---

[40] Peter Goldblatt, *Health Inequalities, Life Cut Short* (London: Institute of Health Equity, 2024).

[41] The legal constitutionalization and adjudication of rights can help support pathways to social justice, among other avenues. See Conor Gearty and Virginia Mantouvalou, *Debating Social Rights* (Oxford: Hart Publishing, 2011); and O'Connell (n 21). In addition, it should be noted that the end result of other avenues may indeed lead to the legalization of SR – for example, where civil society pressure coalescing with political impetus results in human rights reform that embeds SR as legal rights (such as is evident in Scotland and Wales).

[42] For a discussion on accountability in this space, see the leading work of Tom Mullen, 'Access to Justice in Administrative Law and Administrative Justice' in Ellie Palmer et al (eds), *Access to Justice: Beyond the Policies and Politics of Austerity* (London: Bloomsbury Publishing, 2016); O'Brien (n 36); Doyle and O'Brien (n 22); Nick O'Brien and Mary Senevirante, *Ombudsmen at the Crossroads: The Legal Services Ombudsman, Dispute Resolution and Democratic Accountability* (London: Palgrave Macmillan, 2017); Mashaw (n 11); Michael Adler, 'Social Security and Social Welfare' in Peter Cane and Herbert Kritzer (eds), *The Oxford Handbook of Empirical Legal Research* (Oxford: Oxford University Press, 2010); Robert Thomas and Joe Tomlinson, *Current Issues in Administrative Justice: Examining Administrative Review, Better Internal Decisions, and Tribunal Reform* (London: Economic and Social Research Council, 2016); and David Barrett, 'The Regulatory Space of Equality and Human Rights Law in Britain: The Role of the Equality and Human Rights Commission' (2019) 38 *Legal Studies*, pp 247–265.

In relation to the latter, an over-reliance on alternative mechanisms in the UK context immediately falls prey to an insurmountable hurdle. If SR do not enjoy legal status in domestic law, there is no room for substantive enforcement, nor is it the role of such bodies to respond to this gap. So while tribunals, for example, can perform an important fact-finding role in assessing statutory entitlement, they cannot currently assess whether statutory entitlement complies with normative (SR) standards. This can be compared to the transformative potential of alternative routes to justice where SR norms are recognized and upheld. A recent report by the Ombudsman on Housing is indicative of best practice in demonstrating the role that this sector can play in avenues to SR justice.[43] Using the statutory framework for social housing[44] and its powers to examine systemic issues,[45] the Housing Ombudsman examined 410 complaints regarding damp and mould involving 142 landlords over a two-year period and found that there was systemic maladministration in up to 64 per cent of complaints handled.[46] In addition, the report identifies a systemic problem with 'inference of blame' that suggests poor housing standards are a result of 'lifestyle' choice.[47] The report makes a number of recommendations for landlords, including a zero-tolerance approach to damp and mould; an investigative approach to identifying problems (rather than relying on reporting by residents); ensuring that initial response to complaints do not automatically apportion blame on residents; and an improved and effective complaints policy, with clear compensation and redress.[48] While the report does not cover all potential violations (the remit of the ombudsman does not cover the private rental sector, for example), this report is indicative of the potential transformative role that ombuds, regulators and tribunals can play in responding to systemic SR violations when there is a clear mandate and will to do so.

The literature has long dispelled common and pervasive misconceptions that economic, social and cultural rights are of lesser status than civil and political rights.[49] In fact, the operation of economic, social and cultural

---

[43] Housing Ombudsman Service, 'Housing Ombudsman Urges Zero Tolerance Approach on Damp and Mould' (Housing Ombudsman Service Press Release, 2021).

[44] Drawing upon the standards on what is considered to be a decent home, including the Department for Communities and Local Government, *A Decent Home: Definition and Guidance for Implementation* (Department for Communities and Local Government, 2006) and the Homes (Fitness for Human Habitation) Act 2018.

[45] Housing Ombudsman Service (HOS), *Systemic Framework* (Liverpool: Housing Ombudsman Service, 2021).

[46] HOS, *Spotlight on: Damp and Mould, It's Not Lifestyle* (Liverpool: Housing Ombudsman Service, 2021), pp 2 and 53.

[47] Ibid, p 4.

[48] Ibid, pp 5–7.

[49] Boyle (n 5), ch 2; Philip Alston and Gerard Quinn, 'The Nature and Scope of States Parties' Obligations under the ICESCR' (1987) 9(2) *Human Rights Quarterly*, pp 156–229.

rights as enforceable legal rights has been realized in practice in different constitutional and regional settings across the world.[50] Nonetheless, the fact that SR are not made explicit in laws and policies makes them invisible and manifests as challenges in securing SR justice. This not only creates problems for practitioners in adjudicating SR violations, but also robs rights holders of their own power[51] and, by extension, a legitimate voice. It is therefore important to examine which discourses within the broader social and legal context give power to mechanisms of invisibilization, and which counter discourses could be produced to give SR protection its proper place within a human rights framework. Thus, we argue, language or discourse constitutes both the problem *and* potential solutions regarding increasing accountability for SR.

Our theoretical framework: deliberative democracy theory and critical discourse theory

Our approach to analysing the data is underpinned by our understanding that all meaning is created through discourse and, furthermore, that discourse and thought are mediated by power relations that are socially and historically situated.[52] These tenets help us evaluate and better understand how certain groups in society are privileged over others, how to address change in terms of the mechanisms that undermine access to justice and effective remedies, as well as how to empower individuals to disrupt unjust practices. This approach builds on conceptions of rights as constructs of deliberative democracy[53] and rights claiming as a performative act within a deliberative democracy.[54] If rights claiming is an important component of citizenship, then genuine participation in a deliberative framework must address discourses that are constructed to marginalize and exclude. For this reason, deliberative democracy relies on a critical discourse lens. Such a lens illuminates how barriers to social justice are socially and discursively produced and, more importantly, how understanding these dynamics can inform

---

[50] For a discussion on this, see Boyle (n 5).
[51] Hunt (n 27).
[52] Joe Kincheloe and Peter McLaren, 'Rethinking Critical Theory and Qualitative Research' in Norman Denzin and Yvonna Lincoln (eds), *Handbook of Qualitative Research*, 2nd edn (London: Sage Publications, 2000), p 291; Jan Blommaert, *Discourse: A Critical Introduction* (Cambridge: Cambridge University Press, 2005).
[53] For example, see the competing conceptions of rights formation under proceduralism or substantive deliberation in different constitutional settings; Seyla Benhabib, 'Reason-Giving and Rights-Bearing: Constructing the Subject of Rights' (2013) 20(1) *Constellations*, pp 38–50.
[54] Karen Zivi, *Making Rights Claims: A Practice of Democratic Citizenship* (Oxford: Oxford University Press, 2012).

practice and chart ways forward to create legitimacy for SR in the UK. We direct attention to discourses not only because they reflect representations, but also because discourses can be seen as 'practices that systematically form the objects of which they speak'.[55] This Foucauldian perspective recognizes the ways in which knowledge circulates and functions, and it is through discourse that claims to knowledge and truth are produced.

Critiques of social rights adjudication

Our theoretical approach addresses critiques of SR adjudication drawing from principles of deliberative democracy theory.[56] The approach to the qualitative data was framed using these principles to guide our semi-structured interviews. We then analysed and theorized our findings using a critical discourse lens. From the outset of the research project, the theoretical framework recognized the SR accountability gap as an issue in both the literature and practice across the UK. Critiques of SR as legal rights are not unique to the UK jurisdiction and, in many respects, the critiques associated with SR adjudication appear throughout the literature and practice in jurisdictions that grapple with whether or not to constitutionalize or legalize SR as legal rights. We do not seek to (re-)rehearse arguments here in support or against the recognition of SR as legal rights subject to legal adjudication and judicial enforcement. These arguments and counter-arguments are made elsewhere in the literature, including a comprehensive overview of the critiques and the development of principles of deliberative democracy that counteract them.[57] There would be ample opportunity within any book engaging with SR to spend a significant amount of attention addressing SR sceptics. Instead, we point to where these discussions are already rehearsed, and we do so unapologetically. For those engaged in SR research and practice, much time and resources can be exhausted on revisiting the basic foundational arguments and counter-arguments addressing the legal status of the rights. As this book demonstrates, exhausting time and resources at this level inhibits the progression of the discussion beyond those basic sceptical positions and risks perpetuating hegemonic discourses at the expense of new emancipatory perspectives and knowledge.

In brief, the critiques of SR adjudication can be understood as constituting four waves: (i) the anti-democratic critique (that SR are polycentric and the

---

[55] Michel Foucault, *The Archaeology of Knowledge* (A.M. Sheridan Smith, trans.) (New York: Harper & Row, 1972), p 49.
[56] Boyle (n 5) develops principles derived from deliberative democracy to address the critiques of SR adjudication.
[57] Boyle (n 5).

courts are not the appropriate democratic forum for their resolution); (ii) the indeterminacy critique (that SR are indeterminate and that their vagueness hinders effective enforcement); (iii) the incapacity critique (that courts are ill-equipped to deal with complex matters of economic and social policy and lack the expertise to resolve such disputes); and (iv) the pro-hegemonic critique (that SR adjudication in practice results in the court acting as a pro-hegemonic exercise of power, further exacerbating existing inequalities in the distribution of resources).[58]

While addressing these critiques requires careful consideration, they do not present as insurmountable barriers to effective SR adjudication. A response to the anti-democratic critique proposes that while courts should remain a means of last resort, they must perform a democratic function in holding other branches to account when violations of rights occur, and that democratic legitimacy is struck by balancing appropriate weak versus strong[59] forms of review depending on the circumstances. In other words, sometimes courts should adopt deferential roles in the adjudication and development of remedies for breaches of SR, requiring states to justify their approach adopting weak review mechanisms, such as limited tests of irrationality, and ordering declarators that are deferential in nature rather than usurping the role of the legislature or executive. In other circumstances, particularly when there is a violation of a fundamental norm, or where the applicant's dignity or a social minimum is breached, courts can perform more interventionist forms of review and enhanced forms of scrutiny, and can issue outcome-orientated orders. A moderate typology suggests striking a balance and using an aggregate of appropriate remedies as a means of responding to SR violations.[60] This approach is familiar (although arguably underutilized) by the UK judiciary. For example, judicial review can act as an important safeguard in cases of destitution or risk to life, where an aggregate of remedies provides immediate interim relief, together with deferential orders to revisit the decision-making process in a longer timeframe, with courts performing a supervisory role.[61]

Responses to the indeterminacy critique propose that courts, along with other actors in a multi-institutional framework, should perform a role in

---

[58] For a discussion on the vast academic literature examining the waves of ESR critiques, see Boyle (n 5), ch 1.
[59] Mark Tushnet, *Weak Courts, Strong Rights: Judicial Review and Social Welfare Rights in Comparative Constitutional Law* (Princeton: Princeton University Press, 2008), p 23.
[60] César Rodríguez-Garavito and Diana Rodríguez-Franco, *Radical Deprivation on Trial, the Impact of Judicial Activism on Socioeconomic Rights in the Global South* (Cambridge: Cambridge University Press, 2015), p 10.
[61] By way of example, see *QH v Secretary of State for the Home Department* [2020] EWHC 2691 (Admin).

giving meaning and content to rights. Young tells us SR adjudication is nothing more than finding consensus between epistemic communities – including the legislature, executive and judiciary – around the meaning of rights.[62] It is in the dialogue between epistemic communities (legislative, executive and judicial) that SR adjudication can help give meaning to rights, a role that Michelman argues courts should not abdicate.[63] The UK Supreme Court's decision in *SC* risks amounting to a form of abdication in relation to those causes whereby majoritarian politics cannot (by way of representative democracy) provide marginalized[64] or minority groups with routes to justice through the legislative and executive branches.[65] Lord Reed warns against pursuing remedies through the courts for failed political campaigns, urging the judicial branch to maintain a clear distinction between the political and judicial realms.[66] Does this position risk further marginalizing those who do not enjoy majoritarian power? If so, it ultimately risks the court entrenching hegemonic structures of inequality. Rather than completely abdicating its role in this regard, Tushnet argues that courts must strike the right balance so that they do not 'debase dangerously the entire currency of rights and the rule of law' by failing to engage with the meaning and content of SR.[67]

Responses to the indeterminacy critique also argue that courts must have clear instructions on their role, whether in the constitution or in enabling statutory frameworks, as well as having regard to appropriate sources in interpreting SR, including both international human rights law and comparative law, both of which can offer normative frames of reference when interpreting domestic law.[68] Responses to the incapacity critique follow a similar vein; courts must equip themselves with the relevant expertise and evidence to assess compliance with SR, including the deployment of *amicus curiae*, as well as drawing on a broad range of sources. In addition, court procedures must adapt to better facilitate collective responses to systemic problems.

---

[62] Kathrine Young, *Constituting Economic and Social Rights* (Oxford: Oxford University Press, 2012), p 8.

[63] Frank Michelman, 'Socioeconomic Rights in Constitutional Law: Explaining America Away' (2008) 6(3) *International Journal of Comparative Constitutional Law*, pp 663–686, p 683.

[64] The research team acknowledges that marginalized/minoritized groups are not homogeneous and that the nature of challenges, as well as barriers to accessing justice, may differ significantly. Although our empirical data (practitioner interviews) foreground particular groups of people facing certain (unique) challenges, these accounts merely provide glimpses of insight; it is beyond the scope of the project to address the diversity of needs/hurdles of specified groups in a structured and comprehensive manner.

[65] *R (SC) v Secretary of State for Work and Pensions* [2021] UKSC 26.

[66] Ibid.

[67] Tushnet (n 59).

[68] See the South African Constitution, https://www.constituteproject.org/constitution/South_Africa_2012

Responses to the pro-hegemonic critique argue that courts can act as an important mechanism and 'institutional voice' for those who are politically disenfranchised.[69] Legal processes should take steps to embrace countermajoritarian adjudication.[70] This can be constituted along the lines of broader rules around standing, enhanced opportunities for third party or strategic litigation, and enabling collective class actions or group proceedings.[71] More appropriate remedies are required to help the court embrace this role, such as the deployment of structural remedies when systemic issues arise.[72] In other words, the often systemic nature of SR violations requires new remedial responses that go beyond individual relief (structural remedies are a type of hybrid remedy that can offer individual and systemic relief, potentially involving multiple applicants and multiple defendants).[73]

Principles of adjudication

The research suggests that principles of adjudication can offer responses to the critiques of SR. For example, the principles of accessibility, participation, deliberation and fairness can counteract the anti-democratic, incapacity and indeterminacy critiques.[74] The principles of countermajoritarianism can guide responses to the pro-hegemonic critique through enhanced responses to systemic violations. And the principle of effective and appropriate remedial relief can countenance critiques relating to democratic legitimacy

---

[69] Jeff King, *Judging Social Rights* (Cambridge: Cambridge University Press, 2011); Colm O'Cinneide, 'The Constitutionalisation of Economic and Social Rights' and Frank Michelman, 'Constitutionally Binding Social and Economic Rights as a Compelling Idea: Reciprocating Perturbations in Liberal and Democratic Constitutional Visions' in Helena García et al (eds), *Social and Economic Rights in Theory and Practice, Critical Inquiries* (Abingdon: Routledge, 2015), pp 261–262 and 279–280, respectively; Aoife Nolan et al, *The Justiciability of Social and Economic Rights: An Updated Appraisal* (Belfast: Human Rights Consortium, 2007); Virginia Mantouvalou, 'Structural Injustices and the Human Rights of Workers' (2020) 73(1) *Current Legal Problems*, pp 59–87.

[70] David Landau, 'The Reality of Social Rights Enforcement' (2012) 53 *Harvard International Law Journal*, pp 190–247.

[71] See the potential of class actions discussed by Michael Molavi, *Collective Access to Justice: Assessing the Potential of Class Actions in England and Wales* (Bristol: Bristol University Press, 2021).

[72] Landau (n 70); and Rodríguez-Garavito and Rodríguez-Franco (n 60).

[73] Gaurav Mukherjee, 'Effective Remedies & Structural Orders for SR Violations, Nuffield Access to Justice for SR, Addressing the Accountability Gap', Access to Justice for Social Rights, 2022, https://www.nuffieldfoundation.org/wp-content/uploads/2019/11/Boyle-Effective-Remedies-Briefing_18MAY2.pdf

[74] For a discussion on how principles of deliberative democracy help address the critiques of SR adjudication, see Boyle (n 5), ch 1.

and pro-hegemonic critiques. These principles, derived from deliberative democracy theory, offer a lens through which to view the building blocks of access to justice from initial violation through to effective remedy.

The principles of adjudication are one mechanism by which we have scrutinized the data produced (see Table 1.1). This project has also been influenced by the three-dimensional theory of justice.

Table 1.1: Defining principles of adjudication

ACCESS	Barriers of access to legal processes need to be removed, including prohibitive costs, access to legal aid, advice, advocacy, representation and sufficiently broad tests of standing.
PARTICIPATION	Rights holders are often unable to meaningfully participate in complex legal processes and are often excluded from decisions regarding the outcomes of those processes. Even in situations adapted for litigants in person, equality of arms concerns arise when rights holders are often entering into disputes with parties represented with legal representation at tribunal level or summary court.
DELIBERATION	For normative application of rights enforcement, adjudicators need to deliberate on rights with reference to appropriate sources, including international and comparative law in addition to domestic law, as well as between institutions horizontally (the executive, legislative and judicial branches) and vertically (local, devolved, national and international institutions).
FAIRNESS	Adjudication needs to draw on both procedural and substantive concepts of fairness, requiring a more intense engagement with the merits of decisions as well as the decision-making process. In the UK, this means expanding our conception of 'reasonableness' beyond irrationality or *Wednesbury* reasonableness. International human rights law suggests the adoption of proportionality-inflected reasonableness.
COUNTERMAJORITARIAN	Ideally adjudication processes facilitate collective responses to systemic SR violations, meaning processes are adapted to enable third-party, strategic litigation and class actions/ multi-group proceedings in order to avoid the systemic problem falling as a burden on the individual.
REMEDIAL	Effective and appropriate remedies require a rethink in terms of both individual and collective relief, moving beyond individual compensation-based relief to guarantees of non-repetition and wider collective or structural remedies that draw on an aggregate of weak versus strong review and remedial relief.

A three-dimensional theory of justice: distribution, recognition and representation

Theoretically, we find value in Nancy Fraser's three-dimensional theory of justice.[75] Her point of departure is that the most general meaning of justice is parity of participation.[76] Her view of justice as participatory parity goes hand in hand with principles of deliberative democracy. She says that on the one hand, the principle of participatory parity is an *outcome* notion, 'a substantive principle of justice by which we may evaluate social arrangements: the latter are just if and only if they permit all the relevant social actors to participate as peers in social life'. On the other hand, Fraser says, participatory parity is also a *process* notion, which specifies 'a procedural standard by which we may evaluate the democratic legitimacy of norms: the latter are legitimate if and only if they can command the assent of all concerned in fair and open processes of deliberation, in which all can participate as peers'.[77] Embedded in this duality is an inherent reflexivity that allows us to problematize both substance and procedure. In other words, this approach can expose the unjust background conditions that skew decision-making processes and barriers to access to justice, as well as the unjust procedures that generate unequal outcomes. This aligns with Iris Marion Young's theory of structural injustice that situates the role of societal structures and processes that marginalize and place groups in a position of disadvantage from which others benefit.[78]

Fraser's theory of justice entails the economic dimension of distribution, the cultural dimension of recognition and the political dimension of representation.[79] Fraser posits that overcoming injustice means dismantling institutionalized obstacles that prevent people from participating on a par with others, related to two particular types of injustice. On the one hand, full participation can be impeded by economic structures that deny people the resources they need in order to interact with others as peers, constituting distributive injustice or maldistribution. On the other hand, parity may be obstructed by institutionalized hierarchies of cultural value that deny them the requisite standing, in which case people suffer from status inequality

---

[75] Nancy Fraser, *Scales of Justice: Reimagining Political Space in a Globalizing World* (New York: Columbia University Press, 2009), p 16.

[76] The research team acknowledges Fraser's monistic viewpoint, framing justice around the principle of parity in participation. We do not preclude other conceptualizations of justice. For a theoretical critique, see Christopher F. Zurn, 'Review: Scales of Justice: Reimagining Political Space in a Globalizing World by Nancy Fraser' (2012) 38(1) *Social Theory and Practice*, pp 165–172.

[77] Fraser (n 75), p 29.

[78] Iris Marion Young, *Responsibility for Justice* (Oxford: Oxford University Press, 2013).

[79] Fraser (n 75), p 16.

or misrecognition.[80] Fraser defines these as problems of class structure and status. Furthermore, she elaborates a third dimension of justice related to the political constitution of society – representation. Although Fraser presents the dimensions of distribution, recognition and representation as different facets of justice, our data show that they are also closely interlinked.

Another important element of Fraser's theory is 'the politics of framing',[81] which is closely tied to the dimension of 'representation'. Framing is an exercise of boundary setting, of delimiting actions and interpretations; it centres on issues of membership and procedure, relating to matters of social belonging. We have already highlighted how questions relating to the justiciability of SR frame them in a particular manner and limit the ways in which these rights can be adjudicated. The data show that the politics of framing proceeds simultaneously on multiple levels; on one level, there are efforts to redress 'first order' injustices of maldistribution, misrecognition[82] and political misrepresentation. On a second level, movements aim to redress 'meta-level' injustices of misframing by reconstituting the 'who' of justice.[83] Our analysis teases out these injustices and we now direct our attention to discourse, which allows us to examine more closely the frames and misframings that sometimes impede access to justice.

Why discourse?

As stated at the beginning of the chapter, analysing discourse is a pathway to understanding the power inherent in social and historical contexts. By using a methodological approach that allows power to 'appear', the project was able to recognize privilege (of those in power over others), a necessary precursor to remedies that challenge unjust practices, and how access to justice and effective remedies may need to dismantle power. Equally, the project aimed to centre and empower individuals. As identified by Karen Zivi, rights claiming can be a performative act in a deliberative democratic framework and an important component of citizenship: the democratic practice of rights claiming is important, not because it guarantees a certain legal, political or social outcome, but because it involves individuals in developing the skills of citizenship while also reimagining the contours of community and (re)defining who is included.[84]

---

[80] Fraser (n 75).
[81] Young (n 78), p 22; Deborah Tannen, *Framing in Discourse* (Oxford: Oxford University Press, 1993).
[82] See also Bourdieu's notion of *méconnaissance* (misrecognition); Pierre Bourdieu, *Language and Symbolic Power* (Cambridge: Polity Press, 1991).
[83] Fraser (n 75), p 25.
[84] Zivi (n 54).

Language, or discourse, plays a key role in processes of social differentiation and the construction of inequality.[85] The seminal work of Dell Hymes[86] reminds us that language forms may be equal in substance, but there may be significant differences in terms of how language actually works in society. This linguistic inequality and, consequently, much social inequality are the result of an inability to perform certain discourse functions on the basis of available and accessible resources – meaning exclusion from the performative act of citizenship and rights claiming, as defined by Zivi. That is to say that differences in the use of language, or how and which discourses are mobilized, often quite systematically translate into inequalities between individuals.[87] Our data show that not all members of society have access to language or discourse in the same way, resulting in a significant impact on the realization of SR and the ability to access an effective remedy. We examine how practitioners mobilize different discourses in relation to rights claims, and how these forms of knowledge may promote or uphold SR. We seek to better understand which discourses resist and challenge dominant and disenfranchising discourses, and, in contrast, which discourses intersect and potentially undermine access to justice for SR.

Social actors produce and reproduce discourses in ways that correlate with a particular position within social and political structure. The notions of discourse and ideology are often conflated, as it is difficult to explicitly disentangle their close links. In other words, in the mobilization of discourses, certain ideological conceptions are concomitantly invoked, albeit unconsciously or implicitly. However, one benefit of directing attention to how particular discourses (representations) are articulated together in unique ways is that it helps to shed light on the (dis)alignments with specific ideologies. In this sense, ideologies function as 'underlying' conceptual frames that become salient in discourse.[88] Similarly, discourse may be conceived of as a site of ideology[89] or, more concretely, that discourse is the 'most tangible manifestation of ideology'.[90]

---

[85] Susan Gal, 'Language and Political Economy' (1989) 18 *Annual Review of Anthropology* 345; Judith Irvine and Susan Gal, 'Language Ideology and Linguistic Differentiation' in Paul V. Kroskrity (ed.), *Regimes of Language: Ideologies, Polities, and Identities* (Santa Fe: School of American Research Press, 2000).

[86] See, for instance, Dell Hymes, 'Inequality in Language: Taking for Granted' (1992) 8(1) *Working Papers in Educational Linguistics*, pp 1–30.

[87] Blommaert (n 52), p 71.

[88] Kathryn A. Woolard, *Singular and Plural: Ideologies of Linguistic Authority in 21st Century Catalonia* (Oxford: Oxford University Press, 2016), p 16.

[89] Blommaert (n 52).

[90] Jan Blommaert and Jef Verschueren, 'The Role of Language in European Nationalist Ideologies' in Paul V. Kroskrity and Kathryn A. Woolard (eds), *Language Ideologies: Practice and Theory* (Oxford: Oxford University Press, 1998), p 26.

As Alistair Pennycook[91] succinctly explains, discourses are indelibly connected to power, knowledge and truth, but they neither represent nor obscure truth and knowledge in the interests of pre-given powers (as in the case of many versions of ideology). We follow Foucault's interest in directing attention to the processes by which claims to knowledge or truth are produced.[92] His fundamental interest was not in truth, but 'truth claims', seeing 'historically how effects of truth are produced within discourses which in themselves are neither true nor false'.[93] In other words, producing knowledge is never neutral, but is mobilized for specific purposes.

The bifurcation of rights

We are interested, for example, in how the bifurcation of two separate treaties following the Universal Declaration of Human Rights[94] saw civil and political rights enshrined in the International Covenant on Civil and Political Rights[95] (ICCPR), and economic, social and cultural rights enshrined in the International Covenant on Economic, Social and Cultural Rights[96] (ICESCR). This separation led to misconceptions and erroneous 'truth claims' about the lesser status of the ICESCR. As we indicated earlier, the literature has long since dispelled these myths,[97] providing examples of economic, social and cultural rights that are treated as enforceable legal rights in different contexts across the world. Nonetheless, the trajectories of

---

[91] Alistair Pennycook, *Critical Applied Linguistics: A Critical Introduction* (Abingdon: Routledge, 2001).

[92] Foucault rejected the concept of ideology, preferring the term 'discourse'; Michel Foucault, 'Truth and Power' in Michel Foucault, *Power/Knowledge: Selected Interviews and Other Writings 1972–1977* (Colin Gordon, ed.) (New York: Pantheon Books, 1980).

[93] Foucault (n 92), p 118.

[94] UN (General Assembly), Universal Declaration of Human Rights (UDHR), Resolution 217A (III) of 10 December 1948.

[95] UN (General Assembly), International Covenant on Civil and Political Rights (ICCPR), Resolution 2200A (XXI) of 16 December 1966.

[96] UN (General Assembly), International Covenant on Economic, Social and Cultural Rights (ICESCR), Resolution 2200A (XXI) of 16 December 1966, United Nations, Treaty Series, vol. 993, 3. The UDHR, the ICCPR and the ICESCR are collectively known as the International Bill of Rights.

[97] See Boyle (n 5), ch 2; Alston and Quinn (n 49), p 159; Sally-Anne Way, 'The Myth and Mystery of US History on Economic, Social, and Cultural Rights: The 1947 United States Suggestions for Articles to Be Incorporated in an International Bill of Rights', (2014) 36(4) *Human Rights Quarterly*, pp 869–897; Daniel J. Whelan and Jack Donnelly, 'The West, Economic and Social Rights, and the Global Human Rights Regime: Setting the Record Straight' (2007) 29(4) *Human Rights Quarterly*, pp 908–949; Daniel Whelan, *Indivisible Human Rights* (University of Pennsylvania Press, 2010); Mathew Craven, *The International Covenant on Economic, Social, and Cultural Rights: A Perspective on Its Development*, (Oxford: Clarendon Press, 1995).

SR enforcement has had to overcome a major hurdle in that 'much of the doctrinaire debate about economic, social, and cultural rights throughout the second half of the last century sprang from a legal fiction: that of the separation of human rights into two distinct sets'.[98] Many of the remnants of this legal fiction are often invisible and structural in the UK's legal constitutional framing of rights, and thus play out in the everyday setting of individual lived experience, manifesting as challenges in securing SR justice.

A discourse analysis approach helps us to make visible discourses embedded in practice that are linked to structures of authority and executed through a variety of specific techniques, including those discourses that marginalize, undermine or are wielded in order to hinder SR protection. The data show that the realization of SR relates to the operational processes of determining entitlement and eligibility. In addition, there are also processes of valuation and categorization that sort people into predetermined categories by means of various tools and mechanisms. These processes are not neutral but value-laden, influenced by wider sociopolitical currents and, as the data show, (re)produce difference and embed inequalities. Furthermore, these practices are situated at the intersection of different sectors and scales of social structure. It is a fragmented system that interlinks governments, legal frameworks and the third sector. In the UK, there is an even greater level of fragmentation due to different constitutional arrangements and legal frameworks under devolution. The large-scale undertaking of providing public services is also dispersed, provided by nearly half a million civil servants across cities in England, Wales, Scotland and Northern Ireland. This governing 'at a distance'[99] is constituted in various apparatuses, programmes, documents and procedures to give effect to the goals and logics of government. In some instances the empirical data suggests that there are strong links between discourses mobilized by government actors and systemic structural injustice, meaning that violations of SR and the absence of accountability are socially constructed and reproduced deliberately. This formal and informal bureaucracy reflects a form of structural injustice developed by Mantouvalou, which is one in which there is state complicity. In other words, we identify 'state actions that can be viewed as having a *prima facie* legitimate aim, but which create patterns that are very damaging for large numbers of people'.[100] Our tribunal data discussed in Chapter 4 provide clear examples of decision

---

[98] Mónica Feria Tinta, 'Justiciability of Economic, Social, and Cultural Rights in the Inter-American System of Protection of Human Rights: Beyond Traditional Paradigms and Notions' (2007) 29(2) *Human Rights Quarterly*, pp 431–459, p 432.

[99] Nikolas Rose and Peter Miller, 'Political Power beyond the State: Problematics of Government' (1992) 43(2) *British Journal of Sociology*, pp 173–205, p 181; see also Nancy Fraser's discussion on Postfordist modes of regulation: Fraser (n 75), p 118.

[100] Mantouvalou (n 69).

making that deliberately reproduces SR violations where, for example, 75 per cent of Personal Independence Payment (PIP) decisions are overturned, indicating widespread systemic maladministration.

Street-level bureaucracy and governmentality

On an operational level, the system may be best described as 'street level bureaucracy',[101] a term that encapsulates the challenges and often paradoxical reality of the provision of public services that calls for treating all rights holders alike in their claims on government and, at the same time, must be able to respond to individual needs. 'Bureaucracy' thus points to the entailed rules, procedures and structures of authority, while 'street-level' acknowledges that much of the decision making takes place away from a perceived centre of authority in more informal settings.[102] Importantly for our discussion, the rights holders that are clients in street-level bureaucracies are customarily nonvoluntary. So even though potential welfare recipients 'voluntarily' apply for services, this can hardly be considered voluntary if they have no other means to meet their needs. The poorer the person, Michael Lipsky says, the more likely that person will be a nonvoluntary client of not one but multiple street-level bureaucracies.[103]

This resonates with our empirical data that show that rights holders seeking help in accessing a SR or challenging a rights violation generally have many intersecting problems suffering from clustered injustice.[104] The inherent intersectionality of SR is one of the identified challenges in the current operational and legal frameworks, a point to which we will return. Moreover, the fact that an individual client in a street-level bureaucracy is a nonvoluntary participant creates a power imbalance, as they are also subject to potential sanctions and other punitive measures for noncompliance embedded in strict rules and regulations. In addition, our analysis shows that these power inequalities impact greatly on an individual's capacity to create legitimacy for themselves in their fight for an effective remedy for a SR violation.

In order to explain the tensions and conflicts that emerge across the data, it is imperative to be cognizant of how contemporary neoliberal logics and practices have been instrumental in the promotion of new forms of

---

[101] Michael Lipsky, *Street-Level Bureaucracy: Dilemmas of the Individual in Public Services* (New York: Russell Sage Foundation, 2010).
[102] Ibid, p xii.
[103] Ibid, p 54.
[104] Clements (n 8).

identity and subject formation, and thereby new forms of governance and governmentality[105] in the era of neoliberal globalization.[106] Large-scale processes, such as the provision of public services, are inextricably linked to governance and political economy. Directing attention to governmentality helps to make visible the various ways in which power operates. It is multidirectional and relational.[107] It relates to macro-regulations of the state as well as micro-levels of diverse practices.[108] Contemporary scholarship on governmentality and political economy generally conceives of these activities as dynamic, historically situated and often contradictory processes of knowledge mobilization.[109] These dynamics, as we will demonstrate through our analysis, become visible in circulating discourses.

Governmentality and neoliberal rationalities

Despite the vastness of the concept of neoliberalism, it is still a useful analytical term for interpreting the tensions between the governance of the bureaucratic structure providing welfare rights provisions in the UK, on the one hand, and the realization of SR and access to an effective remedy, on the other hand. The neoliberal project represents a specific kind of valorization that is rooted in economics, also referred to as the 'economization of democracy'.[110] Neoliberal rationalities permeate social life in ways that are unconscious and internalized, shaping our norms and conduct. Neoliberalism has been instrumental in promoting new forms of identity and subject formation, moving from collective to individual subjectivities and cultivating individual responsibility.

---

[105] Michel Foucault, 'Governmentality' in Graham Burchell et al (eds), *The Foucault Effect: Studies in Governmentality* (Chicago: University of Chicago Press, 1991).

[106] It is not possible in the context of this report to do justice to the vast literature and research on neoliberalism, globalization, political economy and governmentality. However, we felt it necessary to acknowledge that our discussion on SR is inextricably embedded in the political project of neoliberal globalization, as it results in particular rationales being mobilized in discourse around the notion of SR and the adjudication journey.

[107] Mark C.J. Stoddart, 'Ideology, Hegemony, Discourse: A Critical Review of Theories of Knowledge and Power (2007) 28(1) *Social Thought and Research*, pp 191–225.

[108] Alistair Pennycook, 'Language Policy and Docile Bodies: Hong Kong and Governmentality' in James W. Tollefson (ed.), *Language Policies in Education: Critical Issues* (Abingdon: Routledge, 2002).

[109] Alfonso Del Percio et al, 'Language and Political Economy' in Ofelia García et al (eds), *The Oxford Handbook of Language and Society* (Oxford: Oxford University Press, 2017).

[110] Wendy Brown, 'Who Is Not a Neoliberal Today?', *Tocqueville 21*, 18 January 2018, https://tocqueville21.com/interviews/wendy-brown-not-neoliberal-today/

These neoliberal and capitalist rationalities are intimately connected to the operational arm of the governing system for social welfare. Data around poverty levels are traditionally used (and methodologies reformed to show improvements) by governments to demonstrate their capabilities in supporting citizens. The cost-of-living crisis has substantially increased experiences of poverty, particularly for children in the UK since 2021.[111] In turn, the austerity approach to budget control taken by the previous Conservative government in the UK has systematically removed the welfare 'safety net' from many.[112] The data show that neoliberal values of efficiency, cost reduction, control and compliance become visible in the workings of the system by means of different mechanisms and tools: increased outsourcing of public services, automation and digitization, testing and assessments, audits and (discretionary) funding. The system operates with strict rules, regulations and procedures that determine entitlement to (and distribution of) social security, housing, food and fuel. These determinations are not subject to independent normative value-based standards based on international human rights law to which the state has agreed to be bound, which creates a major accountability gap in the bureaucratic system.

From our perspective, the concept of governmentality also draws our attention to the ways in which power influences the 'self' by the internalization of specific discourses by individuals. We see this in the valuation practices and discourses across the data that frame the 'worthiness' of individuals and particular groups of people in particular ways. In turn, these valuation discourses are sometimes internalized by practitioners and rights holders. This echoes Foucault's interpretation of governmentality as government's approaches to shape human conduct by calculated means.[113] Our data show how this manifests itself, which helps us to understand some of the recurring themes and various discourses that are foregrounded. In our analysis, we show that there are competing logics at play that become visible in local struggles and tensions around conceptions of entitlement, welfare, poverty and justice. Furthermore, we demonstrate how the various ways in which the systematic categorization and filtering of information and people is facilitated by different tools and mechanisms, impacting on the access to justice journey.

---

[111] Guy Skinner, Paul Bywaters and Eilis Kennedy, 'The Cost-of-Living Crisis, Poverty and Child Maltreatment' (2023) 7(1) *The Lancet Child & Adolescent Health*, pp 5–6.

[112] Mary O'Hara, *Austerity Bites: A Journey to the Sharp End of Cuts in the UK* (Bristol: Policy Press, 2015).

[113] '[C]onduire des conduites' [conduct of conduct]; Michel Foucault, *Dits et Écrits IV* (Paris: Gallimard, 1994), p 237.

Our normative framework: access to social justice and the right to an effective remedy

As discussed earlier, access to justice as a field of law and practice can often mean different things to different epistemic communities. This is in and of itself problematic because discourse around the field of study can draw on significantly varying definitions, potentially undermining a common understanding. We widen the access to justice lens to constitute a broader conception of social justice that includes substantive protection of SR, meaning we are interested in both the procedural and substantive components of the access to justice journey and, in particular, whether the outcomes of the journey can be deemed effective.

To borrow from discourse theory – 'access to justice' or 'justice' in and of itself, could be framed as an 'empty signifier', in that it is a pursuit rather than a prescriptive end.[114] Justice, and the means of achieving it, can be understood and framed in different ways as an (impossible) ideal that societies seek to achieve – meaning that while the end is never fully realized, its absence compels an ongoing struggle to achieve it and, in that process, people prescribe different meanings to the end goal: 'even if the full closure of the social is not realisable in any actual society, the idea of closure and fullness still functions as an (impossible) ideal. Societies are thus organized and centred on the basis of such (impossible) ideals'.[115]

This is of course equally applicable to the elusive terminology around 'social justice' as a 'feelgood' term to which everyone can subscribe without any concrete or shared definition as to what it constitutes.[116] Miller warns that among those who support it, 'it is not at all clear what the idea means. Often it seems little more than a rhetorical phrase ... People may be committed to social justice in the abstract, and yet disagree bitterly about what should be done'.[117] Different disciplines lay claim to 'social justice' constituting a form of procedural justice,[118] formal equality,[119] substantive

---

[114] Although the fullness and universality of society is unachievable, its need does not disappear: it will always show itself through the presence of its absence; Ernesto Laclau, *Emancipation* (London: Verso, 1996), p 53.

[115] David Howart et al (eds), *Discourse Theory and Political Analysis: Identities, Hegemonies and Social Change* (Manchester: Manchester University Press, 2000), p 8.

[116] David Piachaud, *Social Justice and Public Policy: A Social Policy Perspective* (Bristol: Policy Press, 2008), p 33.

[117] David Miller, *Principles of Social Justice* (Cambridge, MA: Harvard University Press, 2001).

[118] John Rawls, *A Theory of Justice* (Cambridge, MA: Harvard University Press, 1971).

[119] Rawls (n 118); Ronald Dworkin, 'Keynote Address: Justice for Hedgehogs' (2010) 90(2) *Boston University Law Review*, pp 469–477.

equality,[120] spatial equality,[121] participatory justice,[122] structural justice,[123] (re)distributive justice,[124] and rights realization.[125] Others conceive of it as a process in and of itself defining social justice as empowering disadvantaged groups to collaborate for social change.[126]

It is the pursuit of the (ideal social) justice, including the means of accessing it, that gives rise to an empty signifier where different actors and epistemic communities impose their own meanings and connotations in realizing this ultimate aim, as evidenced in the empirical data. In the meantime, the overall direction of the literature and practice evolves in the context of seeking to achieve justice, giving rise to the access to justice discourse. Different conceptualizations may not be immediately familiar to those working within the access to justice field from different perspectives. There is therefore a conceptual difficulty in framing 'access to social justice'.

There are two important lessons to be taken from this framing. The first is the pitfalls and dangers associated with different epistemic communities attaching different meanings to terminology that is understood and conceived of in different and sometimes opposing ways – potentially to the detriment of those whose marginalization means they are furthest from accessing (some form of) justice. By way of an example, what does access to justice mean for the person who experiences in-work poverty, relying on food banks and living in housing that is uninhabitable? The data reveal that various tiers of advice from street-level bureaucracy through to advice centres, lawyers and barristers each view these SR violations in distinct ways, none of which may ultimately address the complexity of the rights holder's predicament.

---

[120] Sandra Fredman, 'Substantive Equality Revisited' (2016) 14(3) *International Journal of Constitutional Law*, pp 712–738.

[121] Emil Israel and Ammon Frenkel, 'Social Justice and Spatial Inequality: Toward a Conceptual Framework' (2021) 42(5) *Progress in Human Geography*, pp 647–655, p 647.

[122] Nancy Fraser and Alex Honneth, *Redistribution or Recognition? A Political-Philosophical Landscape* (London: Verso, 2003).

[123] Young (n 78).

[124] Fraser (n 75); Amartya Sen, *The Idea of Justice* (Cambridge, MA: Harvard University Press, 2009).

[125] Martha C. Nussbaum, 'Capabilities as Fundamental Entitlements: Sen and Social Justice' (2003) 9(2–3) *Feminist Economics*, pp 33–59; Chris McInerney, 'Exploring the Meaning of Social Justice' in *Challenging Times, Challenging Administration: The Role of Public Administration in Producing Social Justice in Ireland* (Manchester: Manchester University Press, 2014); Carlos Andrés Pérez-Garzón, 'Unveiling the Meaning of Social Justice in Colombia' (2018) 10(2) *Mexican Law Review*, pp 27–66.

[126] Joanne Schulze et al, 'An International Social Justice Agenda in School Psychology? Exploring Educational Psychologists' Social Justice Interest and Practice in England' (2019) 29(4) *Journal of Educational and Psychological Consultation*, p 394; Katherine Abbott, 'Social Justice' in Alex C. *Michalos Encyclopedia of Quality of Life and Well-Being Research* (New York: Springer, 2014).

The second is around managing expectations of achieving what ultimately is a neverending journey. In other words, the empty signifier analogy helps remind the reader that it is the absence of justice and the means of achieving it which creates the empty signifier around which progress is made. Injustice is the absence of justice and while discourses emerge to close the gap, or fill the absence, the struggle to do so never fully materializes. Once again, the data suggest that what is meant by 'justice' or a satisfactory outcome of a legal process will diverge significantly across the experience of rights holders, the advice sector, the legal sector and others. Those closer to the violation are primarily concerned with addressing the violation and securing access to a particular service or provision, while the perspective of those closer to the law reflects an acute awareness of the limitations of the law in relation to SR provision and the limited remedies for a breach.

The tensions in the qualitative data around how to prescribe meaning to SR and access to social justice are also evident in the literature. For example, scholars invoke both narrow and broad definitions that pertain to 'access to justice' and 'effective remedies'. Mullen, for example, argues that a narrow conception of access to justice is when 'remedies' are available or exist, whereas a broader conception is about whether those 'remedies' can be easily accessed.[127] 'Effective remedies', he clarifies, include tribunals, Ombudsman, complaint procedures and various hybrids, including public inquiry-based decision-making processes.[128] Access to justice under this definition concerns the availability of easily accessible remedies to address wrongs.[129] By remedies, Mullen is referring to legal processes rather than the efficacy or remedial relief offered as an outcome of such processes, and an 'effective remedy' is defined as a right to challenge in an independent forum that is truly accessible.[130]

A broader lens on access to justice includes effective access to legal processes that result in effective outcomes. According to Shelton, remedies are the processes by which arguable claims are heard and decided, whether by courts, administrative agencies or other competent bodies (aligning with Mullen's account), as well as the outcome of the proceedings and the relief afforded the successful claimant (addressing Garth and Cappelletti's second aim – leading to results that are individually and socially just).[131] Our reconceptualization

---

[127] Tom Mullen, 'Access to Justice in Administrative Law and Administrative Justice' in Ellie Palmer et al (eds), *Access to Justice, Beyond the Policies and Politics of Austerity* (London: Bloomsbury Publishing, 2016), p 70.
[128] Mullen (n 127).
[129] Ibid.
[130] Ibid, p 71.
[131] Dinah Shelton, *Remedies in International Human Rights Law* (Buckingham: Open University Press, 1999), p 7.

of access to social justice begins with the violation of a right and ends in an effective remedy for that violation. This requires a renewed focus on what is meant both in terms of effective legal processes (international human rights law suggests that they require to be 'accessible, affordable, timely and effective'),[132] and in terms of effective and substantive outcomes of those processes that constitute effective and satisfactory relief.[133]

The international position makes it clear that remedies for violations of SR ought to be available at the domestic level, and that this should include access to justiciable remedies. Judicial remedies are often cited as a prerequisite of the successful application of a right in international law.[134] Many argue that without judicial sanction, a right is without merit.[135] A blanket refusal to acknowledge the justiciable nature of the rights is considered arbitrary:

> The adoption of a rigid classification of economic, social and cultural rights which puts them, by definition, beyond the reach of the courts would thus be arbitrary and incompatible with the principle that the two sets of human rights are indivisible and interdependent. It would also drastically curtail the capacity of the courts to protect the rights of the most vulnerable and disadvantaged groups in society.[136]

The UN Committee on Economic, Social and Cultural Rights (CESCR) has repeatedly urged the UK to give full legal effect to the ICESCR in its domestic law, asking 'that the Covenant rights are made justiciable, and that effective remedies are available for victims of all violations of economic, social and cultural rights'.[137] Examples of appropriate remedies

---

[132] CESCR (n 14), [9].

[133] Remedies should be effective 'in practice as well as in law': Council of Europe, 'Guide on Article 13 of the European Convention on Human Rights, Right to an Effective Remedy', European Court of Human Rights, 31 August 2021, para 44, https://ks.echr.coe.int/documents/d/echr-ks/guide_art_13_eng

[134] For example, Article 2(3) ICCPR provides for an effective remedy determined by judicial, administrative or legislative authorities. UN General Comment No. 9 (see n 14) provides administrative remedies may be adequate with an ultimate right of judicial appeal.

[135] Alston and Quinn (n 49); Hans Kelsen, *Pure Theory of Law* M. Knight (trans.) (Oakland, CA: University of California Press 1960/1967), pp 125–126; EW Vierdag, 'The Legal Nature of the Rights Granted by the International Covenant on Economic, Social and Cultural Rights' (1968) 9 *Netherlands Yearbook of International Law*, pp 69–105.

[136] CESCR (n 14), [10].

[137] Concluding observations of the UN Committee on Economic, Social and Cultural Rights's (CESCR) UNCSECR's Forty-second session, 4–22 May 2009 Consideration of reports submitted by States parties under articles 16 and 17 of the International Covenant on Economic, Social and Cultural Rights (ICESCR), United Kingdom of Great Britain and Northern Ireland, the Crown Dependencies and the Overseas dependencies, 12 June 2009, E/C.12/GBR/CO/5, para 3.

for violations of international human rights law include restitution, compensation, rehabilitation, satisfaction, effective measures to ensure cessation of the violation and guarantees of non-repetition, public apologies, public and administrative sanctions for wrongdoing, instructing that human rights education be undertaken, ensuring a transparent and accurate account of the violation, reviewing or disapplying incompatible laws or policies, and the use of delayed remedies to facilitate compliance, including rights holders as participants in the development of remedies and supervising compliance post-judgment.[138] As discussed in Chapter 4, we explain how practitioners conceive of effective remedies, including the need to move beyond compensation, the importance of an apology for wrongdoing and the need to take steps to stop the violation happening again to anyone else.

Shelton emphasizes the potential for remedies to provide compensatory or remedial justice, to play a part in condemnation of the violation or retribution, as a form of deterrence and as playing a part in restorative justice or reconciliation.[139] Roach suggests that an effective remedy serves three functions: it places the applicant in, as far as possible, the same position as they were prior to the occurrence of the alleged rights violation, it enables ongoing compliance and it ensures that future violations of the right in question do not occur through (a) deterrence, or (b) an attempt at addressing the feature of a legal system that caused the violation in the first place.[140]

We suggest that adjudicators must be equipped to strike a balance and use an aggregate of appropriate remedies as a means of responding to SR violations, including both individual and collective relief.[141] This aligns with calls in the literature and practice to rethink the role of remedies in economic, social and cultural rights cases: 'The challenge of enforcing ESC rights may require some re-thinking of the traditional idea that remedies must be immediate and track the contours of the right and the violation, and that the courts can order one shot remedies that achieve corrective justice.'[142]

---

[138] UN General Assembly, 'Basic Principles and Guidelines on the Right to a Remedy and Reparation for Victims of Gross Violations of International Human Rights Law and Serious Violations of International Humanitarian Law: Resolution', adopted by the General Assembly, 21 March 2006, A/RES/60/147.

[139] Shelton (n 131), pp 10–15.

[140] Kent Roach, *Remedies for Human Rights Violations: A Two-Track Approach to Supra-National and National Law* (Cambridge: Cambridge University Press, 2021), pp 2–5.

[141] Rodríguez-Garavito and Rodríguez-Franco (n 60).

[142] Kent Roach, 'Crafting Remedies for Violations of Economic, Social and Cultural Rights' in John Squires, Malcolm Langford and Bret Thiele (eds), *The Road to a Remedy: Current Issues in the Litigation of Economic, Social and Cultural Rights* (Sydney: University of New South Wales Press, 2005), p 111.

Shelton argues that although the 'remedies for cases involving SR will often be classical remedies, such as compensation and declarations of wrongdoing, more often general and structural remedies will be necessary'.[143] Shelton notes that this is not a novel legal dilemma.[144] And Roach expands on this:

> An oversimplified understanding of the remedies for civil and political rights as simple corrective remedies that have no distributive effects is a barrier to effective remedies for socio-economic rights. Many traditional political and civil rights require complex dialogic relief with distributional implications to be effective. Once this is recognised then the remedial process that is required to enforce socio-economic rights will appear much less anomalous, albeit no less complex.[145]

An innovative approach to remedies is therefore required to fully embrace the potential of SR adjudication.[146] We include an examination of the role of structural remedies in Chapter 4 as an outcome associated with a successful access to justice journey.

Our approach to methods, analysis and theory

Analytically, we examine how the notion of justice as an 'empty signifier' is filled with various, often competing, meanings by employing a critical approach to discourse analysis. This criticality directs attention to the role of power, particularly in terms of outcomes and impact. Jan Blommaert says that: 'The deepest effect of power everywhere is *inequality*, as power differentiates and selects, includes and excludes. An analysis of such effects is also an analysis of the conditions for power – of what it takes to organise power regimes in societies'.[147] He urges us to focus on language as 'an ingredient of power processes resulting in, and sustained by, forms of inequality, and how discourse can be or become a justifiable object of analysis, crucial to an understanding of wider aspects of power relations'.[148]

---

[143] Dinah Shelton, 'Remedies and Reparation' in Malcolm Langford et al (eds), *Global Justice, State Duties: The Extraterritorial Scope of Economic, Social and Cultural Rights in International Law* (Cambridge: Cambridge University Press, 2013), p 380.

[144] Ibid.

[145] Kent Roach, 'The Challenges of Crafting Remedies for Violations of Economic, Social and Cultural Rights', in Malcom M. Langford (ed.), *Social Rights Jurisprudence: Emerging Trends in International and Comparative Law* (Cambridge: Cambridge University Press 2008), p 58.

[146] Roach (n 140, n 142 and n 145), Shelton (n 143) and Boyle (n 5).

[147] Blommaert (n 52), p 2 (emphasis in original).

[148] Blommaert (n 52).

Examples of critical approaches to discourse and power can be found in diverse fields of scholarly enquiry, including sociology, sociolinguistics, critical anthropology, language policy and planning (LPP), discourse studies and others. We highlight here some of the interdisciplinary work that inspired our analysis, as well as theoretical and methodological tenets we found helpful in examining our empirical data.

A variety of critical approaches address questions of inequality and (in)justice by examining the complexity and unfolding processes of a broad range of intersecting social issues and discourses. Research agendas have increasingly paid attention to the relationship between language/discourse and society and its links to social inequalities and injustice, power asymmetry, politics, social privileges and so forth. These areas of scholarly enquiry contribute to our understanding of how relationships of inequality are discursively (re)produced, enacted and organized by institutions and actors, through the mobilization of forms of knowledge, justifying and legitimating particular activities, and resulting in certain outcomes. Dominant narratives and discourses are also challenged by different social actors, showing evidence of resistance and resilience, and offering alternate ways to engage in order to promote social justice and address the needs and concerns of disenfranchised or vulnerable groups.[149]

For instance, ongoing work in critical sociolinguistics investigates the ways in which language and labour/work are intertwined with capitalism and social inequality.[150] Various studies have looked at the role of language and training programmes, and the various tactics, logics and forms of expertise that govern processes of migration and migrant workers.[151] Additional attention has been directed to processes of racialization and

---

[149] Ibid, p 8.

[150] Cf. Elisabeth Barakos, 'Language Policy and Governmentality in Businesses in Wales: A Continuum of Empowerment and Regulation' (2016) 35(4) *Multilingua*; Elisabeth Barakos, *Language Policy in Business: Discourse, Ideology and Practice* (Amsterdam: John Benjamins Publishing Company, 2021); Alfonso Deldel Percio, 'Language, the Political Economy and Labor' in James Stanlaw (ed.), *The International Encyclopedia of Linguistic Anthropology* (Chichester: Wiley, 2020); Mi-Cha Flubacher, Alexandre Duchêne and Renata Coray, *Language Investment and Employability: The Uneven Distribution of Resources in the Public Employment Service* (London: Palgrave Macmillan, 2018).

[151] Cf. Diana Camps, 'Restraining English Instruction for Refugee Adults in the United States' in Emily Feuerherm and Vaideho Ramanathan (eds), *Refugee Resettlement in the United States: Language, Policy, Pedagogy* (Bristol: Multilingual Matters, 2016); Alfonso Del Percio and Sarah van Hoof, 'Enterprising Migrants: Language and the Shifting Politics of Activation' in Mi-Cha Flubacher and Alfonso Del Percio (eds), *Language, Education and Neoliberalism: Critical Studies in Sociolinguistics* (Bristol: Multilingual Matters, 2017); Beatriz Lorente, *Scripts of Servitude: Language, Labor, Migration and Transnational Domestic Work* (Bristol: Multilingual Matters, 2018)

marginalization within the labour market,[152] transnational labour[153] and challenging gendered work identities.[154] More applied branches of sociolinguistic research, such as LPP and studies on bilingualism/multilingualism,[155] also address concerns regarding the distribution of (linguistic) resources in society[156] related to education,[157] nationalism and national identities,[158] minoritized languages[159] and disability.[160] The various works centre on issues such as discourse, language, governmentality, migration and inequality, and provide important insights into how

---

[152] Tina Shrestha, 'Learning English, Speaking Hindi: The Paradox of (Language) Integration among Nepalis in the United States' in Feuerherm and Ramanathan (eds) (n 151).

[153] Beatriz Lorente, 'The Making of "Workers of the World": Language and the Labor Brokerage State' in Alexandre Duchêne and Monica Heller (eds), *Language in Late Capitalism: Pride and Profit* (Abingdon: Routledge, 2012).

[154] Doris Warriner, '"The Days Now Is Very Hard for My Family": The Negotiation and Construction of Gendered Work Identities among Newly Arrived Women Refugees' (2004) 3(4) *Journal of Language, Identity and Education*, pp 279–294.

[155] Cf. Monica Heller (ed.), *Bilingualism: A Social Approach* (Basingstoke: Palgrave Macmillan, 2007).

[156] Blommaert (n 52), p 10.

[157] Cf. Flubacher and Del Percio (eds) (n 151); Monica Heller and Marilyn Martin-Jones (eds), *Voices of Authority: Education and Linguistic Difference* (New York: Ablex Publishers, 2001); Francis Hult, 'Nexus Analysis as Scalar Ethnography for Educational Linguistics' in Marilyn Martin-Jones and Deirdre Martin (eds), *Researching Multilingualism: Critical and Ethnographic Perspectives* (Abingdon: Routledge, 2017); Marie Källkvist and Francis Hult, 'Multilingualism as Problem or Resource? Negotiating Space for Languages Other than Swedish and English in University Language Planning' in Maria Kuteeva, Kathrin Kaufhold and Niina Hynninen (eds), *Language Perceptions and Practices in Multilingual Universities* (London: Palgrave Macmillan, 2020).

[158] Cf. Adrian Blackledge, 'The Discursive Construction of National Identity in Multilingual Britain' (2020) 1(1) *Journal of Language, Identity & Education*, pp 67–87; Leonie Cornips and Ad Knotter, 'De Uitvinding van Limburg: De Territorialisering van Geschiedenis, Taal en Identiteit' in Albert Knotter and Willibrord Rutten (eds), *Studies over de Sociaal-Economische Geschiedenis van Limburg LXI* (Zwolle: WBOOKS/Sociaal Historisch Centrum voor Limburg, 2016); Ruth Wodak, 'Discourses about Nationalism' in John Flowerdew and John E. Richardson (eds), *The Routledge Handbook of Critical Discourse Studies* (Abingdon: Routledge, 2018).

[159] Cf. Diana Camps, 'Legitimating Limburgish: The Reproduction of Heritage' in Pia Lane, James Costa and Haley de Korne (eds), *Standardizing Minority Languages: Competing Ideologies of Authority and Authenticity in the Global Periphery* (Abingdon: Routledge, 2018), p 66; Alexandra Jaffe, 'Minority Language Movements' in Heller (ed.) (n 155); Bernadette O'Rourke and Sara Brennan, 'Regimenting the Gaeltacht: Authenticity, Anonymity, and Expectation in Contemporary Ireland' (2019) (66) *Language & Communication*, pp 20–28.

[160] Christine Ashby, 'Whose "Voice" Is It Anyway? Giving Voice and Qualitative Research Involving Individuals that Type to Communicate' (2011) 31(4) *Disability Studies Quarterly*, https://doi.org/10.18061/dsq.v31i4.1724

notions of access, distribution and participation are constituted through the interplay of complex and dynamic processes, often in subtle ways. These studies inspire our own work, as similar dynamics are also evident in conversations with practitioners around the provision and adequacy of services, allocation of funding and access to effective remedies for SR violations concerning social security, housing, food and fuel.

A closer examination of how various discourses are intertwined provides greater insight into access to justice and the adjudication of SR. The aforementioned studies provide multiple tools and diverse theoretical and methodological angles for the analysis of multilayered phenomena. As such, our multidisciplinary approach is particularly suitable for examining the multifaceted nature of SR protection frameworks across the UK jurisdictions.

Approach to data analysis

Our approach to the qualitative data we collected was not designed with a predetermined aim to prove or disprove any particular hypothesis; rather, in keeping with a critical analytic approach, it developed from the bottom up. We are inspired by qualitative approaches that adopt a self-reflexive stance and recognize the data as (co)-constructed by the researchers and researched,[161] rather than entailing a mere process of 'discovery'.[162] Reflexivity not only requires researchers to be transparent in the decisions they make in the research process, but also to be self-critical in their engagement with complex social phenomena,[163] such as social justice, inclusion and exclusion, by closely reflecting on theory, knowledge (production) and practice.[164] As is common in qualitative research, our data analysis was an iterative and recursive process, which began with a deductive thematic analysis, teasing out general themes from the interview responses.

---

[161] Lucy Pickering and Helen Kara, 'Presenting and Representing Others: Towards an Ethics of Engagement' (2017) 20(3) *International Journal of Social Research Methodology: New Directions in Qualitative Research Ethics*, pp 299–309.

[162] Simone Plöger and Elisabeth Barakos, 'Researching Linguistic Transitions of Newly-Arrived Students in Germany: Insights from Institutional Ethnography and Reflexive Grounded Theory' (2021) 16(2) *Ethnography and Education*, pp 402–419, p 405.

[163] Phillippa Wiseman and Jo Ferrie, 'Reproductive Justice and Inequality in the Lives of Women with Intellectual Disabilities in Scotland' (2020) 22(1) *Scandinavian Journal of Disability Research*, pp 318–329.

[164] Alastair Pennycook, 'Introduction: Critical Approaches to TESOL' (1999) 33(3) *TESOL Quarterly*, pp 329–348.

Thematic analysis

In a deductive approach, the search for themes is theory-driven,[165] in this case primarily centring on the aforementioned principles of adjudication with 'access to justice' framed as a journey (see Chapter 4). The benefit of this approach is that it can assess the access to justice journey in relation to SR, while maintaining the flexibility of thematic analysis which can identify important new lines of enquiry throughout the analysis process and provide in-depth insights into the case studies.[166]

In the first stage of analysis, all the interviews collected were coded and analysed individually, drawing on the 'access to justice' building blocks and principles of adjudication.[167] In addition, the potential impacts from the COVID-19 pandemic were included in the analysis. The principles provided a framework for approaching the data with questions that could tease out how the various concepts materialize in practice. As outlined earlier, these questions informed our field guide and guided the data analysis. We formulated questions for each of the building blocks and principles, as presented in Table 1.2.

A critical approach to discourse and policy

After the thematic analysis was completed, the data were analysed again using a critical discursive perspective in order to draw out specific tensions and contestations. It is precisely at junctures of conflict and struggle that we need to engage with local realities and probe more deeply to uncover exactly what is at stake. A dynamic research approach facilitates examining the protections in place as they relate to SR and not only evaluate what is explicitly stated in legal documents but also consider how the mandate to protect SR is taken up and negotiated by different social actors across UK jurisdictions. This widens the focus from compliance or noncompliance and questions of accountability, which highlight the identified gaps, to a broader understanding of how these gaps are constituted in practice and what will be required to close them. Directing our attention to those specific moments where competing tensions are evident will help us dig deeper in order to better understand the processes that may lie underneath the surface.

Elisabeth Barakos and Johann Unger make a convincing argument advocating for a discursive approach:

---

[165] Jennifer Fereday and Eimear Muir-Cochrane, 'Demonstrating Rigor Using Thematic Analysis: A Hybrid Approach of Inductive and Deductive Coding and Theme Development' (2006) 5(1) *International Journal of Qualitative Methods*, pp 80–92.

[166] Lorelli Nowell, Jill Norris and Nancy Moulesothers, 'Thematic Analysis: Striving to Meet the Trustworthiness Criteria' (2017) 16 *International Journal of Qualitative Methods*, pp 1–13.

[167] Boyle (n 5).

Table 1.2: Thematic analysis

ACCESS	How is accessibility imagined and implemented in relation to housing, social security and food/fuel poverty, and what does access to justice or access to a remedy mean when there are problems with the provision of these services?
PARTICIPATION	Can everyone participate in decisions that impact them when seeking to access justice? What enables participation? What are the barriers to participation? Are those most impacted by issues and/or marginalized across lines of oppression able to participate?
DELIBERATION	Are there clear dialogues occurring within multi-institutional frameworks across the legislative, executive and judicial branches? Is there accessible information about these dialogues? Are they inclusive and do they lead to outcomes that meet people's SR?
COMPLIANCE	How can the issues people face be legally challenged? Are there set mechanisms for doing this? Are these mechanisms satisfactory?
ENFORCEMENT	What does review and enforcement mean in practice in each of the four UK jurisdictions?
FAIRNESS	Are there suitable means to challenge unfairness in the system?
COUNTERMAJORITARIAN	Can the solutions to these issues, legal or otherwise, be utilized for everyone or only a select few? How can systems prevent elite-driven litigation?
ACCOUNTABILITY	How are institutions held to account? Are there adequate mechanisms for this?
EFFECTIVE REMEDIES	Are remedies implemented? Are these remedies effective? By whose standard are they effective?
COVID-19	What impact has the COVID-19 pandemic had on practitioners and on the realization of SR?

in order to account for and analyse the multiple layers of ... policy and its concomitant impact, we need to theoretically, methodologically, and empirically engage with policy in terms of both structure and agency, and this is made possible by applying various forms of critical and discursive analysis to ... policy situations.[168]

Discursive approaches are valuable for analysing how laws and policy governing SR protections in the UK impact on rights holders because

---

[168] Elisabeth Barakos and Johann W. Unger, *Discursive Approaches to Language Policy* (London: Palgrave Macmillan, 2016).

it draws attention to the intertextual and interdiscursive links between discourses, as expressed in legal doctrine and articulated by practitioners in the field.

Several concepts integral to discourse analysis would be helpful at this stage, including notions of entextualization, intertextuality and interdiscursivity. A discursive approach to analysis looks closely at language and how it shapes meaning and understanding. Foucault provides the conceptual frame for understanding how language is a socially constructed object and urges us to reflect on how discourse production is instrumental to social change. A useful tool for analysing discourse/ policy is *entextualization*, which refers to the process by which discourses are taken from one context and transferred to a new context, thereby creating a new discourse.[169] However, in this process, an 'ideology of fixed text' interacts with discourse practices that may extend or alter the original text.[170] These 'reformulations' (re)frame the text through other discursive practices and representations; they may be incomplete and open to interpretation. It is this space for interpretation or possible entextualizations inherent in the original text that gives it validity; any attack on its meaning may be framed as a misinterpretation or misrepresentation rather than a fault with the original text, which is seen as neutral (we provide an example of this in Chapter 3 through a closer examination of the interpretation of section 6 HRA). Policy texts emerge in a variety of political processes, and in this sense entextualization in policy documents represents a discursive trace of political debates. The resulting discourses that circulate are considered metadiscourse or, rather, discourse about the discourse, reflecting the social reality of how SR, in this case, should be perceived. Once again, ideologies become a salient factor in how discourses in policy texts are entextualized.

Thus, text and context must not be treated as mutually exclusive units, but rather must be seen as closely connected. This may be achieved by drawing on the concept of *intertextuality*,[171] referring to the notion that each text is situated in relation to other texts and to the structures of language itself. Essentially, the words we use are already imbued with meaning and value because they have been used countless times before. Simply put, 'intertextuality refers to the fact that whenever we speak we produce the words of others, we constantly cite and re-cite expressions, and recycle meanings that are available. Thus every utterance has a history

---

[169] Blommaert (n 52).
[170] Ibid, p 201.
[171] Mikhail Bakhtin, *The Dialogic Imagination: Four Essays* (Austin: University of Texas Press, 1981).

of (ab)use, interpretation, and evaluation, and this history sticks to the utterance'.[172]

Therefore, our words are not neutral and intertextuality allows us to look beyond the immediate context to see how expressions relate to ways of use, including more implicit ways such as indirect speech.[173] The use of language, constructing thoughts and ideas in specific ways, produces certain types of discourse. Interdiscursivity thus refers to the connections between discourses, such as types of discourses, register or style.[174]

What is important for our discussion here is that on account of inherent power relations and potential inequalities, access to contextual spaces, such as those characterized by professional and social status, are often curtailed. Although meaning making in communication is shared between the speaker and listener, it is not necessarily allocated equally or fairly due to disparities in power relations (we share examples of this in Chapter 3 in relation, for instance, to medical assessment procedures for certain social security benefits). The notion of context and the related term *contextualization*[175] are also key concepts for understanding how meaning is created and how particular linguistic resources, including types of discourse produced, are particularly pertinent in situations where power asymmetries prevail. In this sense, the process of contextualization is not necessarily negotiable if 'somebody [imposes] a particular contextualisation on somebody else's words'.[176] The recognition that not everyone is allocated an equal 'voice' is particularly pertinent in relation to the provision of SR. As the data show, the adjudication journey for SR is fraught with inequality and marginalization, and getting one's voice heard can be very difficult. Discourse, as a social phenomenon, is thus often a site of contestation, where inequalities and differences become visible. Directing attention to discourse also helps to uncover the implicit ideologies that have become submerged in the experiences and practices of different actors, such as practitioners, rights holders and duty bearers.

---

[172] Blommaert (n 52), p 46.
[173] Norman Fairclough, *Analysing Discourse: Textual Analysis for Social Research* (Abingdon: Routledge, 2003).
[174] Blommaert (n 52), p 72.
[175] We draw on John Gumperz's seminal concept of 'contextualization', which accounts for the ways in which people make sense in interaction, as well as a recognition of the links between language form and social/ cultural patterns; cf. John Gumperz, *Discourse Strategies* (Cambridge: Cambridge University Press, 1982); John Gumperz, 'Contextualization Revisited' in Peter Auer and Aldo Di Luzio (eds), *Contextualization of Language* (Amsterdam: John Benjamins Publishing Company, 1992).
[176] Blommaert (n 52), p 45.

Researcher reflexivity and the notion of voice

The notion of 'voice', or rather a lack thereof, became salient in the ways that practitioners spoke about advocating for their clients and helping them address SR violations. In contemporary societies, Blommaert says, 'issues of voice become all the more pressing, they become more and more of a problem to more and more people. Voice is the issue that defines linguistic inequality (hence, many other forms of inequality)'.[177] The silencing of voices is an iterative theme across the data relating to the inability for certain social actors to claim a legitimate voice.[178] Directing attention to discourse is therefore important in terms of gaining a better understanding of how being able to make oneself heard and understood may be prevented, or even purposely undermined, by other dominant discourses and mechanisms.

It also prompted our own reflections as researchers about what it means to 'give voice' to others. Bogdan and Biklen define giving voice as 'empowering people to be heard who might otherwise remain silent'.[179] Christine Ashby urges us to question whether we are really giving voice, if it is ours to give, and asks who benefits from the telling.[180] She offers several critical points of reflection on how we, as researchers, engage with a process of 'giving voice'. She cautions that the practice of giving voice may in fact 'reinforce the very systems of oppression that it seeks to redress'.[181] By the nature of our positions as academics, lawyers and researchers, hierarchies of power and privilege are re-inscribed when we presume to give voice to someone else, regardless of our intentions. Reflexivity means recognizing that as researchers we occupy multiple spaces of privilege and power,[182] bringing our own perspectives to bear on the data. In Kathryn Woolard's words, there is no perspective from 'nowhere',[183] meaning that the voices we present to be heard by others are not objective truths, but are mediated and interpreted in the process of our research and analysis.[184]

---

[177] Blommaert (n 52), p 5.

[178] Jo Ferrie and Philippa Wiseman, 'Interrogating the Body: Exploring What It Means to Live with Motor Neurone Disease Using Phenomenology' (2020) SAGE Research Methods Cases.

[179] Robert Bogdan and Sari Biklen, *Qualitative Research for Education*, 3rd edn (New York: Allyn & Bacon, 1998), p 204.

[180] Ashby (n 160).

[181] Ibid.

[182] Plöger and Barakos (n 162), p 411.

[183] Kathryn A. Woolard, 'Language and Identity Choice in Catalonia: The Interplay of Contrasting Ideologies of Linguistic Authority' in Kirsten Süselbeck, Ulrike Mühlschlegel and Peter Masson (eds), *Lengua, nación e identidad. La regulación del plurilingüismo en España y América Latina* (Madrid: Iberoamericana, 2008).

[184] Joe L. Kincheloe and Peter McLaren, 'Rethinking Critical Theory and Qualitative Research' in Norman Denzin and Yvonna Lincoln (eds), *Handbook of Qualitative Research*, 2nd edn (London: Sage Publications, 2000), p 291.

We return to this point with suggestions on how to reclaim the narrative for SR, and how to move from 'giving' voice to facilitating voice and agency. In line with others, we adopt the view that our role as researchers is 'not necessarily in giving a voice to somebody or advocating for someone, but rather in integrating oppressed and marginalised voices into dominant discourses'[185] and to make visible the policy mechanisms and practices that perpetuate a system of inequality.

Structure of the book

This chapter has set out our field of enquiry, situating it at the intersection of various disciplinary perspectives and critical theoretical lenses. The next chapter looks at the international legal framework with a particular focus on the ICESCR and the rights to housing, food, social security and fuel. The purpose of this overview is to equip those new to the international legal framework with the necessary tools to lay claim to social rights as legal rights. Chapter 3 explores our empirical data by setting out what we learned from our various case studies across the UK and the themes that began to emerge in our analysis. Chapter 4 builds on this analysis by reframing access to social justice as a journey from rights violation to effective remedy, drawing on our empirical evidence and international human rights law as a normative framework. Our final chapter deepens our theoretical analysis as we weave strands of emerging data to provide greater clarity on the gaps in accessing social justice in practice and the power dynamics that inhibit progress in this space. We provide recommendations to close this gap and point to future research agendas to continue the discussion. Ultimately we urge those engaged in the field to reclaim the narrative of SR as legal rights in order to counteract discourses that marginalize and exclude those who carry the heaviest burden in the protracted access to social justice journey.

---

[185] Plöger and Barakos (n 162), p 414.

2

The International Human Rights Framework for Economic, Social and Cultural Rights

The rights to housing, social security, food, fuel and an adequate standard of living are rights that form part of the UK's international legal obligations to respect, protect and fulfil economic, social and cultural (ESC) rights. In 1976, the UK government voluntarily ratified the ICESCR, which requires states, including the UK, to progressively realize ESC rights in their domestic legal systems. The rights it contains are broad and range from the rights to housing, food, health, education, social security, labour rights and the right to cultural identity. The international legal framework for human rights is based on the principle of indivisibility recognizing the interdependency of one right being dependent on the enjoyment of another. Often the nature of the obligations under this treaty are misunderstood and erroneously sidelined as being of lesser status than civil and political (CP) rights, such as the right to vote or the right to a fair trial.[1] Other international treaties to which the UK has signed up also include protections for ESC rights, but the focus of this chapter is to better understand the obligations under the ICESCR as the first of the treaties to set out specific obligations for ESC rights.[2] In so doing, it becomes

---

[1] This erroneous sidelining of ESC rights is outdated and the remnants of a 'legal fiction' as found in Mónica Feria Tinta, 'Justiciability of Economic, Social, and Cultural Rights in the Inter-American System of Protection of Human Rights: Beyond Traditional Paradigms and Notions' (2007) 29(2) *Human Rights Quarterly*, pp 431–459, p 432. For a full discussion on the misunderstood separation of rights into separate categories, see Katie Boyle, *Economic and Social Rights Law, Incorporation, Justiciability, and Principles of Adjudication* (Abingdon: Routledge, 2020).

[2] The rights protected in international law fall under international treaties such as the UN (General Assembly), International Covenant on Economic, Social and Cultural Rights (ICESCR), Resolution 2200A (XXI) of 16 December 1966, United Nations,

easier to navigate the broader international and regional framework in connection with ESC rights and the steps that are required to ensure their protection and realization at the domestic level.

This chapter should be read alongside the empirical research and is designed with a non-expert audience in mind. Moreover, it is intended for those who are becoming newly acquainted with the international human rights framework engaging with ESC rights (noting of course the discussion on the right to fuel/energy is a new contribution to this discourse). For those readers who have expertise in ESC rights and are keen to explore the nuanced empirical research and the deeper theoretical explorations of our data, we would direct you to Chapters 3–5 where our discussions on the case studies and theorization of our findings using critical discourse analysis takes place. For those who are interested in a deeper dive into the rights discussed here, including food, social security, fuel and housing, we would also signpost you to the briefings on ICESCR obligations and each of the rights produced under the Nuffield Foundation funded study 'Access to justice for social rights: addressing the accountability gap'. These briefings include wider treaty engagement (beyond the ICESCR), a closer look at the devolved context and a comparative analysis in terms of how these rights are protected in other countries. The focus of this chapter is to explain the international legal obligations and query whether the UK is in compliance with these.

Progressive realization

The duty to progressively realize, or to progressively achieve, ESC rights is derived from international law.[3] Article 2(1) ICESCR states that:

> Each State Party to the present Covenant undertakes to *take steps*, individually and through international assistance and co-operation,

---

Treaty Series, vol. 993, 3; the Council of Europe, European Social Charter (Revised), 3 May 1996, ETS 163; UN (General Assembly), Convention on the Rights of the Child (UNCRC), Resolution 44/25 of 20 November 1989, United Nations, Treaty Series, vol. 1577, 3; UN (General Assembly), Convention on the Elimination of Discrimination Against Women (CEDAW), Resolution 34/180 of 18 December 1979, United Nations, Treaty Series, vol. 1249, 13; UN (General Assembly), Convention on the Elimination of Racial Discrimination, Resolution 2106 (XX) of 21 December 1965, United Nations, Treaty Series, vol. 660, 195; and UN (General Assembly), Convention on the Rights of Persons with Disabilities (UNCRPD), A/RES/61/105 of 24 January 2007, 76th plenary meeting; issued in GAOR, 61st sess., Suppl. No. 49, 'Annex: Convention on the Rights of Persons with Disabilities', 2–29.

[3] The UK has signed up to a number of international treaties which espouse the need to progressively realize rights, including the ICESCR, the UNCRPD and the UNCRC. See (n 2) for full details.

especially economic and technical, to the *maximum of its available resources*, with a view to *achieving progressively* the full realisation of the rights recognised in the present Covenant by all appropriate means, including particularly the adoption of legislative measures.[4] (Emphasis added)

The nature of state party obligations has been further elaborated in documents supplementary to the treaty, in particular General Comment 3 (1990), which was preceded by the Limburg Principles (1986) and reaffirmed by the Maastricht Guidelines (1997).[5] Progressive realisation can be understood as the need to move as expeditiously and effectively as possible towards the full realization of rights.[6] In closer detail, it constitutes a multitude of interlinked obligations which work in tandem to ensure that ESC rights are gradually realized over time. Unpacking the 'subduties' of progressive realisation provides a complete framework from which to analyse both current performance of the state and its commitment to realizing ESC rights over time.

The duty to 'take steps'

Article 2(1) requires states to 'take steps' towards the full realization of ESC rights. Taking steps can be understood as a duty to design strategies and programmes to achieve the full realization of ESC rights.[7] The steps taken must be deliberate, concrete and targeted.[8] This is an immediate and process-based obligation, meaning that the obligation gives rise to the right to a process and the development of a policy to achieve a rights-compliant outcome. It is considered an immediate duty as it is expected that any state, in whatever level of development, can put in place basic steps to progress ESC rights realization. Thus, while the full realization of a particular right might not always be possible immediately, a component of the duty to progressively realize ESC rights is that there is a plan, process or policy

---

[4] ICESCR (n 2), art 2(1).
[5] UN Committee on Economic, Social and Cultural Rights (CESCR), 'General Comment No. 3: The Nature of States Parties' Obligations (Art. 2, Para. 1 of the Covenant)' (1990) E/1991/23; UN Commission on Human Rights, 'Note Verbale Dated 5 December 1986 from the Permanent Mission of the Netherlands to the United Nations Office at Geneva Addressed to the Centre for Human Rights' ('Limburg Principles') (1987) E/CN.4/1987/17; and the International Commission of Jurists (ICJ), Maastricht Guidelines on Violations of Economic, Social and Cultural Rights (1997).
[6] CESCR General Comment No. 3 (n 5).
[7] Ibid, [2].
[8] Ibid.

in place to achieve fulfilment. A violation of this duty can be understood as a failure to reasonably plan, adopt strategies and implement policies or programmes to achieve a specific ESC right. International law applies 'proportionality inflected reasonableness' in assessing whether reasonable steps have been taken, learning from the established practice in the South African Constitutional Court.[9]

The duty to respect, protect and fulfil

States are under an obligation to *respect*, *protect* and *fulfil* all rights.[10] This approach suggests that:

> the individual be protected from interference by the state in the exercise of certain freedoms [respect]; that the state protect the individual from interference by other actors, whose conduct the state is in a position of control [protect]; and that the state provide certain public goods that would be undersupplied if their provision were left to marker mechanisms [fulfil].[11]

The duty to respect requires states to refrain from acting in a way that would undermine the right – that is, taking any action that results in a reduction of the right in law (de jure) or in practice (de facto). The duty to protect requires action to prevent others from interfering with the enjoyment of the right, including private third parties that may be responsible for operationalizing the right – for example, in cases of private actors delivering services that are central to realizing ESC rights, such as housing or the care sector. Finally, the duty to fulfil can be understood as a need to facilitate, promote and provide for ESC rights by taking the necessary steps to ensure they can be enjoyed by all within the maximum available resources of the state. This means that states should take concrete steps to progressively improve ESC

---

[9] This is the test adopted by the UN Committee on ESC Rights under the Optional Protocol. See UN General Assembly, 'Optional Protocol to the ICESCR', A/RES/63/117 of 10 December 2008.

[10] This categorization was first developed by Asbjørn Eide in 1989 and was then later adopted in General Comment No. 12. See Asbjørn Eide, 'Realisation of Social and Economic Rights and the Minimum Threshold Approach' (1989) 10(1) *Human Rights Law Journal* 35; and UN CESCR, 'General Comment No. 12: The Right to Adequate Food (Art. 11 of the Covenant)' (1999) E/C.12/1999/5, [15].

[11] See the discussion in Olivier de Schutter, *Economic, Social and Cultural Rights as Human Rights*, 2nd edn (Cheltenham: Edward Elgar, 2014).

rights to the maximum of their available resources (that is, the amount of revenue the state generates).[12]

The duty to gather and deploy maximum available resources

The duty to gather and deploy the maximum available resources (MAR) to achieve progressive realization can be broken down into subcategories. First, there is an expectation that states will prepare and plan budgetary allocation in advance in order to realize ESC rights. This does not mean that a state must use all of its resources on meeting ESC rights, but rather that it must use the MAR that can be expended for a particular purpose without sacrificing other essential services.[13] In order to meet this obligation, states must ensure that resources are generated in a manner that reflects national economic growth – in other words, that there is a correlation between overall national wealth and the generation of revenue through tax resources.[14] If, for example, government spending on the realization of ESC rights is dropping relative to gross domestic product (GDP) or other government expenditures, while not an immediate violation, it is a 'strong indication that there are available resources but that a particular right has not been prioritised' and thus risks falling short of the MAR obligation.[15]

Second, according to the international framework, the allocation of resources must be *effective* (achieve its aim), *efficient* (achieve the highest quality with minimum waste/effort), *adequate* (sufficient to meet the thresholds of dignity/progressive realization) and *equitable* (prioritization of the most marginalized with the aim of achieving substantive equality). Adequacy can be further broken down into subcategorizations of *availability*, *accessibility*, *acceptability* and *quality* (the AAAQ framework).[16] Third, an important point to note is that resources should not be viewed as purely financial, but human,

---

[12] UN Committee on Economic, Social and Cultural Rights (CESCR), 'General Comment No. 4: The Right to Adequate Housing (Art. 11(1) of the Covenant)' (1991) E/1992/23, [14].

[13] Rory O'Connell, Aoife Nolan, Colin Harvey, Mira Dutschke and Eoin Rooney, *Applying an International Human Rights Framework to State Budget Allocations: Rights and Resources* (Abingdon, Routledge, 2016); see also Philip Alston and Gerard Quinn, 'The Nature and Scope of States Parties' Obligations under the ICESCR' (1987) 9(2) *Human Rights Quarterly*, pp 156–229.

[14] Philip Alston and Nikki Reisch, *Tax, Inequality, and Human Rights* (Oxford: Oxford University Press, 2019).

[15] O'Connell et al (n 13), at 76; see also Alston and Quinn (n 13).

[16] The Danish Institute of Human Rights provides more detail on using the AAAQ framework as a toolbox from which to guide states into practical action. See the Danish Institute for Human Rights, *The Availability, Accessibility, Acceptability and Quality (AAAQ) Toolbox: Realising Social, Economic and Cultural Rights through Facts Based Planning, Monitoring and Dialogue* (2015).

social, technological, informative, natural and administrative resources can also be considered.[17] States can demonstrate how each of these resources is deployed as part of any national strategy/policy. Importantly, compliance with the obligations is largely left to the discretion of state parties to demonstrate what steps it has taken to deploy resources in order to realize ESC rights.

In short, there is no singular framework from which to monitor the use of MAR. Assessment of whether the state is meeting its obligations would be dependent on whether the state can demonstrate and justify that its approach is reasonable. This in turn requires budgetary decision making to be transparent, participatory and accountable, and there remain numerous practical steps that states can take to better realize human rights through their budgets and demonstrate compliance with MAR.[18] As an example, by disaggregating data to better understand how money is spent, uncovering potential hidden gaps in the allocation of funding can illuminate how different groups are impacted, including those groups specifically protected under international human rights law and who face potential intersectional inequality (including women, children, disabled persons and ethnic minorities). This type of budget analysis is already well underway across the UK from the perspective of gender justice, but is also increasingly of interest to human rights practitioners and advocates both internationally and within the UK.[19]

The duty to ensure nondiscrimination

States must ensure nondiscrimination so that access to and delivery of rights occurs in a way that does not exclude groups, particularly those who are marginalized and possibly 'hidden' from the system. Before designing and implementing an inclusive system to deliver/provide a right, decision makers should explore and understand those who are disadvantaged and excluded, including what their needs and vulnerabilities are.[20] The ICESCR

---

[17] Olivier de Schutter, *The Rights-Based Welfare State: Public Budgets and Economic and Social Rights* (Berlin: Friedrich Ebert Stiftung, 2018). See also the concept of resources as developed by Joseph E. Stiglitz et al, *Report by the Commission on the Measurement of Economic Performance and Social Progress* (Paris: Stiglitz-Sen-Fitoussi Commission, 2009).

[18] O'Connell et al (n 13).

[19] For an international perspective on human rights and resources, see OHCHR with the International Budget Partnership, *Realising Human Rights through Government Budgets* (New York and Geneva: OHCHR, 2017). For a gender perspective explored in the UK, see the work of the Women's Budget Group, the Scottish Women's Budget Group, the Wales Women's Budget Group and the Northern Ireland Women's Budget Group under the Women's Resources and Development Agency.

[20] Magdalena Sepúlveda, 'Ensuring Inclusion and Combatting Discrimination in Social Protection Programmes: The Role of Human Rights Standards' (2017) 70(4) *International Social Security Review*, pp 13–43, p 37.

obliges states to guarantee the rights without discrimination of any kind as to race, colour, sex, language, religion, political or other opinion, national or social origin, property, birth or other status (Article 2(2)). To fulfil this obligation, states need to gather and generate disaggregated data across various characteristics, including gender, age, geographical location, ethnicity, health status and economic status. It is important that a reliable evidence base is developed to ensure that people are not denied access to the system or inadvertently excluded from the government's strategy. This approach means that a 'deeper evidence base can improve the understanding of how programmes can best address structural and societal power imbalances, while also encouraging greater equity and empowerment for society's most disadvantaged members'.[21]

The duty to provide a minimum core

The minimum core obligation (MCO) for each ESC right acts as a basic minimum threshold below which no one should fall. It is the absolute minimum criteria that is immediately applicable to all states in the fulfilment of ESC rights. It should be understood as complementary to progressive realization rather than as an alternative. This is important in order to ensure that the MCO of the right remains a floor of realization and does not risk becoming a 'ceiling'.[22] International law suggests that a MCO is legally binding and most likely nonderogable (meaning states cannot justify noncompliance).[23] However, what it means in practice is not necessarily always clear. Some of the UN General Comments elaborate minimum core entitlements, but they do not carry this out in a consistent manner across all ESC rights.[24] Those in favour of the doctrine argue that it is necessary

---

[21] Sepúlveda (n 20), p 36.

[22] Geraldine van Bueren, 'Of Floors and Ceilings: Minimum Core Obligations and Children' in Daniel Brand and Sage Russell (eds), *Exploring the Core Content of Socio-economic Rights: South African and International Perspective* (Pretoria: Protea Boekhuis, 2002).

[23] Amrei Müller, 'Limitations to and Derogations from Economic, Social and Cultural Rights' (2009) 9(4) *Human Rights Law Review*, pp 557–601, p 601.

[24] UN Economic and Social Council, *General Comment No. 13: The Right to Education (Art. 13 of the Covenant)*, E/C.12/1999/10, UN Committee on Economic, Social and Cultural Rights (CESCR), 8 December 1999, para 57; UN Economic and Social Council, *General Comment No. 14: The Right to the Highest Attainable Standard of Health (Art. 12 of the Covenant)*, E/C.12/2000/4, UN Committee on Economic, Social and Cultural Rights (CESCR), 11 August 2000; UN Economic and Social Council, *General Comment No. 15: The Right to Water (Arts. 11 and 12 of the Covenant)*, E/C.12/2002/11, UN Committee on Economic, Social and Cultural Rights (CESCR), 20 January 2003, para 37; UN Economic and Social Council, *General Comment No. 17: The Right of Everyone to Benefit from the Protection of the Moral and Material Interests Resulting from any Scientific, Literary or Artistic Production of Which He or She is the Author (Art. 15, Para. 1 (c) of the Covenant)*, E/C.12/

to ensure that, at the very least, minimum criteria are in place to avoid destitution and that the obligations of progressive realization is not overly flexible. Critics of the MCO doctrine fear that by setting minimum criteria, states will be concerned with achieving minimum standards rather than reaching beyond minimum criteria to progressive standards. There is also disagreement as to what the MCO constitutes in both the literature and practice.[25] By way of a brief summary, these arguments centre on whether the obligation requires all states to meet the same minimum absolute standards or whether a relative standard should apply.[26] Put more simply, should all countries be expected to meet the same core standards or are states parties to the ICESCR free to adopt their own 'core' for ESC rights which better reflect the basic needs, culture and resources of the state? Some prominent commentators question its value to the legal framework as a whole due to the complexity of considerations it raises when implemented.[27]

In practice, the UN legal position has been to place the onus on states themselves to determine what actually constitutes an MCO in any given context, depending on a number of variables such as the right in question, the resources available, the measures taken and the prevailing social, economic, cultural, climatic, ecological and other conditions.[28] Best practice would suggest that states adopt both absolute and relative criteria to assess MCO compliance.[29] Adopting both means ensuring there is an international minimum core entitlement to survival, while also enabling individual states to be able to set a higher standard of core obligations domestically in accordance

---

GC/17, UN Committee on Economic, Social and Cultural Rights (CESCR), 12 January 2006, para 39; UN Economic and Social Council, *General Comment No. 18: The Right to Work (Art. 6 of the Covenant)*, E/C.12/GC/18, UN Committee on Economic, Social and Cultural Rights (CESCR), 6 February 2006, para 31; UN Committee on Economic, Social and Cultural Rights (CESCR), *General Comment No. 19: The right to social security (Art. 9 of the Covenant)*, E/C.12/GC/19, 4 February 2008, para 59.

[25] For a philosophical overview of the tensions which exist in application of the MCO, see John Tasioulas, *Minimum Core Obligations: Human Rights in the Here and Now* (Washington, DC: World Bank, 2017).

[26] David Bilchitz, 'Towards a Reasonable Approach to the Minimum Core: Laying the Foundations for Future Socio-economic Rights Jurisprudence' (2003) 19(1) *South African Journal on Human Rights*, pp 1–26, p 15.

[27] Katharine Young, 'The Minimum Core of Economic and Social Rights: A Concept in Search of Content' (2008) 33(1) *Yale Journal of International Law* 113.

[28] CESCR General Comment No. 12 (n 10), [7]. See also the views of Oxford University's Bonavero Institute in Manuel Cepeda et al, *The Development and Application of the Concept of the Progressive Realisation of Human Rights: Report to the Scottish National Taskforce for Human Rights Leadership* (Oxford: Bonavero Institute of Human Rights, 2021).

[29] Katie Boyle, 'Constitutionalising a Social Minimum as a Minimum Core' in Toomas Kotkas et al (eds), *Specifying and Securing a Social Minimum in the Battle against Poverty* (Oxford: Hart Publishing, 2019).

with their particular constitutional arrangements and individual capacity. Current discussions in the UK on the incorporation of international human rights treatises, most notably in Scotland, have led to novel approaches to defining MCO via participative and deliberative approaches, the development of which has, for example, notably included the voices of those most marginalized and disadvantaged in Scottish society.[30]

Limitations and the duty of nonregression

Rights can be limited according to the principles of legality, legitimacy, and proportionality. States are under a duty to avoid measures which reduce access to or delivery of the right (nonregression). The principle of nonregression, also referred to as the duty not to take retrogressive steps, is key to decision-making frameworks for governments. It imposes a duty on states to ensure that there is no 'backsliding' on rights provision and that progressive realization is not subject to periods of decline, even in the most difficult of circumstances, including national or international crises.[31] Indeed, it is in times of crisis that states must do all they can to avert any backsliding in the realization of ESC rights, as a failure to do so may result in longer-term damage.[32] The UN Committee on Economic, Social and Cultural Rights (CESCR) suggests regressive measures that amount to a 'general decline of living and housing conditions directly attributable to policy and legislative decisions by State Parties, and in the absence of accompanying compensatory measures, would be inconsistent with the obligations under the Covenant'.[33]

In other words, backward steps in the provision of rights are counterproductive to progressive realization. In international law, any deliberate retrogressive measure requires the most careful consideration.[34] Any violation of a right because of a deliberate retrogressive measure can only be justified in the most exceptional of circumstances and states must be able to explain that the action is reasonable, proportionate, nondiscriminatory, temporary and does not breach the MCO, as well as demonstrating that all other potential alternatives were considered.[35] Further, as recent work by Liebenberg on nonretrogression in South Africa has demonstrated, the

---

[30] Aidan Flegg, 'Minimum Core Obligations under the UN Convention on the Rights of the Child: A Scottish Perspective' (2021) 25(2) *Edinburgh Law Review*, pp 238–245.
[31] O'Connell et al (n 13), p 70.
[32] Ibid.
[33] CESCR General Comment No. 4 (n 12), [59].
[34] CESCR General Comment No. 3 (n 5), [9].
[35] Letter from CESCR Chairperson to State Parties, CESCR/48th/SP/MAB/SW (16 May 2012).

doctrine provides a potential tool from which to hold states accountable for regressive budgetary allocations.[36]

Access to an effective remedy

States are under a duty to provide access to an effective remedy if there is a failure to meet the obligations imposed by progressive realization. Effective remedies are discussed in more detail in Chapter 5. Effective remedies include facilitating access to a legal remedy in court if necessary, implying the existence of both a substantive and procedural duty towards rights bearers on the part of state parties.[37] Remedies may also include administrative, judicial and legislative actions.

The three potential functions of a remedy are:

a) its capacity to place the right holder in the same place as was the case prior to the SR violation (restitution);
b) ensuring ongoing compliance with a SR (equilibration); and
c) engaging with the feature of the legal system that caused the rights violation (nonrepetition).[38]

Remedies should also be appropriate, sufficient and accessible in terms of meeting these aims.[39] Domestic remedies for SR violations usually take three broad forms: individual (they help address a violation for one person), programmatic (they address a systemic issue that impacts lots of people) and hybrid (they achieve a mixture of both individual and systemic relief). A singular focus on any one of these could result in problems. For example, courts that focus solely on individual cases may jeopardize relief for a broader class of petitioners, while leaving intact a systemic feature of a legal system that may require attention, thereby being unable to ensure nonrepetition of the rights violation. Likewise, delivering only system-wide relief may leave individual petitioners without access to a remedy. Hybrid remedies that combine individual and systemic relief have been the most 'effective' kind, while also being capable of engaging

---

[36] Sandra Liebenberg, 'Austerity in the Midst of a Pandemic: Pursuing Accountability through the Socio-economic Rights Doctrine of Non-retrogression' (2021) 37(2) *South African Journal on Human Rights*, pp 181–204.

[37] CESCR General Comment No. 4 (n 12), [17]; Dinah Shelton, *Remedies in International Human Rights Law*, 3rd edn (Oxford: Oxford University Press, 2015).

[38] Kent Roach, *Remedies for Human Rights Violations: A Two-Track Approach to Supra-National and National Law* (Cambridge: Cambridge University Press, 2021), pp 2–5.

[39] *Jawara v The Gambia* (2000) ACHPR 147/95 and 149/96, [32].

with structural constitutional principles like the separation of powers and parliamentary sovereignty that seek to constrain judicial power in jurisdictions like the UK.

Hybrid remedies of the kind referred to earlier may also take the form of collective litigation in situations involving multiple complainants and multiple duty bearers. Such 'dialogic' forms of judicial remedies are especially suited to claims involving ESC rights, which may often require an institutional expertise that courts may not have. In such cases, courts may consider the meaning and content of rights, but defer back to the decision maker in relation to the remedy. The court can also play an important role in mitigating interinstitutional confrontation where there may be more than one department responsible (this can include between executive departments at the national level or indeed disputes about obligations between the national and devolved levels). Dialogic forms of judicial remedies can be innovative in nature in an exploration of how best to address systemic issues. In such kinds of remedies, courts can act as an intermediary between different rights holders and duty bearers to find an effective remedy that requires multiple duty bearers to respond as part of a structural interdict (a hybrid remedy that can offer individual and systemic relief potentially involving multiple applicants and multiple defendants). Structural remedies are discussed in more detail in Chapter 5.

Thus far we have explored, in brief, the outlines of the obligation to progressively realize ESC rights and the interlinked multitude of subduties to which this gives rise. Understanding this framework not only provides further clarity to states as to the expected actions in relation to ESC rights, but also a toolkit for advocates, practitioners and rights holders with which to hold states and domestic public institutions to account. The following discussion focuses on unpacking this in relation to the well-established ESC rights to food, housing, social security and fuel. Each has a wealth of international guidance and accompanying academic commentary which cannot exhaustively be covered in this chapter. The aim is therefore to set out key aspects of the rights normative content and explore how other jurisdictions have provided domestic legal protection.

The right to food

The CESCR, the body responsible for overseeing compliance with the right to food (Article 11 ICESCR), provides helpful guidance on this right. General Comment No. 12 provides a comprehensive overview of what is required to respect, protect and fulfil the right, defining the right to food as being met when 'every man, woman and child, alone or in community with others, have physical and economic access at all times to adequate food or means for its procurement'.[40] Similarly, the UN Special Rapporteur on the Right to Food has defined the right as having 'regular, permanent and free access, either directly or by means of financial purchases, to quantitatively and qualitatively adequate and sufficient food corresponding to the cultural traditions of the people to which the consumer belongs, and which ensures physical and mental, individual and collective, fulfilling and dignified life free of fear'.[41]

Additionally, the CESCR highlights 'the right to adequate food indivisibly links to the inherent dignity of the human person and is indispensable for the fulfilment of other human rights', further elaborating that it is inclusive and must not be interpreted in a narrow or restrictive sense[42] – for example, equating it with a 'minimum package of calories, proteins and other specific nutrients'.[43]

A key term used when analysing the right to food is food security, which exists when all people, at all times, have physical and economic access to sufficient, safe and nutritious food to meet the dietary needs necessary for an active and healthy life.[44] The CESCR has outlined the right to food to normatively raise and require the progressive realization of the availability, accessibility and adequacy of food.

Availability

Availability 'refers to the possibilities either for feeding oneself directly from productive land or other natural resources, or for well-functioning distribution, processing and market systems that can move food from the site of production to where it is needed in accordance with demand'.[45] Therefore, it:

> requires on the one hand that food should be available from natural resources either through the production of food, by cultivating land or animal husbandry, or through other ways of obtaining food, such as fishing, hunting or gathering. On the other hand, it means that food should be available for sale in markets and shops.[46]

---

[40] CESCR General Comment No. 4 (n 12), [6].
[41] Jean Ziegler, 'Report of the Special Rapporteur on the Right to Food' [2008] A/HRC/7/5/Add.2, [17].
[42] CESCR General Comment No. 4 (n 12), [4].
[43] Ibid, [6].
[44] UN Food and Agriculture Organization (UNFAO), *Rome Declaration on Food Security and World Food Summit Plan of Action* (Quebec City: UNFAO, 1996), [1].
[45] Ibid, [5].
[46] OHCHR, *The Right to Adequate Food: Factsheet No. 34* (New York and Geneva: OHCHR, 2011).

The Food and Agriculture Organization (FAO) have taken this further and elucidated the need for, at a national level, the facilitation of stable and sustainable food supplies. Sustainability is now a key feature of the right to food and has been further cemented by the Sustainable Development Goals (Goal 2: End hunger, achieve food security and improved nutrition and promote sustainable agriculture),[47] which stretches the definition to encompass a state's overall agricultural production and its place in global food markets.[48]

Accessibility (physical and economic)

The accessibility of food captures both physical and economic realities. The Committee has provided that:

> economic accessibility implies that personal or household financial costs associated with the acquisition of food for an adequate diet should be at a level such that the attainment and satisfaction of other basic needs are not threatened or compromised. Socially vulnerable groups such as landless persons and other particularly impoverished segments of the population may need attention through special programmes[49] ... [while] physical accessibility implies that adequate food must be accessible to everyone, including physically vulnerable individuals.[50]

Adequacy

Explicitly mentioned within the ICESCR, the adequacy of food has been slowly unpicked and is commonly understood as:

> Food must satisfy dietary needs, taking into account the individual's age, living conditions, health, occupation, sex, etc. For example, if children's food does not contain the nutrients necessary for their physical and mental development, it is not adequate. Food that is energy-dense and low-nutrient, which can contribute to obesity and other illnesses, could be another example of inadequate food. Food should be safe for human consumption and free from adverse substances, such as contaminants from industrial or agricultural processes, including residues from

---

[47] UN Department of Economic and Social Affairs, 'The Sustainable Development Goals Report 2023: Special Edition' (DESA, 2023), Goal 2.
[48] UNFAO, *Voluntary Guidelines to Support the Progressive Realisation of the Right to Adequate Food in the Context of National Food Security* (Quebec City: UNFAO, 2004).
[49] CESCR General Comment No. 4 (n 12), [13].
[50] CESCR General Comment No. 4 (n 12).

pesticides, hormones, or veterinary drugs. Adequate food should also be culturally acceptable. For example, aid containing food that is religious or cultural taboo for the recipients or inconsistent with their eating habits would not be culturally acceptable.[51]

From here, the adequacy of food can be broken down into three key components, each providing its own layer of protection:

1) Adequate food must satisfy dietary requirements.
2) Adequate food must be safe for human consumption.
3) Adequate food should be culturally appropriate.

The minimum core requires a minimum essential level of benefits to all individuals and families that will enable them to acquire at least essential healthcare, basic shelter and housing, food, water and sanitation, and the most basic forms of education.[52] With regard to the right to food, states have a core obligation to take all necessary action to 'mitigate and alleviate hunger'.[53] Moreover, if any significant number of individuals within the state is suffering from acute hunger or starvation, it is *prima facie* failing to meet the core obligation of the right. If the state fails to meet these obligations owing to resource constrains, it must demonstrate that every possible effort has been made to use all available resources to satisfy the minimum core.

UK compliance with the right to food

Currently, due to the lack of domestic legal protection for the right to food, alongside rising food insecurity and food bank usage, and a failure to fully implement the UK right to food strategy,[54] it has been widely argued the UK is not complying with the right to adequate food.[55] This is emphasized by the fact that the number of UK food banks in use in the last ten years has grown from fewer than 30 to now well over 2,000.[56] The need for food

---

[51] OHCHR (n 46).
[52] CESCR General Comment No. 3 (n 5).
[53] CESCR General Comment No. 12 (n 10), [6].
[54] Department for Environment, Food & Rural Affairs, *National Food Strategy: Independent Review – The Plan* (London: DEFRA, 2021).
[55] Just Fair Consortium, *Going Hungry? The Human Right to Food in the UK* (London: Just Fair, 2014). See also Nourish Scotland, *Report to UN CESCR: The Right to Food* (58th Sess.) (Edinburgh: Nourish Scotland, 2016).
[56] Glen Bramley et al, *State of Hunger: Building the Evidence on Poverty, Destitution, and Food Insecurity in the UK* (Salisbury: Trussell Trust, 2021).

charity is now widespread across all four nations of the UK.[57] While Scotland and Wales have acted within their devolved competencies to mitigate the worst effects of austerity policies, food bank usage has continued to grow.[58] Other issues with the food system range from the existence of 'food deserts', where there is lack of access to nutritional food, to issues within sustainability of food production and a reliance within the UK on food imports and international trade.[59]

To provide more context, the UK's approach to the right to food has been increasingly raised and criticized by the UN treaty monitoring and reporting as well as by UN Special Rapporteurs. In its concluding observations in 2016, the CESCR raised its concerns 'about the lack of adequate measures adopted by the State party to address the increasing levels of food insecurity, malnutrition, including obesity, and the lack of adequate measures to reduce the reliance of food banks'.[60]

The CESCR also urged the UK to restore the link between the rates of state benefits and the costs of living and guarantee that 'all social benefits provide a level of benefit sufficient to ensure an adequate standard of living, including access to health care, adequate housing and food'.[61] The UN Committee on the Rights of the Child (UNCRC) has recommended that the state should regularly monitor and assess the effectiveness of policies and programmes on child food security and nutrition, including school meal programmes and food banks, and programmes addressing infants and young children, as well as to systematically collect data on food security and nutrition for children.[62] Further concerns were raised by the Special Rapporteur for Extreme Poverty in 2019, with the report identifying 'a shocking increase in the number of food banks' across the UK.[63] The report brought to light the inadequacy of the UK's social security system to meet

---

[57] Hannah Lambrie-Mumford, *Hungry Britain: The Rise of Food Charity* (Bristol: Policy Press, 2017).

[58] UN Human Rights Council (UNHRC), 'Visit to the United Kingdom of Great Britain and Northern Ireland – Report of the Special Rapporteur on Extreme Poverty and Human Rights' (2019) A/HRC/41/39/Add.1.

[59] Tomaso Ferrando and Kath Dalmeny, *A UK right to food law could tackle food poverty and environmental degradation* (Policy Briefing 63) (Bristol: Policy Press, 2018). See also Anna Taylor and Rachel Loopstra, *Too Poor to Eat: Food Insecurity in the UK* (London: Food Foundation, 2016).

[60] UN CESCR, 'Concluding Observations on the Sixth Periodic Report of the United Kingdom of Great Britain and Northern Ireland' (2016) E/C.12/GBR/CO/6.

[61] Ibid, [41].

[62] UN CESCR, 'Concluding Observations on the Fifth Periodic Report of the United Kingdom of Great Britain and Northern Ireland' (2016) CRC/C/GBR/CO/5, [67].

[63] UNHRC (n 58).

the needs of people who are food insecure. This has been echoed by a range of reports.[64]

Further still, the Special Rapporteur on the Right to Food wrote a letter to the UK government concerning 'the deepening level of food insecurity among low-income households, particularly families with children, and the lack of comprehensive measures to ensure their access to adequate food'.[65] Evidently, there is strong international concern that the UK is not complying with the right to food as laid out by international human rights law.

The right to adequate housing

General Comment Nos. 4 and 7 of the CESCR give a comprehensive overview of what is required to respect, protect and fulfil the right to adequate housing (Article 11 ICESCR).[66] General Comment No. 4 defines adequate housing as the right of all persons, regardless of their income or economic resources, to 'live somewhere in security, peace and dignity'.[67]

Applying the AAAQ framework

The following points give a summary of the right discussed earlier and what exactly it involves:

- *Availability*: The availability of services, material, facilities, and infrastructure. In particular, access to natural and common resources, safe drinking water, energy for cooking, heating and lighting, sanitation and washing facilities, means of adequate housing storage, refuse disposal, site drainage and emergency services.
- *Cultural adequacy*: The way in which housing is constructed, the building materials used and the policies supporting these must appropriately enable the expression of cultural identity and diversity of housing to reflect different housing needs.
- *Habitability*: Adequate space and protection from cold, damp, heat, rain, wind or other threats to health, structural hazards, and disease vectors must be ensured. The physical safety of occupants must also be guaranteed.

---

[64] See, for example, Human Rights Watch, *Nothing Left in the Cupboards: Austerity, Welfare Cuts, and the Right to Food in the UK* (New York: Human Rights Watch, 2019). See also Food Foundation, *A Crisis within a Crisis: The Impact of Covid-19 on Household Food Security* (London: Food Foundation, 2021).

[65] Letter from Special Rapporteur to the OHCHR, AL/GBR/8/2020 (5 August 2020).

[66] CESCR General Comment No. 4 (n 12); and UN CESCR, 'General Comment No. 7: The Right to Adequate Housing (Art. 11(1)): Forced Evictions' (1997) E/1998/22.

[67] CESCR General Comment No. 4 (n 12), [7].

- *Affordability*: Personal or household financial costs associated with housing should be at such a level that the attainment and satisfaction of other basic needs are not threatened or compromised. Housing costs should be commensurate with income. There should be protection from unfair rent and unfair rent increases.
- *Accessibility*: To be accessible for all disadvantaged groups.
- *Security of tenure*: For example, legal protection against forced eviction.
- *Appropriate location*: Adequate housing must be in a location which allows access to employment options, healthcare services, schools, childcare centres and other social facilities.
- *Adoption of a national housing strategy*: This strategy should reflect extensive genuine consultation with, and participation by, all of those affected, including the homeless, the inadequately housed and their representatives.

In January 2018 the UN Special Rapporteur on the Right to Housing introduced a set of key principles on which effective rights-based housing strategies should be based.[68] In 2019, this was elaborated upon with 16 guidelines being provided in order to enable states to implement the right to housing.[69] These principles and guidelines, alongside the normative content outlined earlier, provide states with adequate direction to realizing the right to housing domestically. The minimum core, as outlined by the CESCR, requires states to take action to address homelessness and inadequate housing within their jurisdictions.[70] Forced evictions are considered to breach the right to housing and are only allowed in limited circumstances. When a forced eviction does occur, due process should be followed, there should be consultation in advance and an opportunity to seek a remedy, and those being evicted must be offered alternative accommodation.[71]

UK compliance with the right to adequate housing

The right to housing is currently not recognized in law in the UK, despite it being recognized commonly in other jurisdictions. States across Europe have recognized the right to housing in their constitutions.[72] Alongside the

---

[68] Leilani Farha, 'Report of the Special Rapporteur on Adequate Housing as a Component of the Right to an Adequate Standard of Living, and on the Right to Non-discrimination in This Context' [2017] A/HRC/34/51.

[69] Leilani Farha, 'Guidelines for the Implementation of the Right to Adequate Housing' [2019] A/HRC/43/43.

[70] CESCR General Comment No. 4 (n 12), [13].

[71] CESCR General Comment No. 7 (n 66).

[72] The Belgian Constitution provides a right to decent accommodation. The Finnish Constitution imposes a duty on public authorities to promote the right of everyone to housing and the opportunity to arrange their own housing. The Swedish Constitution

expected treaty monitoring on the right to housing, in 2013, the UK was subject to scrutiny by the UN Special Rapporteur on housing, who raised significant concerns about access to the right, including the adverse impact on disadvantaged groups such as those living in poverty, homeless persons, the disabled, the elderly, young people, the Gypsy Traveller community, migrants, Roma and the Catholic community in Northern Ireland (NI).[73] The UK has for a long time provided welfare and benefits through a number of different statutory schemes and when asked about implementing the right to housing, the UK government refers to the broad base of welfare-based legislation that constitutes the structure of the welfare state.[74] However, the legislation, whether derived from Westminster or the devolved level, is not necessarily designed to comply with international standards, which can create a housing rights accountability gap.

In 2016, the CESCR raised concerns about the 'persistent critical situation in terms of the availability, affordability and accessibility of adequate housing … in part as a result of cuts in State benefits'.[75] The Committee also raised concerns about the lack of social housing, forcing households to move into the private rental sector, which is also not adequate in terms of affordability, habitability, accessibility and security of tenure.[76] It noted the significant rise in homelessness, particularly in England and NI affecting mainly single

---

provides that 'public institutions shall secure the right to employment, housing and education, and shall promote social care and social security, as well as favourable conditions for good health'. In Switzerland, the Constitution encourages the development of suitable housing to ensure that any person seeking accommodation for themselves, or their families can find suitable accommodation and that housing schemes should account in particular for the interests of families, elderly persons, persons on low incomes and persons with disabilities. In Spain citizens are entitled to decent and adequate housing. In Ukraine the right to housing includes providing those in receipt of social protection with housing free of charge or at a price that is affordable for them, in accordance with the law. The Portuguese Constitution states that everyone shall possess the right for themselves and their family to have an adequately sized dwelling that provides them with hygienic and comfortable conditions and preserves personal and family privacy. In Poland public authorities are under a constitutional duty to pursue policies conducive to satisfying the housing needs of citizens, in particular combating homelessness, promoting the development of low-income housing and supporting activities aimed at the acquisition of a home by each citizen. In the Netherlands, the Dutch Constitution provides that authorities should provide sufficient living accommodation.

[73] Raquel Rolnik, 'Report of the Special Rapporteur on Adequate Housing, as a Component of the Right to an Adequate Standard of Living, and on the Right to Non-discrimination in This Context' [2013] A/HRC/25/54/Add.2.

[74] UN International Human Rights Instruments (IHRI), 'Common Core Document Forming Part of the Reports of States Parties: United Kingdom of Great Britain and Northern Ireland' [2014] HRI/CORE/GBR/2014; and CESCR (n 60), [122]–[123].

[75] CESCR (n 60), [49].

[76] CESCR (n 60).

persons, families with children, victims of domestic violence, persons with disabilities and asylum seekers. It also raised concerns about the adverse impact that reforms of social security and reductions in financial support to local authorities have had on the right to adequate housing, especially with regard to the criminalization of rough sleeping.[77]

Recent evidence submitted to the CESCR in early 2023 has demonstrated that many of the issues raised in 2016 are still prevalent throughout UK society, and in some instances have deteriorated further. As a UK-wide non-governmental organization promoting economic, social and cultural rights, Just Fair is responsible for preparing the UK parallel civil society report to CESCR as part of the Committee's review of UK compliance. Just Fair has collated a range of evidence from across civic society in England and Wales, and raised a plethora of issues covering the right to housing. To provide some insight into the key areas raised, Just Fair's evidence demonstrates concerns over the extensive use of the 'private rental sector to meet public housing needs and address homelessness' and an overall 'lack of adequate affordable housing and inadequate support to meet unregulated rental costs'.[78] These are structural issues with the delivery of public housing policies which lead to further issues of overcrowding in accommodation and adversely impact the habitability of the housing in question. Furthermore, homelessness remains a significant issue in the UK, where 'families experiencing homelessness are left in temporary accommodation for long periods of time'.[79] Specific groups still suffer far more acutely from a lack of adequate housing, with the evidence providing the insight that the 'accessibility of culturally appropriate housing for Gypsy and Traveller people persists as an inadequately address[ed] issue'.[80]

In relation to Scotland specifically, the Committee highlighted the chronic shortage of social housing particularly for the most disadvantaged and marginalized, such as persons with disabilities.[81] The UNCRC has urged Scotland, as well as other parts of the UK, to strictly implement the legal prohibition of prolonged placement of children in temporary accommodation by public authorities, to reduce homelessness and to ensure that children have access to adequate housing that provides physical safety, adequate space, protection against threats to health and structural hazards, (including cold, damp, heat and pollution and accessibility for children with disabilities), and to introduce a statutory duty for local authorities to

---

[77] Ibid, [51].
[78] Just Fair, *Submission to UN CESCR: Pre-sessional Working Group Submission on Behalf of Civil Society in England and Wales* (London: Just Fair, 2023), p 12.
[79] Ibid, p 13.
[80] Ibid.
[81] CESCR (n 62).

provide safe and adequate sites for travellers.[82] In relation to NI, the CESCR echoed the findings of the UN Special Rapporteur and encouraged the NI Assembly to 'intensify its efforts to address the challenges to overcoming persistent inequalities for Catholic families in North Belfast, including through meaningful participation by all actors in decision-making processes related to housing'.[83]

In 2019 the UN Special Rapporteur on contemporary forms of racism, racial discrimination, xenophobia and related intolerance identified key state failings in the right to adequate housing for different minority groups. For example, the Special Rapporteur's UK report noted that children from Pakistani or Bangladeshi households (28.6 per cent) and Black households (24.2 per cent) were more likely to live in substandard accommodation than those in White households (18.6 per cent).[84] The report noted that the Race Disparity Audit found that in England in 2015–2017, Black African and Black Caribbean households were the ethnic groups most likely to rent social housing (47 per cent and 45 per cent respectively).[85] The Special Rapporteur also drew attention to the 2013 Scottish Parliament Equalities Committee report, which set out that Gypsies and Travellers lived in 'horrendous conditions'. For example, the Committee observed that families paying rent to their local council were 'expected to bathe young children in freezing cold amenity blocks with extortionate heating costs'. It also observed unacceptable conditions in some settlements, including 'a putrid overflowing septic tank', and wrote 'that elderly and disabled people might have to go outside to a toilet block in the middle of a cold, winter's night'. The Special Rapporteur's own consultations with Gypsy, Roma and Traveller communities revealed that access to adequate housing solutions that respect ancestral nomadic traditions remains a major challenge across the UK, especially in Wales.[86] The UN Special Rapporteur on Poverty also identified key state failings in relation to housing stating: 'In England, homelessness rose 60 per cent between 2011 and 2017 and rough sleeping rose 165 per cent from 2010 to 2018.'[87]

---

[82] Committee on the Rights of the Child (CRC), 'Concluding Observations on the Fifth Periodic Report of the United Kingdom of Great Britain and Northern Ireland' (2016) CRC/C/GBR/CO/5, [71(e)].

[83] CESCR (n 62), [50].

[84] Tendayi Achiume, 'Visit to the United Kingdom of Great Britain and Northern Ireland: Report of the Special Rapporteur on Contemporary Forms of Racism, Racial Discrimination, Xenophobia, and Related Intolerance' (2019) A/HRC/41/54/Add.2, [22].

[85] Ibid.

[86] Ibid.

[87] National Audit Office, *Homelessness: Report – Value for* Money (London: Department for Levelling up, Housing & Communities, 2017), p 14. See also Ministry of Housing,

In our study, practitioners highlighted issues with access to justice mechanisms where people do not receive adequate advice or representation in adversarial eviction processes (where often the landlord is represented and the tenant is not). Practitioners also raised concerns with regard to the adequacy of housing standards and insufficient legal rights to ensure adequate heating and ventilation in order to address issues like mould and damp or to ensure habitability of housing – several practitioners noted those in housing need relying on charity to provide gas, electricity, furniture and white goods. Concerns were raised about the lack of accountability in the private sector, including both poor standards of housing and processes of eviction without due process. There are significant barriers faced by different groups – for example, a practitioner reported that the minority Catholic population in north Belfast still constitutes 94 per cent of those in housing need (NI, Esther, Housing activist, NGO for human rights). Likewise, research in Scotland highlighted the implications of the hostile immigration environment, where those seeking asylum are faced with precarious housing conditions (including eviction without notice and unrealistic demands on tenants remaining in accommodation, unable to stay overnight with friends or family and unable to have visitors stay with them). There is sufficient evidence to suggest that even if there are examples of good practice in the provision of adequate housing, the UK is not meeting its international obligation to provide for the right to housing in a manner that is compliant with its international human rights obligations.

The right to social security

Article 9 ICESCR (the right to social security) encompasses the right to

> access and maintain benefits, whether in cash or in kind, without discrimination in order to secure protection, inter alia, from (a) lack of work-related income caused by sickness, disability, maternity, employment injury, unemployment, old age, or death of a family member; (b) unaffordable access to health care; (c) insufficient family support, particularly for children and adult dependents.[88]

The right to social security is of 'central importance in guaranteeing human dignity for all persons when they are faced with circumstances that deprive them of their capacity to fully realise their Covenant rights'.[89] General

---

Communities and Local Government, *Rough Sleeping Statistics, Autumn 2018, England (Revised)* (London: Ministry of Housing, Communities and Local Government, 2019).

[88] UN CESCR, 'General Comment No. 19: The Right to Social Security (Art. 9 of the Covenant)' (2008) E/C.12/GC/19, [2].

[89] Ibid, [1].

Comment No. 19 gives a comprehensive overview of what is required to respect, protect and fulfil the right to social security.[90]

Availability

The right to social security requires the state to introduce a scheme, or a variety of schemes, which are available and in place to ensure that benefits are provided for the relevant social risks that people face in their everyday lives. This includes protection in the areas of: (a) lack of work-related income caused by sickness, disability, maternity, employment injury, unemployment, old age or death of a family member; (b) unaffordable access to healthcare; or (c) insufficient family support, particularly for children and adult dependants.

Adequacy

The right to social security must include the distribution of benefits, whether in cash or in kind, which are adequate in terms of amount and duration in order that everyone may realize their rights to family protection and assistance, an adequate standard of living and adequate access to healthcare. This means that the level at which benefits are set should be enough to ensure a life of dignity.

Affordability

If a social security scheme requires people to make financial contributions, then those contributions should be communicated to people in advance of a scheme being set up. The direct and indirect costs and charges associated with making contributions must be affordable for all and must not compromise the enjoyment of other rights, such as access to housing, food, healthcare or education. Normally there will always be a need to have a noncontributory scheme so that those who cannot generate income through employment will still have access to a social security system to protect them.

Accessibility

All persons should be covered by the social security system, especially individuals belonging to the most disadvantaged and marginalized groups, without discrimination on any of the grounds of race, colour, sex, age, language, religion, political or other opinion, national or social origin, property, birth, physical or mental disability, health status, sexual orientation,

---

[90] CESCR General Comment No. 19 (n 88).

or civil, political, social or other status. Social security services must allow for physical access for those who require it. They should not be provided in a way that excludes certain groups.

In meeting the MCO of the right to social security, the CESCR has outlined specific core obligations as follows:

- To ensure access to a social security scheme that provides a minimum essential level of benefits to all individuals and families that will enable them to acquire at least essential healthcare, basic shelter and housing, water and sanitation, foodstuffs and the most basic forms of education. If a state party cannot provide this minimum level for all risks and contingencies within its MAR, the Committee recommends that the state party, after a wide process of consultation, should select a core group of social risks and contingencies.
- To ensure the right of access to social security systems or schemes on a nondiscriminatory basis, especially for disadvantaged and marginalized individuals and groups.
- To respect existing social security schemes and protect them from unreasonable interference.
- To adopt and implement a national social security strategy and plan of action.
- To take targeted steps to implement social security schemes, particularly those that protect disadvantaged and marginalized individuals and groups.
- To monitor the extent of the realization of the right to social security.[91]

UK compliance with the right to social security

The UK provides social security under various statutory schemes, which the UK government has long argued meets the state's obligations in international law to provide for the right.[92] However, as laid out previously, merely providing a scheme is not enough in and of itself to ensure compliance with the right. The right to social security requires that any scheme provided is available, accessible, affordable and adequate. States must take account of and meet the interlinked duties of progressive realization laid out at the beginning of this chapter. Taking account of this broader set of requirements to satisfy the UK's obligations on the right to social security, the CESCR through its treaty monitoring role has consistently raised concerns that the

---

[91] Ibid.
[92] IHRI (n 74); and CESCR (n 60), [122]–[123].

UK is not complying with the right to social security. In its 2016 review, the CESCR raised concerns in relation to:

> The various changes in the entitlements to, and cuts in, social benefits introduced by the Welfare Reform Act 2012 and the Welfare Reform and Work Act 2016, such as the reduction of the household benefit cap, the removal of the spare-room subsidy (bedroom tax), the four-year freeze on certain benefits and the reduction in child tax credits. The Committee is particularly concerned about the adverse impact of these changes and cuts on the enjoyment of the rights to social security and to an adequate standard of living by disadvantaged and marginalized individuals and groups, including women, children, persons with disabilities, low-income families and families with two or more children. The Committee is also concerned about the extent to which the State party has made use of sanctions in relation to social security benefits and the absence of due process and access to justice for those affected by the use of sanctions.[93]

The 2016 CESCRs concluding observations on the UK outlined some steps it can take to ensure closer compliance with the right to social security, which demonstrates the types of actions the CESCR is seeking. For example, in relation to working conditions in the UK, the CESCR stated: 'Ensure that the labour and social security rights of persons in part-time work, precarious self-employment, temporary employment and "zero-hour contracts" are fully guaranteed in law and in practice.'[94] More specifically in relation to social security, the CESCR called on the UK to:

- review the entitlement conditions and reverse the cuts in social security benefits introduced by the Welfare Reform Act 2012 and the Welfare Reform and Work Act 2015;
- restore the link between the rates of state benefits and the costs of living, and guarantee that all social benefits provide a level of benefit sufficient to ensure an adequate standard of living, including access to healthcare, adequate housing and food;
- review the use of sanctions in relation to social security benefits and ensure that they are used proportionately and are subject to prompt and independent dispute resolution mechanisms;

---

[93] CESCR (n 60), [40].
[94] Ibid, [32].

- provide in its next report disaggregated data on the impact of the reforms to social security on women, children, persons with disabilities, low-income families and families with two or more children.[95]

In addition, the European Committee on Social Rights has concluded that the UK is not in conformity with the right to social security as required by the European Social Charter, which requires states to establish, maintain and progressively improve their social security system.[96] The Committee concluded in January 2018 that the level of statutory sick pay and long-term incapacity benefits are inadequate, as are the minimum levels of employment support allowance and unemployment benefits.[97] Thus, drawing from international monitoring would suggest that currently the UK is not meeting its international obligations in relation to social security provision.

The UK is undergoing a CESCR review at the time of writing, with evidence submitted to the Committee from a range of civic society, including Scotland's National Human Rights Institution (NHRI).[98] The concluding observations and recommendations remain outstanding at the time of writing. However, the evidence submitted gives a strong insight into the plethora of issues that remain in relation to the UK's approach to social security. According to Just Fair's collective evidence on social security in England and Wales, '[s]ocial security is not adequate: both in terms of the underlying level not being enough to meet essential needs, and the failure to update provision to keep parity with inflation and rises in cost-of-living'.[99] The report goes on to discuss a wealth of issues, from the regressive measures of removing the £20 uplift to Universal Credit, to the significant impact of the benefit cap freeze alongside rising prices during a stubborn cost-of-living crisis. Further still, it has been shown that a lack of rights-compliant social security provisions has a direct impact on areas like 'in-work' poverty, which rose 13 per cent between 1996/1997 and 2019/2020. Due to the importance of adequate social security in alleviating poverty, this has led to an increase of children in poverty in the UK, with Just Fair reporting that in some areas of the

---

[95] CESCR (n 60), [41].
[96] European Social Charter (n 2), art 12(1)–(3).
[97] European Committee of Social Rights, *European Social Charter: Conclusions XXI-2* (Strasbourg: Council of Europe, 2018).
[98] For example, Just Fair (n 78). See also Scottish Human Rights Commission (SHRC), 'Submission to the UN's CESCR: Pre-sessional Working Group' (Scottish Human Rights Commission, 2022); and HRW, 'Submission to the CESCR: Review of the United Kingdom of Great Britain and Northern Ireland' (Human Rights Watch, 2023).
[99] Just Fair (n 78).

UK 'the number of children in in-work poverty has risen by 91 per cent since 2014/15'.[100]

It is also increasingly clear that those hit hardest by the inadequacy of the system are often from ethnic-minority backgrounds, raising the discriminatory impacts of social security policy and provision. Significant issues with the overall operability of the system have also been shown, with Just Fair's report identifying further issues of: insufficient capacity to minimize administrative delays, which creates cycles of debt and hardship; the five-week delay for first Universal Credit payments pushing people into debt; the need for further access to adequate advice and an emergency response scheme to help with essential living costs; and the inadequacy of disability benefits to meet the additional costs of living with an impairment.[101] These represent bleak circumstances for many and are merely a selective insight into the extent of issues with social security provision in the UK. This would suggest that significant action is needed by the state to meet its requirements under Article 9 ICESCR.

The right to fuel: an emerging economic, social and cultural right

In our empirical research, we focused on the right to an adequate standard of living (Article 11 ICESCR) and, although not explicitly protected under this right, the concept of the right to fuel was identified as a key component of our research, alongside housing, food and social security. Inherent to the realization of many ESC rights,[102] a right to fuel itself is not made explicit in international human rights law. This means that it is first important to assess the grounding for such a right in the international human rights system. There are brief treaty provisions alluding to its existence which can provide some direct insights. For example, Article 11(1) of the Additional Protocol to the American Convention on Human Rights provides that '[e]veryone shall have the right to live in a healthy environment and to have access to basic public services', including energy services.[103] More pertinently, the Convention on the Elimination of Discrimination Against Women (CEDAW) also raises the need for electricity access for adequate

---

[100] Ibid.
[101] Ibid.
[102] For the connection between fuel poverty and the human right to health, see Marmont Review Team, *The Health Impacts of Cold Homes and Fuel Poverty* (London: Friends of the Earth, 2011); and Michael Marmont et al, *Health Enquiry in England: The Marmont Review 10 Years on* (London: Health Foundation, 2020), pp 84–85.
[103] Organization of American States (OAS), Additional Protocol to the American Convention on Human Rights in the Area of Economic, Social and Cultural Rights ('Protocol of San Salvador') (1999) A-52, art 11.

living conditions in rural areas[104] to combat a range of violations for women living in rural poverty.[105] These provisions provide some footing from which to build; however, when compared to the explicit nature of other human rights, the guidance from treaties themselves is undoubtedly limited. They do not provide an explicit framework for how a right to fuel could be formulated, enacted or enforced in line with a human rights-based approach. Nonetheless, treaty bodies refer to the right to fuel and energy interchangeably, indicating there is a normative right engaged under the treaty. For example, the CESCR and the UN Special Rapporteur have called on efforts to tackle fuel poverty.[106] The UN Special Rapporteur on Extreme Poverty has identified that families are forced to make a choice between heating their homes and feeding their children.[107] The UN Committee on the Rights of the Child and the UN Special Rapporteur on the Right to Food have recognized the importance of fuel for cooking[108] and fuel for transport[109] respectively in connection with the right to food. Several treaty bodies and UN Special Rapporteurs have engaged with 'energy poverty'[110] and discuss energy as a component of the right to an adequate standard of living,[111] the right to health[112] and the right to housing.[113]

---

[104] CEDAW (n 2) discusses the need for electricity in relation to rural women. Article 14(2)(h) states that women should 'enjoy adequate living conditions, particularly in relation to housing, sanitation, electricity and water supply, transport and communication'.

[105] The Committee has commented further on a 'right to electricity' by stating that rural women have 'various energy needs' for cooking, heating, cooling and transportation which require to be met. CEDAW, 'General Recommendation No. 34 on the Rights of Rural Women' (2016) CEDAW/C/GC/34.

[106] CESCR, 'Consideration of Reports Submitted by States Parties under Articles 16 and 17 of the Covenant' (2009) E/C.12/GBR/CO/5. See also Leilani Farha, 'Report of the Special Rapporteur on Adequate Housing as a Component of the Right to an Adequate Standard of Living, and on the Right to Non-discrimination' [2020] A/HRC/43/43/Add.2.

[107] Olivier de Schutter, 'Visit to Spain – Report of the Special Rapporteur on Extreme Poverty and Human Rights' [2020] A/HRC/44/40/Add.2.

[108] CRC, 'Concluding Observations on the Combined Second and Third Periodic Reports of Timor-Leste' (2015) CRC/C/TLS/CO/2–3.

[109] Jean Ziegler, 'Report of the Special Rapporteur on the Right to Food' [2007] A/HRC/7/5/Add.3.

[110] CESCR, 'Concluding Observations on the Sixth Periodic Report of Germany' (2018) E/C.12/DEU/CO/6.

[111] CEDAW, 'Concluding Observations on the Fifth Periodic Report of Kyrgyzstan' (2021) CEDAW/C/KGZ/CO/5. See also HRC (n 58); and CESCR, 'Concluding Observations on the Fifth Periodic Report of Belgium' (2020) E/C.12/BEL/CO/5.

[112] CRC, 'Concluding Observations on the Combined Third and Fourth Periodic Reports of Kyrgyzstan' (2014) CRC/C/KGZ/CO/3–4.

[113] CESCR, 'Concluding Observations on the Third Periodic Report of the Bolivarian Republic of Venezuela' (2015) E/C.12/VEN/CO/3.

Similar trends are developing comparatively. A wide range of countries from Spain, France and Greece to Colombia, South Africa, India, Pakistan and the Philippines recognize or are moving towards recognition of the right to energy/electricity.[114] In 2015, the Colombian Supreme Court concluded that while the 'right to electricity [was] not an autonomous right', it did find that the Colombian Constitution could be read as providing 'a right to receive electricity' through guarantees to a right to life and a right to health.[115] With further direct reference to ESC rights obligations, the Colombian court has also ordered reconnections of households to minimum 'subsistence' (*minimio vital*) amounts of electricity supply to ensure that particularly disadvantaged groups, such as children and the elderly, have access to basic energy services.[116]

The South African Constitutional Court has also provided protection for the provision of electricity. In recognizing its central importance to the realization of rights guaranteed by the South African Constitution, the court opined that 'electricity is one of the most common and important basic municipal services [and] virtually indispensable, particularly in urban society'; its provision is 'a cardinal functions, if not the most important functions, of every municipal government'.[117] Municipalities in South Africa have the constitutional duty to develop a service capacity that can 'meet the basic needs of all inhabitants of South Africa' and secure access in manner that is:

(a) equitable and accessible;
(b) conducive to:
   - the prudent, economic, efficient and effective use of available resources, and
   - the improvement of standards of quality over time;
(c) financially sustainable;
(d) environmentally sustainable; and

---

[114] Marlies Hesselman, 'Energy Poverty and Household Access to Energy Services in International, Regional and National Law' in Martha M. Roggenkamp et al (eds), *Energy Law, Climate Change and the Environment* (Cheltenham: Edward Elgar, 2021). See also Panos Merkouris, 'Disaster Management in EU Law: Solidarity among Individuals and among States' in Marlies Hesselman et al (eds), *Socio-economic Human Rights in Essential Public Services Provision* (Abingdon: Routledge, 2017).

[115] Constitutional Court of Colombia, *María Yamilde Martínez Córdoba v las Empresas Municipales de Cali EMCALI Empresa Industrial y Comercial del Estado. E.S.P.* (Sentencia T-761/15), 11 December 2015. See also a discussion on the case in Marlies Hesselman, 'Right to Energy' in Christina Binder (ed.), *Elgar Encyclopaedia of Human Rights* (Cheltenham: Edward Elgar, 2022).

[116] *Córdoba* (n 115), [4.1].

[117] *Joseph and Others v City of Johannesburg and Others* [2009] ZACC 30, [34]–[39], [47].

(e) regularly reviewed with a view to upgrading, extension and improvement.[118]

Identifying the right to fuel

This section will consider the theoretical basis for a right to fuel. This can be carried out in a range of ways and from differing perspectives.[119] Hesselman's exploration of international, regional and national laws in relation to energy access concludes that fuel and energy are integral to realizing the right to an adequate standard of living.[120] Her work suggests that there is a clear legal basis from which to understand and build a human rights approach to energy access, in which, we argue, fuel plays an integral part.

The iterative approach to developing and defining, or uncovering, the right to fuel echoes the first steps taken towards recognizing a right to water and sanitation,[121] leading to the subsequent adoption of General Comment No. 15.[122] This, we propose, would suggest the right to fuel is a derivative right 'by way of the existence of duties (or other Hohfeldian rights-correlatives) in others'.[123] A similar exploration of the basis for a right to electricity has been carried out by Lofquist, where the conclusion is drawn that like fuel, a right to electricity exists as a derived right from the right to an adequate

---

[118] *Joseph* (n 117). See also Hesselman (n 114).

[119] For example, many explorations of the nexus between fuel/energy and human rights use environmental law as a basis. See Damilola S. Olawuyi, *The Human Rights-Based Approach to Carbon Finance* (Cambridge: Cambridge University Press, 2016); Ross Gillard et al, 'Advancing an Energy Justice Perspective of Fuel Poverty: Household Vulnerability and Domestic Retrofit Policy in the United Kingdom' (2017) 29 *Energy Research & Social Justice*, pp 53–61; Martha C. Nussbaum, 'Capabilities and Human Rights' (1997) 66(2) *Fordham Law Review*, pp 273–300; Amartya Sen, 'Human Rights and Capabilities' (2005) 6(2) *Journal of Human Development*, pp 151–166; Giovanni Frigo et al, 'Energy and the Good Life: Capabilities as the Foundation of the Right to Access Energy Services' (2021) 22(2) *Journal of Human Development and Capabilities*, pp 218–248.

[120] Hesselman (n 114). See also Marlies Hesselman et al, 'Energy Poverty in the COVID-19 Era: Mapping Global Responses in Light of Momentum for the Right to Energy' (2021) 81 *Energy Research & Social Science*, pp 1–11.

[121] For an overview of the development of the right to water and a recent discussion of the basis for derivative rights, see Dovilė Stankevičiūtė, 'The Legal Ground for the Right to Water: Between a Derivative and an Independent Human Right' (2019) 2(20) *Law Review*, pp 26–43; and Jaakko Kuosmanen, 'Repackaging Human Rights: On the Justification and the Function of the Right to Development' (2015) 11(3) *Journal of Global Ethics*, pp 303–320.

[122] CESCR, 'General Comment No. 15: The Right to Water (Art. 11 and 12 of the Covenant)' (2003) E/C.12/2002/11 states that the 'human right to water is indispensable for leading a life in human dignity. It is a prerequisite for the realisation of other human rights'.

[123] Lawrence C. Becker, 'Three Types of Rights' (1980) 13 *Georgia Law Review*, pp 1197–1220, p 1200.

standard of living.¹²⁴ Lofquist concludes: 'We should therefore understand electricity as a derived right. A right to electricity is often necessary to protect our basic rights, for example, to life and to such material things as adequate housing, healthcare, and education. Still, it is life, housing, health care and education that are essential, not electricity.'¹²⁵ With a similar line of reasoning, a right to fuel is better understood in the human rights framework as a derived right from its essential nature to the realization of a plethora of ESC rights and, in cases of more extreme deprivation, some CP rights. Moreover, the Human Rights Committee (HRC) responsible for monitoring the ICCPR provides that 'the duty to protect life also implies that states parties should take appropriate measures to address the general condition in society that may give rise to direct threats to life or prevent individuals from enjoying their right to life with dignity'.¹²⁶ The HRC continues to provide the following:

> The measures called for addressing adequate conditions for protecting the right to life include, where necessary, measures designed to ensure access without delay by individuals to essential goods and *services such as food, water, shelter, health-care, electricity and sanitation*, and other measures designed to promote and facilitate adequate general conditions such as the bolstering of effective emergency health services, emergency response operations (including fire-fighters, ambulances and police forces) and social housing programs'.¹²⁷

From this guidance, not only does the HRC emphasize the need for positive action in relation to protecting the CP right to life and once again undermine the poorly conceived, but once widely held understandings of negative and positive human rights duties, it also establishes electricity alongside other essential basic services explicitly or implicitly recognized as human rights within the ICESCR. The ECHR has also demonstrated willingness to protect CP rights due to deprivation caused by lack of access to fuel. A successful challenge of the right to life on the grounds of destitution, of which fuel was an aspect, was found in *Nencheva v Bulgaria*.¹²⁸ In this case, the court found the State of Bulgaria had failed to

---

[124] Lars Lofquist, 'Is There a Universal Human Right to Electricity?' (2020) 24(6) *International Journal of Human Rights*, pp 711–723.
[125] Ibid, at 721. See also Stephen Tully, 'Access to Electricity as a Human Right' (2006) 24(4) *Netherlands Quarterly of Human Rights*, pp 557–587.
[126] HRC, 'General Comment No. 36: Art. 6 (Right to Life)' (2019) CCPR/C/GC/36, [26].
[127] HRC General Comment No. 36 (n 126) (emphasis added).
[128] *Nencheva and Others v Bulgaria* [2013] ECHR 554.

act sufficiently in relation to a care home where its residents were facing destitution, without access to nutritious food, sufficient heating and general basic care. Fifteen children and young adults lost their lives in the state institution, despite warnings about the risks residents were facing. In its reasoning, the court laid out that due to the vulnerability of the children, their role in providing care, and knowledge of the conditions the institution was facing, there had been a clear breach of Article 2 ECHR (the right to life).[129] While *Nencheva* provides the clearest example of violated ESC rights giving rise to a breach of Article 2, there are several other important cases in which the court has raised the impact poor heating (or a lack of it altogether) can have on patients of hospitals and inmates of state prisons.[130] While these cases do not discuss fuel directly, or a right to it, the willingness of the court to associate heating as a core element of securing a person's basic needs would suggest that in very serious cases of fuel poverty, where it is so severe that here is a risk to life, the court could find a violation of Article 2. As a different example, in the Netherlands, the Supreme Court recognized that Article 2 and Article 8 (the right to private and family life) require the state to undertake more ambitious climate action, with significant implications for national energy policies.[131] As a result of the case, the government announced a €3 billion spending package to subsidize, among other things, renewable energy projects and home refits.[132]

Meaning and content of the right to fuel

Having discussed viewing fuel as a derivative right necessary for the realization of many ESC rights, our attention must now turn to defining what the core elements of such a right would be. As a derivative right without clear international guidance, these elements must be derived from elaborations of other rights, such as the right to an adequate standard of living and health. The right to an adequate standard of living acts essentially as a precondition for a life lived with dignity and consists of the right to housing, food, clothing, water and sanitation.[133] We can therefore assess

---

[129] Ibid.
[130] *Câmpeanu v Romania*, Application No. 47848/08 ECHR 2014. See also *Muršić v Croatia*, Application No. 7334/13 ECHR 2016.
[131] *Uganda Foundation v State of the Netherlands* [2015] HAZA C/09/00456689, [2.1]. See also Margaretha Wewerinkle-Singh, 'A Human Rights Approach to Energy: Realising the Rights of Billions within Ecological Limits' (2021) 31(1) *Review of European, Comparative & International Environmental Law*, pp 16–26.
[132] *Uganda* (n 131).
[133] Asbjørn Eide, 'Adequate Standard of Living' in Daniel Moeckli et al (eds), *International Human Rights Law* (Oxford: Oxford University Press, 2022).

the relationship between fuel and these rights to establish its basis in the international legal framework. Here we will focus on fuel and the right to adequate housing due to how the issue is defined and measured within the UK;[134] however, it is important to recognize that a similar process could be carried out in relation to the right to health or the right to food.[135]

The right to adequate housing has been provided plenty of international guidance, with General Comment Nos. 4 and 7 setting out a comprehensive overview of the right.[136] General Comment No. 4, for example, espouses the need for the availability of services in relation to adequate housing. The CESCR provides:

> An adequate house must contain certain facilities essential for health, security, comfort and nutrition. All beneficiaries of the right to adequate housing should have sustainable access to natural and common resources, safe drinking water, energy for cooking, heating and lighting, sanitation and washing facilities, means of food storage, refuse disposal, site drainage and emergency services.[137]

Here, General Comment No. 4 emphasizes the need for the 'availability of services', of which fuel will be an integral part. This language is echoed by the European Social Charter, which provides that adequate housing requires 'all basic amenities, such as water, heating, waste disposal, sanitation facilities, [and] electricity'.[138] Thus, availability forms our first key element. Affordability is another key component underpinning the right to fuel. General Comment No. 4 discusses the need for 'personal or household financial costs associated with housing to be at such a level that the attainment and satisfaction of other basic needs are not threatened or compromised'.[139] With most UK households heated by fuel, gas or electricity, its affordability will primarily dictate the overall affordability of maintaining an adequate home. Finally, General Comment No. 4 lays out the condition of habitability in meeting the right to adequate housing. Housing must have 'adequate space and protection from cold, damp, heat, rain, wind or other threats to health'.[140] In colder climates, access to

---

[134] Andrew Burlinson et al, 'The Elephant in the Energy Room: Establishing the Nexus between Housing Poverty and Fuel Poverty' (2018) 72(c) *Energy Economics*, pp 135–144.
[135] Ben Christman and Hannah Russell, 'Readjusting the Political Thermostat: Fuel Poverty and Human Rights in the UK' (2016) 2(2) *Journal of Human Rights in the Commonwealth*, pp 14–31.
[136] CESCR General Comment No. 4 (n 12) and CESCR General Comment No. 7 (n 66).
[137] CESCR General Comment No. 4 (n 12), [8(b)].
[138] European Social Charter (n 2), art 31.
[139] CESCR General Comment No. 4 (n 12), [8(c)].
[140] Ibid, [8(d)].

fuel means access to heating, which is an essential tool in staving off the cold and the inevitable creep of damp which follows. This leads to the conclusion that fuel must be accessible to homes in a sufficient quantity to meet the condition of habitability, such as in particularly cold or more rural conditions.

The following key criteria can be understood as constituting the right to fuel:

Availability: Fuel must be made reliably available to all through the development of suitable infrastructure, facilities and delivery.

Accessibility: Fuel must be made accessible to all without discrimination, including for all included in disadvantaged or marginalized groups, in sufficient quantities so as to ensure the adequate habitability of their home.

Affordability: Fuel must be made affordable for all. Where fuel is unaffordable or prices rise suddenly, support mechanisms should be made available to those who are vulnerable to fuel poverty. The cost of fuel should be at such a level that the attainment and satisfaction of other basic needs are not threatened or compromised.

These elements of the right are clearly interlinked, but there is a further important element to consider which is not directly derived from an ESC right. Through its nexus with Goal 7 of the Sustainable Development Goals, which dictates access to 'affordable, reliable, sustainable and modern energy for all',[141] the right to fuel must also have an element of sustainability included. Again, delving into debates on energy rights and justice, it is clear that further action is required to ensure obligations around the provision of fuel do not present a choice between heating your home and reducing your carbon footprint.[142]

Sustainability: The availability of fuel should not come at the expense of sustainable development. Where there is a transition from fossil fuels to more renewable sources of energy, this must be carried out in a manner which does not undermine the availability, accessibility or affordability of fuel. In short, the cost of energy transitions cannot be footed by those least able to afford it.

---

[141] UN Department of Economic and Social Affairs, (n 47), [Goal 2].

[142] See Jan Rosenow et al, 'Fuel Poverty and Energy Efficiency Obligations: A Critical Assessment of the Supplier Obligation in the UK' [2013] *Energy Policy*, pp 1194–1203 for a discussion on the tension in alleviating fuel poverty.

Progressive realization of the right to fuel

As explored at the outset of this chapter, the nature of the progressive realization obligation requires a multitude of interlinked duties to be met, including that states respect, protect and fulfil the right to fuel. This means that states should progressively achieve the right to fuel to the maximum of their available resources. They must take steps to refrain from acting in a way that would undermine the right to fuel – that is, take any action that results in reducing the right (the duty to respect). For example, the state must not interfere with the production and distribution of fuel in a manner which would undermine the realization of the right. It must also take action to prevent others from interfering with enjoyment of the right, including private third parties that are responsible for the production and delivery of fuel in the UK (the duty to protect). This requires the UK to have appropriate regulatory mechanisms in place to ensure that private ownership of fuel production does not interfere with the realization of fuel as a human right. Finally, the state must facilitate, promote and provide the right to fuel by ensuring that the right can be enjoyed by all to the maximum of its available resources (the duty to fulfil). Fulfilling the right to fuel could take many forms, from the expansion of renewable infrastructure, to putting in place appropriate social security schemes to ensure that the worst consequences of global markets and private companies fuel price rises do not fall on those who can least afford it.

Furthermore, the UK must demonstrate how it is using the maximum of its available resources to deliver upon the right. Where the violation of an ESC right is evident throughout a state, there is an increased justificatory burden for the state to show that the violations took place despite its use of MAR. Evidently connected to budgetary decision making, the duty requires the UK government to adequately generate, allocate and spend resources to the maximum extent possible in order to ensure that people have access to and can afford fuel. This obligation generally requires the allocation of further financial resources from the central government. As the CESCR's recent concluding observations on Belgium reiterate: 'The Committee recommends that the State party take the measures necessary to ensure a minimum supply of energy, even when a meter is installed. It also recommends that the State party expand coverage for beneficiaries of the social tariff, by allocating more financial resources to the Gas and Electricity Fund.'[143] The CRC too has raised the need for transparency of financial resources being allocated to deliver basic services for children in Greece in relation to energy.[144] When considering these concluding observations

---

[143] CESCR (n 111).
[144] CRC, 'Concluding Observations of the Committee on the State Report on Implementation of the CRC' (2012) CRC/C/GRC/CO/2–3.

and taking into account the many other instances where guidance has been provided on the MAR duty,[145] it is clear that the generation, allocation and expenditure of a state's resources should adequately account for the need to divert resources to ensuring the right to fuel is being progressively realized.

There is a further area to consider. The obligation to spend MAR within a state is often discussed purely in relation to financial resources. However, with a right to fuel, questions can be raised in relation to a state's natural resources, and these being used to the maximum extent possible to ensure the realization of the right to fuel. De Schutter notes that 'a State's population has a right to enjoy a fair share of the financial and social benefits that natural resources can bring'.[146] Also coined natural capital in wellbeing economics, natural resources can refer to a state's environmental assets, biodiversity, soil and ecosystems. The use of natural resources, particularly in relation to the transition to renewable energy, should therefore also be considered when assessing whether a state has maximized all its resources to ensure the availability and affordability of fuel. The potential for renewable energy production in Scotland, as explored by the government and a plethora of private companies,[147] provides a good example of the opportunities available for producing sustainable fuel at a better price for the population and consequently maximizing its use of resources beyond the confines of finance.

In short, the right to fuel can be progressed in a plethora of ways and should not be viewed restrictively as simply requiring an increase in fuel social security payments or regulation of energy companies. Progressive realization of the right to fuel should be directly focused on and captured within the many actions taken to ensure the accessibility, availability, affordability and sustainability of fuel for all now and in the future.

The MCO for the right to fuel might include access to sufficient fuel, without discrimination, to protect against dangerously cold weather conditions. When viewed through the lens of the right to food, it is evident there would be an MCO to ensure adequate fuel for cooking and adequate refrigeration. The CESCR in its concluding observations on Belgium did raise the need to ensure everyone has a 'minimum supply of energy', with concerns raised over energy services being switched off due to a lack of payment.[148] While this is not an explicit mention of MCOs, it does provide a nod to the understanding that there is a minimum essential level of fuel required within a household in order for people to live a dignified life.

---

[145] Farha (n 68).
[146] De Schutter (n 17).
[147] Scottish Affairs Committee, *Renewable Energy in Scotland Report* (London: House of Commons, 2021).
[148] CESCR (n 111).

UK compliance with the right to fuel

Fuel poverty in the UK has been raised on several occasions by these monitoring mechanisms, with significant concerns raised over both the extent of fuel poverty and its impact. In 2009, the CESCR's concluding observations on the UK laid bare the issue, stating that 'poverty and fuel poverty, especially among children, remain widespread in the State party, despite the level of its economic development'.[149] The CESCR also raised the need to 'intensify the efforts to combat poverty, fuel poverty, and social exclusion, in particular with regard to the most disadvantaged and marginalized individuals and groups and in the most affected regions and city areas'.[150] However, it is interesting that in 2016, when the CESCR delivered its next concluding observation on the UK, there was no reference to fuel poverty.[151] While there was widespread acknowledgement of poverty, including its many manifestations and their ramifications for ESC rights realization, the CESCR overlooked the specific issue of fuel poverty. Fuel poverty was again raised in 2019 in relation to the privatization of energy companies and its impact on the affordability of fuel. Since the late 1980s, energy companies in the UK have been privatized. In fact, there have been no publicly owned energy companies in the UK since 1990. In 2019 Alston reported:

> The United Kingdom was a pioneer in privatizing previously public services across a wide range of sectors. In 2018, the National Audit Office concluded that the private finance initiative model had proved to be more expensive and less efficient than public financing in providing hospitals, schools, and other public infrastructure. Studies of the results of privatization in sectors such as water, energy and public transportation suggest that prices have been raised excessively while access for low-income households has been restricted and capital investments have been inadequate.[152]

These comments came before the fuel poverty crisis developing in the UK.

Fuel poverty is driven by three key factors: a household's income, its fuel costs, and its energy consumption, which is affected by the energy efficiency of the home.[153] This means that when discussing fuel poverty, research can range from the inefficiency of the UK's housing stock (for example, cladding and

---

[149] CESCR (n 62), [28].
[150] Ibid.
[151] CESCR (n 60).
[152] UNHRC (n 58).
[153] Suzanna Hinson, Paul Bolton and Steven Kennedy, *Fuel Poverty in the UK* (London: House of Commons Library, 2024).

insulation) to the proportion of people's income spent on heating their home to a safe standard. Fuel poverty is defined and measured differently across England, Wales, Scotland, and Northern Ireland, partly because energy is a devolved area, meaning different legal and policy frameworks apply.[154] This is not to say that wider UK policy is not the main driver for fuel poverty within each nation, with, for example, the inadequacy of social security payments playing a pivotal role. The use of different definitions and measures throughout the UK creates the problem of providing decisive figures relating to fuel poverty throughout the whole of the UK. Each nation is therefore dealt with in turn subsequently. Whatever figures are relied upon, the once rarely raised issue of fuel poverty in the UK has grown to be recognized widely as an epidemic afflicting millions of households across the UK's nations. While not every case of fuel poverty would necessarily give rise to the violation of ESC rights, it certainly serves as a strong indication that the UK is not meeting its obligations. Where the government has brought in mitigation packages, such as Winter Fuel Payments, the Committee on Fuel Poverty has highlighted how much of the money spent on these policies is not reaching those who need it. The Committee in 2021 reported:

> It is unacceptable that out of a current total budget of over £2.55 billion per year allocated to improving energy efficiency and assisting householders to pay their fuel bills, only about £0.4 billion per year is received by fuel poor households. It is also unacceptable that although there are current plans to increase the total budget to circa £3 billion per year, it is only proposed to allocate circa £0.6 billion per year to the fuel poor.[155]

Thus, while large figures of money can be pointed to as action on fuel poverty by the UK government, it is clear that those who need the most help are not always receiving it. This suggests that while steps are being taken, they are not adequately targeted, concrete and deliberate as would be required when using a human rights approach to tackling fuel poverty.

The evolution of changing definitions for fuel poverty in England has been well documented and need not be reiterated in full here.[156] What is important to grasp is that, since Boardman's 1991 book defined it as covering households whose fuel expenditure on all energy services exceeded 10 per cent of their income, the definition has moved several times,[157] the most

---

[154] Ibid.
[155] Committee on Fuel Poverty, *Annual Report* (London: Committee on Fuel Poverty, 2021).
[156] Richard Moore, 'Definitions of Fuel Poverty: Implications for Policy' [2012] *Energy Policy*, pp 19–26.
[157] Brenda Boardman, *Fuel Poverty: From Cold Homes to Affordable Warmth* (London: Belhaven Press, 1991).

notable changes being the introduction of the Low Income High Costs (LIHC) measure in 2013[158] and the recently introduced Low Income Low Energy Efficiency (LILEE) measure in 2021. Both use the English Housing Survey data to assess the extent of fuel poverty.[159] It is an anonymized survey which adds to the difficulty in prioritizing or targeting resources for those most in need. The LIHC measure defined a household as fuel poor if the amount they would need to spend to keep their home at 'an adequate standard of warmth' was above the national median level and if they spent that amount, their leftover income would be below the poverty line.[160] It was criticized on a range of grounds, from its complexity to the fact that it placed an emphasis on the energy efficiency of homes over the ability of people to afford basic energy.[161] According to Middlemiss, it had the overall impact 'to further entrench the idea that reform of the energy market and addressing income inequality are policy options that are outside the realms of possibility'.[162] Importantly, the change in measure helped skew the reality faced by households in England: '[the] numbers of households officially recognised as experiencing fuel poverty were approximately halved by this change in measure'.[163] This is further compounded by the fact that the fuel poverty targets in England are not based on alleviating families from fuel poverty, but are set on the households' Energy Performance Certificates.[164] The devolved governments in the UK have not adopted the same measures or targets. This reflects the difficulty in truly assessing the extent of the issue in England; however, recent data have been released in relation to the new LILEE measure and provide some insight.

The current LILEE measure defines a household as fuel poor if 'they are living in a property with an energy efficiency rating of band D, E, F, or G' and their 'disposable income (income after housing costs and energy needs) would be below the poverty line'.[165] It is thus a continuation of

---

[158] For further information on research examining and proposing the LIHC measure for fuel poverty, see John Hills, *Getting the Measure of Fuel Poverty* (London: Hills Fuel Poverty Review, 2012).

[159] Department for Energy Security & Net Zero, *Fuel Poverty Methodology Handbook (LILEE)* (London: Department for Energy Security & Net Zero, 2023).

[160] Hinson et al (n 153).

[161] Lucie Middlemiss and Ross Gillard, 'Fuel Poverty from the Bottom-up: Characterising Household Energy Vulnerability through Lived Experience of the Fuel Poor' (2015) 6 *Energy Research & Social Science*, pp 164–154; and Moore (n 156).

[162] Lucie Middlemiss, 'A Critical Analysis of the New Politics of Fuel Poverty in England' (2017) 37(3) *Critical Social Policy*, pp 425–443, p 426.

[163] Middlemiss (n 162).

[164] Energy Performance of Buildings (Certificates and Inspections) (England and Wales) Regulations (2007).

[165] Hinson et al (n 153).

the approach of LIHC with a priority focus on energy efficiency over the percentage of income spent on fuel. According to this measure and the latest statistical data available, there is an estimated 3.16 million households living in fuel poverty in England.[166] According to official statistics and trends, fuel poverty in England has declined steadily since 2010, despite austerity policies.[167] Questioning official figures further, the government projected fuel poverty levels would fall to 12.5 per cent of households in 2022, despite the extortionate rise in energy prices. Instead, fuel poverty remained consistent with the previous three years. Unsurprisingly, these figures lie in direct conflict with those estimated using the original 10 per cent measure. Under this measure, the figure jumps to around 4.5 million households living in fuel poverty, and that does not yet take into account the 54 per cent price increase due to the lifting of the energy cap in 2022. Further clarity on the true scale of fuel poverty can be sought from assessing the fuel poverty gap.

The fuel poverty gap is a further measure that is used and is defined as the reduction in required spending which would take a household out of fuel poverty. It is thus more intimately tied to the proportion of income spent on fuel. According to official figures, the fuel poverty gap was expected to rise from £223 in 2020 to £258 in 2022; however, it reached £348 in 2022, and rose a further 20 per cent to £417 in 2023.[168] The UK government's assertion that fuel poverty is in decline in England while the fuel poverty gap has increased is indicative of the methodological challenges. There are also concerns that the strategies and policies brought in to reduce fuel poverty in England specifically, such as energy rebates, may be leading already low-income households into further debt.[169] While the idea of support is welcome, more cynically, the way in which some of the targeted policies have been designed would suggest that the government is more focused on short-term reductions of fuel poverty figures over dealing with its underlying causes or long-term entrenchment within society.

Across the UK's four nations, Scotland faces the most challenges in ensuring the availability, accessibility and affordability of fuel for all. Cold weather conditions require increased spending on heating homes. The cost of heating rural households across the highlands and islands of Scotland add further to the mounting concern about how to heat Scotland's homes as fuel

---

[166] Department for Energy Security & Net Zero, *Fuel Poverty Statistics* (London: Department for Energy Security & Net Zero, 2021).
[167] Ibid.
[168] Ibid.
[169] Rachel A. LaFortune, 'UK Energy Price Hike Threatens to Worsen Poverty Crisis' [2022] *Human Rights Watch*, 9 February.

prices continue to rise.[170] Up to 2019, Scotland used Boardman's original 10 per cent measure to ascertain the extent of fuel poverty throughout the population. For many years under this measure, Scotland's fuel poverty steadily increased to a peak of 39 per cent of the population in 2011 before beginning to fall to around 25 per cent in 2018.[171] The failure to alleviate fuel poverty in Scotland, despite devolved powers, targets and strategies, led to the establishment of two working groups tasked with assessing the definition of fuel poverty in Scotland, with England having recently adopted the LIHC measure, as well as designing policy responses for its alleviation.[172] This led to the unanimous passing of the Fuel Poverty (Targets, Definition and Strategy) (Scotland) Act in 2019, which brought in an updated measure for fuel poverty.

Under the Fuel Poverty Act, a household is considered fuel poor if after housing costs have been deducted, more than 10 per cent (20 per cent for extreme fuel poverty) of its net income is required to pay for its reasonable fuel needs and if after further adjustments are made to deduct childcare costs and any benefits received for a disability or care need, its remaining income is insufficient to maintain an acceptable standard of living, which is defined as being at least 90 per cent of the UK Minimum Income Standard (MIS).

There are several notable aspects of the new definition. First, the measure clearly differs from that adopted in England and continues to have a primary focus on expenditure on fuel over energy efficiency. This means that the measure used is much more sensitive to changes in energy prices as these have a direct impact on the proportion of income spent on fuel within a household. As the primary cause of increasing fuel poverty is currently related to fuel prices, this measure would seem better suited to capturing the full extent of the problem. Additionally, the measure discusses the need for income for an 'adequate standard of living'. While a right to fuel is not explicitly recognized in Scotland, this measure makes the connection between adequate fuel and an adequate standard of living, and could be built upon to reflect the standards set by the right to an adequate standard of living as espoused by the UDHR and the ICESCR.

Despite some positives in Scotland in relation to the new measure, current statistics and forecasts do not make for easy reading. Official statistics from the Scottish House Condition Survey only give an indication as to fuel poverty in 2019 and fail to capture the recent changes to the fuel price cap in 2021

---

[170] For issues specific to Scotland, see Scottish Fuel Poverty Strategic Working Group, *A Scotland without Fuel Poverty Is a Fairer Scotland: Report* (Edinburgh: Scottish Government, 2016).
[171] Hinson et al (n 153).
[172] Initially, there was the Fuel Poverty Forum that advised the government on fuel poverty. This developed into the Scottish Fuel Poverty Advisory Panel.

and April 2022. Still, in 2019 fuel poverty under Scotland's new measure affected 613,000 households – around 24.6 per cent of all households in Scotland.[173] Without official figures, it is difficult to fully understand the full extent of the problem, but Energy Action Scotland, a leading fuel poverty charity, has estimated that the fuel price rise will lead to a further 211,000 households suffering from fuel poverty. This means that fuel poverty could exceed 40 per cent of all households in Scotland, with over 50 per cent of households in fuel poverty in the Western Isles.[174] With the impact of fuel poverty on a range of factors that are important to basic standards of living, these figures are truly devastating and suggest widespread violations of ESC rights. Despite the actions taken by the Scottish government to alleviate fuel poverty and reduce its persistence, the figure reported would strongly indicate that further targeted action and resources are required.

Wales too suffers from high levels of fuel poverty. In Wales, fuel poverty is measured in relation to whether a household must spend more than 10 per cent of its income on maintaining a satisfactory heating regime.[175] It is a simple measure, but continues to provide a focus on income and is thus likely to capture many of the difficulties caused by rising fuel prices. However, the Welsh measure does not have an income cap built into it, meaning that some high-earning households can be captured inadvertently.[176] This is the benefit of the Scottish measure using the MIS as a baseline. Under the Welsh measure, there was a peak of fuel poverty in 2008 according to official data, with just over 25 per cent of all households in Wales living in fuel poverty. This had reduced to 12 per cent (or 155,000 households) in the last round of official data in 2018. However, as with the other nations, these figures do not capture the reality faced by thousands more households in 2022. The Welsh government has recently released updated estimates which provide

---

[173] Hinson et al (n 153).

[174] Energy Action Scotland has produced a range of publications, including reports and briefings, demonstrating the extent of fuel poverty in Scotland generally, but also with a focus on rural areas. See also Mark Shucksmith et al, 'Costs of Living Crisis Will Push More into Rural Poverty', *Centre for Rural Economy*, 1 April 2022, https://blogs.ncl.ac.uk/cre/2022/04/01/cost-of-living-crisis-will-push-more-into-rural-poverty/#:~:text=Mark%20Shucksmith%2C%20Polly%20Chapman%2C%20Jayne,by%20increases%20in%20energy%20costs

[175] A 'satisfactory heating regime' is 23°C in the living room and 18°C in other rooms, required for 16 hours in a 24-hour period in households with older (a person aged 60 and over) or disabled (a person living with a long-term limiting illness or who is disabled) people. For all other households, 21°C in the living room and 18°C in other rooms is required for nine hours in every 24-hour period on weekdays, and 16 hours in a 24-hour period on weekends.

[176] National Energy Action, 'Fuel Poverty Statistics Explainer' (2021), https://www.nea.org.uk/wp-content/uploads/2022/02/Fuel-Poverty-explainer.pdf

further insight. As of October 2021, 196,000 households in Wales (14 per cent of all households) were living in fuel poverty, with 38,000 in severe fuel poverty (spending 20 per cent of their income on fuel). Furthermore, the April 2022 price increase left charities warning that this figure could rise hugely to up to 45 per cent of all households and 8 per cent in severe fuel poverty. The extent of these estimates is disturbing given the knock-on impact it can have on the realization of ESC rights generally, but also on enabling people to live a life with basic human dignity. The only silver lining being the figures likely represent an accurate depiction of the difficulties faced by households in Wales in relation to fuel price rises and thus the government's task in its alleviation is better understood.

In NI, a household is considered to be in fuel poverty if, in order to maintain a satisfactory level of heating (21°C in the main living area and 18°C in other occupied rooms), it is required to spend in excess of 10 per cent of its household income on all fuel use, and a household is considered to be in severe fuel poverty if it needs to spend more than 15 per cent of income on all fuel use.[177] At the time of carrying out this research, the latest figures in 2024 were reliant upon data collected in 2016, meaning that the data may not capture the full extent to which people suffer from fuel poverty in NI today, particularly since the cost-of-living crisis has worsened since the COVID-19 pandemic. The data collected in 2016 by the House Condition Survey found that 22 per cent of households in NI were classified as fuel poor under the NI measure.[178] This figure has also been used by the NI Department for Communities and is therefore well recognized as a baseline of fuel poverty in NI. However, as we have found in all other parts of the UK, the real figure is likely to be higher, with recent price rises for fuel alongside other financial pressures. The National Energy Action charity has suggested that as of 2022, up to 45 per cent of all homes in NI could be considered to be in fuel poverty.[179] In recent years, the NI government has made some efforts to alleviate the impact of fuel poverty on the most vulnerable through policies such as the Emergency Fuel Payment Scheme. This scheme was aimed at supporting up to 20,000 households with the cost of energy through the provision of one-off support in the form of up to £100 worth of electricity, gas or oil to 20,000 households across NI that were experiencing an emergency fuel crisis during the winter of 2021/2022. However, without up-to-date data on fuel poverty, it is difficult to know

---

[177] Jack Hulme and Claire Summers, *Measuring Fuel Poverty in Northern Ireland* (Watford: Building Research Establishment, 2016).
[178] Building Research Establishment, *Estimates of Fuel Poverty in Northern Ireland in 2019* (Watford: Building Research Establishment, 2016).
[179] National Energy Action, 'How Is Fuel Poverty Defined in Northern Ireland?', 2023, https://www.nea.org.uk/fuel-poverty-map/fuel-poverty-in-ni

whether the scheme was effective in its aim of ensuring those households who needed it most were adequately supported throughout the winter.

Conclusions

This chapter provides an overview of the SR legal framework for the purposes of informing the discussions in the following chapters. The UK's international obligations include compliance with ESC rights. The rights to housing, food, social security and fuel are not currently protected within the domestic framework and there is an accountability gap when violations occur. The normative content of these rights involves continuing processes of interpretation across UN governance structures, including treaty interpretation by the CESCR as well as UN Special Rapporteurs engaged across ESC rights. In addition, there is a significant degree of subsidiarity indicating that it is for states themselves to address indeterminacy using the normative framework as skeletal foundation. The normative framework suggests that there must be efforts to ensure that service provision for social rights is made available across the state and across different demographics within the state (using up-to-date disaggregated data to determine varying need). Likewise, we know that social rights provision should be culturally inclusive, enabling people to live, cook, eat and enjoy home life in ways that respect cultural traditions and practices. We know that rights should not be treated as separate objectives, but should be treated holistically so that the provision of one right supports, and balances, the provision of another. We know that structures, processes and outcomes should be designed to ensure a level of quality in services and national strategies that aim to monitor and improve provision. Likewise, we know that service provision should be non-discriminatory and seek to address historical structural injustices through substantive equality. We also know that social rights provision should prioritize those most in need, should use equitable and efficient ways of delivering resources, and that any process of privatization, automation or outsourcing should not detract from the quality of the service provided. And when provision falls short of these general principles on availability, adequacy, accessibility and quality, there should be mechanisms in place to scrutinize and interrogate provision and ensure that remedies are available to address any violations. The domestic incorporation, or legalization, of ESC rights is not about enforcing absolute rights; rather, it is about creating an accountability framework to assess whether normative standards are upheld and whether processes of service provision relating to social rights are performed in a way that is reasonable and justifiable.

This legal analysis also provides a lens through which to understand our empirical data. Importantly, there are a number of themes that emerge in the legal data that re-emerge in the qualitative interviews with practitioners.

International human rights law creates a framework that recognizes the indivisibility of rights – in other words, that the enjoyment of one right is entirely dependent on the enjoyment of others or, alternatively, that the absence of one right or gaps in its fulfilment undermines the broader set of rights. The domestic legal system siloes legal needs into separate categories, or justice pathways, rather than treating them as indivisible human needs and human rights. For example, our empirical research identifies that when something goes wrong in one area of life, there is a 'spiral' or 'cluster' of issues that appear and when this 'snowball effect' occurs, you 'just keep going around in circles and you can't quite get off the train'. One practitioner explained, in relation to a client she was supporting, that there are

> clusters of problems, because [name redacted] lost her job … she had to claim Universal Credit. Her job was about making ends meet, so she was able to pay her rent. She was able to feed herself, you know, basic heat and electricity … So whenever she lost that income, she became destitute. I have had to give her money to get the bus to her relative's house. And because of this housing issue … she's had to go from relative to relative. She doesn't have the money to pay for transport, pay for electricity, pay for food. She said to me I have been out my home for the last eight weeks, it has worn me down so much that I am now not mentally able to look for a new job. And of course she isn't, because she doesn't have a house.

This insight from the empirical data highlights the interrelated dimension of the human rights framework and the importance of acknowledging the indivisibility of rights. It also highlights the importance of a legal recognition of the rights and value that human rights offer in terms of addressing social injustice. The absence of human rights from the domestic system means that the siloed access to justice framework is ill-equipped to respond to indivisibility. In addition, the absence of meaning and content of rights, the elaboration of what rights mean in practice, is also missing from those cases that do come before an adjudicator. This creates a system in which the burden of seeking justice is placed on the individual, who is already most likely facing a multitude of issues and cannot make a claim with reference to human rights as legal obligations, meaning that much of the evidence related to the social rights claim is not engaged under whichever route to justice is sought. We turn now to our empirical data generated via four UK-wide case studies that provide insights into the everyday reality of this justice gap in practice.

3

What Our Case Studies Told Us about Social Rights in Each Part of the UK

This chapter sets out the data generated from our empirical research and provides insights into the experience of practitioners with direct quotes to support the analysis. We explored a specific SR legal case study from three of the four UK jurisdictions, with a more general approach adopted to understanding access to justice for SR issues for Wales. Case studies of live legal court proceedings were used to help focus our research and help our team identify potential similarities, commonalities and differences across jurisdictions, meaning that we could explore various levels of the justice journey, from the frontline services that may or may not refer a case on to the barristers representing rights holders in the higher courts.

The Scottish case study focused on the cases surrounding government contractor Serco changing the locks on the homes of asylum seekers in the *Ali*[1] case. The English case study looked at the access to justice journey in the *Pantellerisco*[2] judgments concerning algorithmic capping of benefits that operated according to when the claimant is paid each month. In NI, both social security and housing were discussed in the *Cox*[3] case concerning access to Personal Independence Payment (PIP) for people with a terminal illness. The Welsh case study addressed a range of SR issues, with the main focus being access to food, revealing that the absence of strategic litigation made it an outlier to the comparable case studies.

There were 26 interviews conducted across the four geographical case studies with practitioners who worked on an identified legal case or SR

---

[1] *Ali v Serco Ltd* [2019] CSIH 54.
[2] *R (Pantellerisco and Others) v SSWP* [2020] EWHC Admin 1944.
[3] *Cox, Re Application for Judicial Review* [2020] NIQB 53.

issue (to capture those issues that do not proceed to a legal case). Rather than relying on our own interpretations, we draw on the practitioners' words and insights to illustrate various challenges encountered in differing 'access to justice' journeys.

This chapter covers layers of analysis. First, we used theory-driven analysis in relation to the access to justice journey and used principles of deliberative democracy theory to frame our enquiry. Our thematic analysis was then further developed as we theorized our findings using critical discourse analysis to help us identify specific areas of tension surrounding access to justice for SR. This analysis was then used to define and develop the key findings and recommendations.

Scotland: lock-change evictions of those seeking asylum in Glasgow

In July 2018, Serco, the private company contracted by the UK Home Office to provide accommodation to people seeking asylum living in Glasgow, announced a new evictions policy. This policy entailed changing the locks on asylum seekers' homes if they were no longer eligible for asylum support, which would, in turn, force them into street homelessness. Serco's actions raised public outcry and mobilized the legal sector and frontline agencies to advocate for those impacted by the punitive practice.

The research team interviewed seven practitioners who all played an active and supportive role in the legal cases that were raised to challenge the lock-change evictions, as well as being engaged in work tied more broadly to the SR context in Scotland. The interviewees (or participants) included five legal practitioners (solicitors), an evictions caseworker working with an NGO advocating for asylum seekers, as well as a consultant with a grassroots organization (see Table 3.1).

Table 3.1: Scotland case study participants

Name	Role
Carole	Consultant and activist, NGO for human rights
Kelly	Solicitor specializing in women/children/immigration, NGO delivering legal services
Julie	Solicitor specializing in asylum/immigration, NGO delivering legal services
Freya	Solicitor, NGO for housing
Erica	Solicitor, human rights public body
Jonas	Solicitor related to the *Ali* case
Abigail	Evictions caseworker, NGO for asylum seekers

The solicitors we interviewed generally specialized in either housing or immigration law, but given that the rights holders impacted were asylum seekers, the Serco-related cases brought together the migration and housing sectors around a shared aim (Julie, Freya). Serco's actions rapidly mobilized the creation of a coalition of lawyers and nonlawyers to work together to address the pressing challenges that suddenly caused more than 300 already-vulnerable individuals to face homelessness, destitution and despair (or assault to dignity). Julie, a solicitor who specializes in asylum and immigration, called it 'a social justice collaboration', as all involved were inspired by a collective dedication to addressing the human rights violations. Another solicitor, Jonas, said: 'I think, principally, on the face of it, they are housing cases, but they are just so inextricably linked with asylum law and asylum support, etc etc, such that, effectively, the way that I view them is as human rights cases, rather than one or the other.'

Ali[4] and *Saeedi*[5] were both relevant legal cases for the purposes of this case study and we looked at these from the practitioners' perspectives, gaining insights at different stages of the adjudication journey, as well as various viewpoints due to their expertise in either immigration or housing law or other professional background. *Ali* was an ordinary action raised in the Court of Session in August 2018 arguing that it was unlawful for Serco to evict people without first obtaining a court order, contravening Scots housing law as well as human rights law. *Saeedi* was a judicial review lodged with the Court of Session shortly after *Ali* in October 2018, arguing that the lock changes were unlawful because of noncompliance with human rights law and the Equality Act 2010.[6]

The Serco cases effectively challenged two separate issues: first, Serco's decision to enact evictions by lock change without obtaining an eviction order; and, second, arguing that Serco, as a private company, should be treated as a public authority for the purposes of section 6 HRA because its functions, providing accommodation for those within the asylum system, were of a public nature. The *Ali* case represents the contested interpretation of section 6 HRA, which sought to ensure that private bodies performing public functions would be required to comply with the ECHR. The contested nature of section 6 can be best understood through jurisprudence that has sought to clarify its scope. In 2007, in the case of *YL*,[7] the House of Lords held that a private care home did not perform functions of a public

---

[4] *Ali* (n 1).
[5] A separate legal case sisted pending the outcome of *Ali* (ibid).
[6] *Saeedi* was settled out of court in the intervening period, as Mr Saeedi was granted leave to remain.
[7] *YL v Birmingham City Council* [2007] UKHL 27.

nature and was not a 'hybrid' public authority for the purposes of the Act.[8] The UK Parliament responded by enacting section 145 of the Social Care Act 2008 to clarify that private care homes exercise a function of a public nature when providing accommodation and personal care. This is a narrow expansion of the test, meaning any other service beyond the scope of residential care would be subject to the narrow test applied in *YL*. The *YL* test has prevailed in subsequent case law.[9]

The *YL* precedent has been reinterpreted and can be understood as constituting 'no single test of universal application'.[10] Case law has focused on four overarching factors[11] in the determination of whether a private provider performs a public function for the purposes of section 6 HRA, thus constituting a 'hybrid' public authority. First, is the service publicly funded (if yes, it may engage section 6, but does not include a commercial contract where the motivation of the service provider is to secure profit)?; second, does the service relate to the performance of a statutory function (if yes, it may engage section 6, but does not include publicly funded contracts of a private nature such as for religious or commercial purposes)?; third, is the private provider taking the place of central government or local authorities in providing a public service (if yes, it may engage section 6, but must be 'governmental in nature')?; and, fourth, is the provision of the service a public service (if yes, it may engage section 6, but does not cover services provided by 'private schools, private hospitals, private landlords and food retailers')?[12] The *YL* precedent means that there is a focus on the motivation of the service provider in the determination of the act. Thus, ultimately, in *Ali* the motivation of the service provider to make a profit superseded the performance of the public function to provide housing in a human rights-compliant way.[13] An appeal to the Supreme Court was made, but permission for appeal was refused. The 'motivation' aspect of the test sets a worrying precedent.

---

[8] Ibid.
[9] Section 145 of the 2008 Act was repealed and replaced by s 73 of the Care Act 2014. In Scotland, s 73 of the 2014 Act provides that personal care in residential accommodation paid for by the local authority under ss 12, 13A, 13B and 14 of the Social Work (Scotland) Act 1968 meets the threshold of a function of a public nature and therefore engages s 6 HRA. This provision does not apply to children under 18 and excludes adults facing destitution subject to s 115 of the Immigration and Asylum Act 1999 (exclusion from benefits)
[10] Lord Nicholls, *Aston Cantlow and Wilmcote with Billesley Parochial Church Council v Wallbank* [2003] UKHL 37, [12].
[11] See *R (Weaver) v London and Quadrant Housing Trust* [2010] 1 WLR 363 [35]–[38].
[12] Ibid.
[13] *Ali* (n 1), [23].

A tentatively broader definition of the four-factor approach in *YL* (2007) (drawn from *Aston Cantlow* [2004][14] and applied in *R (Weaver)* [2010])[15] is found in *TH* (2016)[16] and applied in *Cornerstone* (2020).[17] In *TH* the court expands the four factors to include a further two questions: fifth, to what extent is the body democratically accountable?; and, sixth, would the allegations, if made against the UK, render it in breach of its international law obligations? This expanded test would provide a much broader basis for human rights compliance when obligations of the state are contracted out. However, *Ali* did not explicitly refer to *TH* in the judgments of the Outer or Inner House of the Court of Session.

In the first of two judgments in April 2019, the Outer House of the Court of Session considered that Serco's service to provide housing to destitute asylum seekers was 'the implementation by the UK of its international obligations to provide essential services to destitute people seeking asylum'.[18] The Court held that the provision of housing formed a function that is 'governmental in nature' (satisfying the third factor) and that Serco therefore constituted a hybrid body under the HRA, meaning a successful outcome for the petitioner. However, on appeal in November 2019, the Inner House of the Court of Session (Scotland's highest civil court) did not consider the international obligations dimension either in relation to the governmental nature of the duties or in relation to whether the allegations would render the UK in breach of its international obligations. Instead, Lady Dorrian concluded that:

> [T]he State cannot absolve itself of responsibility for such public law duties as the provision of accommodation to asylum seekers by delegating its responsibility to private bodies. If arrangements are made with a private company to provide accommodation, responsibility for the exercise of the public law duty is not delegated, but remains with the Home Secretary.[19]

While it is correct that responsibility remains with the state, the state has also sought to extend obligations to private actors under section 6 HRA.

---

[14] Lord Nicholls, *Aston Cantlow* (n 10), [75].
[15] *Weaver* (n 11).
[16] *TH v Chapter of Worcester Cathedral* [2016] EWHC Admin 1117.
[17] *R (on the Application of Cornerstone (North East) Adoption and Fostering Service Ltd) v Office for Standards in Education, Children's Services and Skills* [2020] EWHC Admin 1679 7 July 2020 This judgment was affirmed on appeal on 24 September 2021.
[18] *Ali v Serco Ltd* [2019] CSOH 34 [31].
[19] *Ali* (n 1).

In other words, the judgment fails to acknowledge the legislative aim of regulating the private body when performing a public function. This 2019 judgment adopts a much narrower definition of the 2007 *YL* precedent than in subsequent case law, including *Cornerstone* (2020), *TH* (2016) and *LW v Sodexo* (2019).[20] In the last of these cases, the court found that the Secretary of State had failed in his duty to provide adequate or effective supervision monitoring of strip searching of female and transgender prisoners to ensure compliance with Article 8 and Article 3 ECHR. In this case, the private contractor[21] Sodexo Ltd had already settled out of court, conceding that it owed the claimants positive obligations to ensure compliant search procedures under the ECHR. Thus, both the private contractor (the hybrid public authority) and the Secretary of State for Justice had obligations under the ECHR by virtue of the HRA and, in relation to the latter, as a state party to the ECHR treaty. This approach would have seen the *Ali* judgment acknowledge that both the Secretary of State for Justice and the private provider of accommodation were required to act in a human rights-compliant way thus rendering the eviction of the asylum seekers unlawful. This case therefore provided us with a unique opportunity to better understand the experience of practitioners seeking to support asylum seekers and their right to adequate housing in what is very much a contested legal space, where devolved housing law and reserved immigration law coalesce around a contested interpretation of section 6 HRA.

Jonas, a solicitor, explained that from his perspective, the unfortunate issue was that *Ali* was quite narrow in scope. By comparison, he considered *Saeedi*, by way of judicial review, to be much wider and a forum in which additional evidence could be lodged:

> The beauty of raising proceedings in that format is that additional evidence regarding, for example, prevalence of mental health issues in asylum seekers can be founded upon, rather than effectively a black letter interpretation of how the law *is* written, it's more a case of how the law *should* be. And so, I think the Saeedi case would have been a good vehicle for achieving what was sought for this vulnerable client base.

Unfortunately, *Saeedi* was sisted (paused) to await the outcome of *Ali*, as it was the leading case, which ultimately concluded that the lock changes were deemed lawful. In the intervening period, Mr Saeedi was granted leave to remain and so his case was not continued following the outcome

---

[20] *LW v Sodexo Ltd, Secretary of State for Justice* [2019] EWHC Admin 367.
[21] Ibid, [4].

of *Ali*. This was a criticism of the practitioners who noted that the process of sisting *Saeedi* was fatal to the success of that case, which was in turn frustrating because the judicial review could have included a much broader set of evidence than the ordinary action under *Ali*. Despite accepting the outcome of the case, practitioners disagreed with the court's interpretation of section 6 HRA in relation to accountability for upholding human rights.

Despite judgment in favour of Serco and the Home Office, the lock-change evictions appear to have stopped. This may be largely attributed to public outcry, which led Mears Group, now the designated entity to house asylum seekers in Glasgow, to publicly state that it does not have a policy of changing locks. Practitioners noted that this does not mean that evictions have stopped altogether; it merely means that the lock-change style of evictions is unlikely to be happening at the moment, which may provide asylum seekers some with more space to seek support when faced with eviction. This is an example of SR adjudication with 'symbolic impact' where, despite the applicants losing the case, there has been a longer-term symbolic or material change beyond the judgment itself.[22]

Importantly, the broader issues of housing rights and evictions for those seeking asylum have not been fully addressed in law. However, the campaigning and coalition of practitioners associated with the cases led to greater awareness and potential attitudinal changes over time, linking to Zivi's argument about the importance of rights claiming as a performative act, even when success is not immediate.[23] Indeed, it is an example of rights claiming that has helped reshape the narrative and redistribute power incrementally, leading to empowerment in other rights-claiming moments. For example, in Glasgow in May 2021, an impromptu protest following a Home Office attempt to evict two Indian nationals during Eid saw a stand-off between the Home Office and a crowd of local residents who would not let the immigration van leave. This civic-led zero-tolerance policy to forced evictions of asylum seekers made headlines globally.[24]

---

[22] For a discussion of this, see César Rodríguez-Garavito and Diana Rodríguez-Franco, *Radical Deprivation on Trial, the Impact of Judicial Activism on Socioeconomic Rights in the Global South* (Cambridge: Cambridge University Press, 2015), pp 17–21.

[23] Karen Zivi, *Making Rights Claims: A Practice of Democratic Citizenship* (Oxford: Oxford University Press, 2012).

[24] Libby Brooks, '"A Special Day": How a Glasgow Community Halted Immigration Raid', *The Guardian*, 14 May 2021; Antoria Noori Farzan, 'Hundreds of Protesters Block Immigration Van, Forcing Scottish Officials to Release Men Detained in Raid', *Washington Post*, 14 May 2021; Pablo 'Pampa' Sainz, 'Un muro humano en Glasgow frena la deportación de solicitantes de asilo', *El Salto*, 14 May 2021; 'Écosse. Une manifestation contre les services d'immigration pour empêcher des expulsions', *Ouest-France*, 13 May 2021. The protest was named as one of the ten most influential protests to make a difference in 2021 – see https://news.upday.com/uk/10-protests-from-2021/

Practitioners' perspectives on section 6 of the Human Rights Act

Section 6 HRA refers to the acts of public authorities. It was argued that the HRA should apply to those carrying out public functions, such as the housing of asylum seekers, regardless of being a public or private body. This argument was based on section 6 HRA, which states '[i]t is unlawful for a public authority to act in a way which is incompatible with a Convention right' (section 6(1)) and that 'a "public authority" includes any person certain of whose functions are functions of a public nature' (section 63(b)). Erica, a practitioner, explained the operation of this principle as follows:

> Private bodies, when they are performing functions of a public nature, are also caught by the Human Rights Act. And that is basically to fulfil the principle that a state can't contract out of its human rights obligations and that the principle is really like when you're standing in the shoes of the state then you also must comply with their human rights obligations.

As discussed earlier, the Court of Session (in the Outer House judgment) had, in fact, determined that *Serco* was exercising functions of a public nature and therefore would have to meet human rights standards, which were violated by the lock-change evictions. The Home Office, however, appealed that point with what is referred to as a cross-appeal and the Inner House overturned the decision of the Outer House. The Inner House concluded that due to being a private company, Serco was not exercising a public function and therefore was not obliged to comply with the HRA (Erica). The court relied on an interpretation of public authority that excluded private bodies whose motivation was primarily for profit.[25] An attempt was made to appeal the verdict with the Supreme Court, which was refused. No reasons for the refusal were given as part of the legal process, which was disappointing for the practitioners involved in the case.

We asked Erica, who works as a solicitor for a human rights public body, to explain how the decision was overturned. Erica appreciated that the provision in the HRA is relatively uncontroversial, but how the provision has been applied and interpreted over the years by the courts has been problematic. She said:

---

[25] This is a contested position and arguably erroneously applies previous precedent on the interpretation of s 6. For a discussion of this, see Katie Boyle, 'The Right to an Effective Remedy and Accountability in the Privatisation of Public Services: United Nations Convention on the Rights of the Child (Incorporation) (Scotland) Bill' (2020) 6 *European Human Rights Law Review*, pp 610–623.

The whole idea of it ... everything in the intention of Parliament at the time when the Human Rights Act was going through, is that you should look at the function. So it doesn't matter, if this company is a private company and if they're for-profit and they have shareholders and essentially they look very much like a private entity ... if they look at a function, so in this case it would be the provision of accommodation and other support to asylum seekers, if that function is of a public nature then in exercising that function they are obliged to comply with the Convention.

These arrangements are also referred to as 'hybrid public authorities'. Erica thought that it was quite clear that the provision in the HRA was specifically intended to hold companies such as Serco to account, but unfortunately the court in this instance took a very restrictive approach to the provision of the HRA. Rather than taking a functional approach, the court adopted a motivational approach that looked at Serco's institutional nature as a for-profit company, rather than looking at the functions Serco was performing. Drawing on our critical discourse lens, we can see that the reinterpretation of section 6 of the HRA is problematic. This recontextualization introduces a new policy position on the scope of private bodies' responsibilities that does not extend universally. The recontextualization of section 6 HRA in the *Ali* case provides an example of how legitimacy is afforded to the outcome of one case that differs from the outcomes of other contemporaneous legal processes (where the interpretation is broader). Ms Ali and others affected by the narrower interpretation are marginalized by the discourse of the Scottish case without recourse to a remedy to draw on broader discourses in *Cornerstone* (2020), *LW v Sodexo* (2019) and *TH* (2016).

The practitioners we interviewed did not agree with the court's approach and analysis in the Scottish case law. Erica would have liked an opportunity for the public authority point to have been argued in the Supreme Court because she believes that it is an issue of 'massive public importance', particularly because of the prevalence of outsourcing and privatization[26] in the delivery of public services. She thinks that it would have been helpful for the Supreme Court to look at the issue again 'in [a] fresh light' to clarify how section 6 HRA should be interpreted.

---

[26] Outsourcing and privatization are similar terms that are often used interchangeably, but are fundamentally different. When governments engage a nongovernmental unit (for-profit or nonprofit) to provide services or carry out functions that the government would normally do itself, such as through a contract with an external provider, this is called outsourcing. To avoid confusion and ambiguity, we will primarily use the term 'outsourcing' here to refer to the ways in which government engages with other (private) actors to perform government functions, such as medical assessments.

Another solicitor, Freya, who specializes in housing issues, reiterated Erica's concern about the potential broader implications of the verdict, saying that what may be more widely problematic 'is the finding that Serco was not a public authority for human rights purposes, and in the context of housing when public authorities increasingly contract out … all of those things are brought into question. So that decision on that front is quite alarming'.

The following subsections further explicate the expressed concerns, particularly as they relate to the outsourcing of public services.

Not an automatic waiver of human rights, but cause for concern

The key concern here was that the government could avoid its human rights obligations by outsourcing public functions to private bodies. However, Erica noted that although the Serco decision was disappointing and she disagreed with the court's analysis, she felt that the court was looking at Serco in a particular context and that did not necessarily mean wide-reaching human rights implications for all private providers that may be exercising public functions. In other words, although the law sided with Serco in this instance, it did not mean that all private companies executing public functions would be granted an automatic waiver on their accountability for human rights. Nonetheless, the verdict is still disconcerting because, as Erica said:

> It definitely creates uncertainty and confusion, which is not good, particularly from an individual person perspective. It could potentially create a two-tier human rights system whereby if whatever you need is provided directly by the state then there's no question that they *have to* comply with human rights obligations. But then if you happen to be in a different postcode … or in some other situation whereby, through no fault of your own, that service that you need that the state is obliged to provide you, is provided by a private company, then there's less clarity over that.

She goes on to explain that if a body is unsure as to whether or not they are caught by the HRA, then that will surely impact on how they actually provide their services and functions: 'It's not just about redress to the courts, human rights should come in way upstream and actually influence what you do and influence how you deliver those services … they're there so that you create better services, you create better policy.'

Although the Serco judgment does not have universal application, it can still have a wide-ranging impact and create greater confusion surrounding human rights obligations and less influential power over the behaviour of private organizations, which has a longer-term material impact. In other words, the verdict creates a space that does not inherently support and promote SR.

Erica feared that it has created a situation where organizations will act as if human rights do not apply to them and will see if they will be challenged, acknowledging that 'that's not a sustainable and acceptable situation'.

Rather than encouraging and advancing a human rights-based approach, based on international human rights standards, which includes principles of equality and nondiscrimination, participation and accountability, the court's decision creates an opening for private companies to 'see what they can get away with' rather than developing the capacities of 'duty bearers' to meet their obligations. As both Erica and Freya indicated, it causes great concern with respect to increased outsourcing of government public functions, embedding potential inequalities in the system, depending on your postcode or individual circumstances.

Abigail, one of the practitioners who worked directly with asylum seekers facing evictions due to Serco's lock-change policy, also expressed concern about the practices of private companies without sufficient regulation and oversight. In discussing concerns relating to asylum support and the importance of it for people to buy basic needs such as food, she shared examples of how some asylum seekers had their support stopped due to mistakes on the part of the Home Office or housing provider, but that there was no recognition or apology for the mistakes that had a massive impact on the lives of individuals:

> This system is kind of constructed in such a way – or the fact that the contracts are by private bodies with very little oversight, kind of means that [half sighs] if they were left to their own devices, I think it would just spiral into these very unfair and very cruel and inhumane systems. And that's why I can really see the continuity between how the housing system works normally and to ... things like putting people in barracks now under COVID ... there is a continuity between those things and also how housing managers operate when they basically have to carry out these very cruel decisions and they're the ones that have to deal face to face with people and they're probably not paid very well, it is a recipe for cruelty.

Abigail raises the point that the implementation of 'the system' is undertaken by individuals who themselves are likely underpaid and merely performing a job.[27] Combined with inherent discrimination, it is not difficult to understand how current practices reproduce the inhumane treatment of individuals. *Ali* addressed the inhumane treatment of asylum seekers, challenging any

---

[27] Michael Lipsky, *Street-Level Bureaucracy: Dilemmas of the Individual in Public Services* (New York: Russell Sage Foundation, 2010).

justification of that treatment on the grounds of a person's immigration status. The asylum seekers in question are referred to as 'refused' or 'failed' asylum seekers, although a more neutral description would be to say that it refers to a person seeking asylum whose asylum application has been unsuccessful and whose subsequent appeals have also been unsuccessful. This is also referred to as 'appeal rights exhausted'.

However, the reality is that many of those categorized as 'failed asylum seekers' will ultimately be granted refugee status. Julie explains:

> This drives my conviction … mostly when people tell me that they're refugees, I believe that mostly that is probably true, even if they're failed asylum seekers because their case is stalled and with enough time and the right lawyer, almost all of them will be granted refugee status. And so, what does that mean? It isn't that the lawyers are lying, it's a lack of resource at the right time. It's a lack of representation.

She further explained that under international law they may still be refugees, which means that the state still has obligations. 'It's our British rules', she says, 'that have kind of broken up the system, if you like, in this way and then created barriers to access, to support.'

Freya highlighted that a claim for asylum is in itself 'a human rights and access to justice issue'. She explained that often months would pass between a person being appeal-rights-exhausted and being in a position to submit a further claim, usually due to trying to find an immigration lawyer and getting the required evidence. Proving their status is also closely tied to having the necessary resources and appropriate legal representation.

The asylum seekers who faced eviction following Serco's lock-change announcement had no recourse to public funds, were not allowed to work and had no other sources of support. Erica discussed the implications of this within the context of the Serco case through an international human rights lens. She states that in *Ali*, arguments were made invoking Article 8 ECHR, which is the protection of the right to private and family life. In addition, Erica goes on to say that the argument made by Ms Ali's lawyers was that Serco's actions and threat of destitution combined with circumstances that prevent a person from access to work, access to homelessness services and other supports amount to a contravention of Article 3, which protects against torture and inhumane and degrading treatment, constituting a grievous human rights violation. Erica felt that the nature of them being asylum seekers actually made them more vulnerable to human rights abuses. Jonas, echoed this, stating:

> I think the fallout of the *Ali* case is that there are so many individuals here that are effectively relying on friends or are vulnerable to

exploitation, the Home Office doesn't necessarily have any proposal to remove them or detain them, they will effectively just leave them and it's inhumane I feel ... if an individual is in this country and you're not going to remove them, then to suggest that it's their own fault that they're in destitution, to me, is barbaric and I think the reality is that the state should do more to safeguard the individual's rights, to avoid breach of their human rights, particularly when you're considering Article 3 considerations. But I think that very powerful points are almost lost in rhetoric, this rhetoric of 'we've got someone who is safe to return to their country and they're just simply choosing not to', a judge has said that they're not credible. These are the observations that I find that are led to, justify effectively, just leaving people to starve.

The label of 'failed asylum seeker' is neither an objective nor a permanent category yet immigration status has been used as a justification for the rights-violating treatment of asylum seekers. We take up the point relating to immigration legal status and associated framings in Chapter 5.

Jonas expressed regret that *Saeedi* did not get heard, recognizing that there were some matters, particularly in relation to the Equality Act, that simply could not have been raised in the context of *Ali* because of its nature as an ordinary application. Jonas said that '*the* principal basis of the petition in *Saeedi* was founding upon a breach in terms of public sector equality duty'. Namely, the argument was that there had been a failure to have due regard to the need to advance equality of opportunity, as would have been the case in relation to persons with the protected characteristic of disability and those without that protected characteristic.

One of the fundamental issues, Jonas said, is that the public sector equality duty is nondelegable. He went on to explain:

Within the context of this case, what we experienced was that effectively [sighing] the Home Office are contracting out their obligations to asylum seekers. That the principal obligation is on the Home Office, may choose to contract out privately and then effectively try to distance themselves from the decisions that would breach an individual's rights in terms of the Equality Act by suggesting that they had nothing to do with it. The law is such that it's a non-delegable duty and so it wouldn't have been a defence. And throughout that particular case there were calls upon Serco, calls upon the Home Office, to provide information about any form of assessment that was carried out, and the effect that it would have on people with a protected characteristic prior to the introduction of the policy – radio silence! was effectively the response. That was single-handedly the most unfortunate aspect of this case, that there was quite clearly a policy, from our perspective, which was unlawful. However, because Saeedi sisted, there was no opportunity to ventilate those particular arguments.

The test-and-sist approach – that is, where all related cases are paused while the lead case is heard – presents a significant hurdle in access to justice when dealing with a systemic issue in which many people are impacted by a structural failure, but their cases are not heard simultaneously. One of the key contributions of the literature in response to systemic issues is that more attention should be paid to designing justice systems that can respond to a systemic issue collectively.[28] Indeed, in Scotland, the deployment of structural orders for systemic issues forms part of the recommendations of the First Minister's Advisory Group and National Taskforce on Human Rights Leadership.[29] Boyle has also recommended new procedures for collective cases such as class actions when multiple applicants experience violations as a result of a systemic issue, something which may be made possible under the new group proceedings framework.[30] We will discuss the potential of structural remedies for systemic cases in Chapter 4.

Conflicts between reserved and devolved power

As observed in other jurisdictions, the Serco case drew attention to the inherent tensions and conflicts between reserved and devolved powers in terms of the ways that asylum/immigration law intersected with housing law. It was generally accepted by the practitioners we interviewed that there is a will to make things better in Scotland, which contrasts with the 'hostile environment' being promoted by the UK government's Home Office, and that Scotland is more progressive in housing law compared to England, but that, as Julie said, 'the UK government is making immigration policy which is constraining the powers of the government or causing really bad outcomes in Scotland where the Scottish government is legally responsible'.

---

[28] Katie Boyle, *Economic and Social Rights Law, Incorporation, Justiciability and Principles of Adjudication* (Abingdon, Routledge, 2020), pp 38–39; Rodríguez-Garavito and Rodríguez-Franco (n 22); and David Landau, 'The Reality of Social Rights Enforcement' [2012] 53 *Harvard International Law Journal* 189.

[29] See *First Minister's Advisory Group on Human Rights Leadership* (2018), https://humanrightsleadership.scot/wp-content/uploads/2018/12/First-Ministers-Advisory-Group-on-Human-Rights-Leadership-Final-report-for-publication.pdf; and the *National Taskforce for Human Rights Leadership Report* (2021), https://www.gov.scot/publications/national-taskforce-human-rights-leadership-report/documents/

[30] Boyle (n 28); Katie Boyle, 'Models of Incorporation and Justiciability of Economic, Social and Cultural Rights', Scottish Human Rights Commission (2018), https://www.scottishhumanrights.com/media/1809/models_of_incorporation_escr_vfinal_nov18.pdf

Conditions for asylum seekers: insights from practitioners on the ground

The final key point to highlight about the Scottish case study concerns the living conditions and broader challenges individuals seeking asylum face on a day-to-day basis. Although *Ali* revolved around the injustices of the lock-change eviction policy, it became clear from speaking to practitioners that the lock changes were merely the tip of the iceberg. Some of the other issues that were highlighted in the interviews were that asylum seekers are only allowed up to £1,000 of possessions in their home, losing asylum support after 28 days of a claim being refused or accepted, money being provided via a card that can only be used at certain locations, often not including public transport, and not being allowed to leave their homes for more than six days at a time. These constraints make life for asylum seekers more difficult and create barriers to accessing justice. Abigail stated that:

> There's the kind of large overarching injustices but then there's all these tiny examples and sometimes those to me are what really speak to the larger injustices of the situation, because the tiny ones are so absurd and so petty and have to be built on so many different things of policy kind of meeting together that stop people in all these tiny ways from just being a normal human being.

A better understanding of the difficult living conditions of asylum seekers helps to underscore that SR should not be categorized as luxuries, but as minimum requirements for treating people with humanity and dignity. This sentiment is expressed strongly by practitioners, but is currently absent from many policies and service provisions, causing justice for SR to be eluded.

The Scotland case study provided insights into some of the broader dynamics observed across the data that include challenges relating to the outsourcing of government functions and the intersections of reserved and devolved frameworks, in this instance immigration and housing. Significant concerns were also raised regarding the inhumane treatment of those seeking asylum. Despite a commitment in Scotland to treat people in ways that honour their humanity and dignity, UK Home Office policy and ideology curb efforts to realize these goals.

England: digitization, algorithms and the direct impact on social security provisions

In 2013, the UK government introduced a benefit cap, which imposed a limit on the total amount of benefit a person can receive. In September 2019, judicial review proceedings were issued on behalf of Sharon Pantellerisco, a lone parent, and her three children. The judicial review challenged the

WHAT OUR CASE STUDIES TOLD US

Table 3.2: England case study participants

Name	Role
Andrea	Welfare benefits advisor related to the *Pantellerisco* case
Roland	King's Counsel related to the *Pantellerisco* case
Miles	Welfare rights advisor, NGO to combat child poverty
Jane	Welfare rights advisor, NGO to combat child poverty
Claire	Solicitor related to the *Pantellerisco* case
Tobias	Barrister related to the *Pantellerisco* case

approach adopted by the Secretary of State for Work and Pensions (SSWP) to the calculation of the benefit cap in the Universal Credit statutory scheme. The case was heard in May 2020. (See Table 3.2.)

In order to be exempt from the cap, claimants must be working at least 16 hours per week earning the national living wage. Despite meeting the designated threshold, Ms Pantellerisco's benefits were still capped as she was paid on a four-weekly basis rather than by calendar month. As the judgment[31] explains:

> A year has 13 4-week periods in it, but 12 monthly assessment periods. Therefore ... everyone paid on a 4-weekly cycle will, each year, have 11 Universal Credit assessment periods in which they receive one thirteenth of their annual salary, and one assessment period in in which they receive two thirteenths of their salary.

Thus, as the assessment period for Universal Credit is calculated as a calendar month, and Ms Pantellerisco was paid on a four-week cycle rather than monthly, the Department for Work and Pensions (DWP) computer system undercounted her wages in 11 out of 12 assessment periods, subjecting her to the benefit cap.

Judgment was given in July 2020, with the court finding in Ms Pantellerisco's favour – in other words, that the algorithm used to calculate entitlement was flawed, irrational and therefore unlawful. At the time that the interviews were conducted, the SSWP was in the process of appealing to the Court of Appeal and the practitioners awaited the next steps. In a very disappointing outcome, the appeal was heard and judgment was given in October 2021, allowing the SSWP's appeal. Permission to appeal to the Supreme Court was refused by the Court of Appeal, a point we will return to at the end of this section.

---

[31] *Pantellerisco* (n 2).

This case study highlights some unique aspects of the case by drawing on insights from practitioners at different stages of the adjudication journey, ranging from frontline advice to King's Counsel (KC). We interviewed six practitioners, four of whom were directly involved in the case, including a welfare benefits officer who supported Ms Pantellerisco, a solicitor, a barrister and a KC recognized for their legal expertise in social security. In addition, we gained perspectives from two additional welfare rights advisors.

The judicial review case is only one component of Ms Pantellerisco's journey to address the violation of her SR. Insights from the welfare rights advisor Andrea shed light on the processes and procedures that preceded the judicial review proceedings. Andrea was Ms Pantellerisco's first point of contact when she attended the food bank where Andrea works. Andrea describes the situation as follows:

> It was a lady that had attended the food bank and through no fault of her own ... she was on working and child tax credits. She had a breakup and had to apply for Universal Credit because of that change in circumstances, and the way Universal Credit is calculated is that they calculate it as a monthly income. And with this particular client, she was paid every four weeks, so while she was working the required hours and earning the minimum wage that meant she should be exempt from the benefit cap. Due to the way that Universal Credit [is] calculated, they calculated her four-weekly earnings as a monthly earning, so they determined she actually fell under the cap, and she lost initially because there were four children on the original claim.[32] She was losing £700 a month and they applied that instantly to her, so all of a sudden she found herself £700 a month in finance worse off.

Mandatory reconsideration and tribunal hearings

When the DWP initially (mis)calculated Ms Pantellerisco's hours and wages, and determined that she would be subject to the benefit cap, it immediately applied the cap and thereby reduced her income by £700 per month overnight, even though she should have been exempt. The DWP's regulations indicate that a person should be given a nine-month grace period, so that there is time to prepare for their earnings to be reduced. However, in Ms Pantellerisco's case, the grace period was not granted because, using the same monthly income calculation, the DWP determined that she did

---

[32] When the judicial review was issued, Ms Pantellerisco's eldest child was 19 and had finished school; she still lived at home with her three younger siblings.

not meet the earnings threshold in the 12 months prior and was therefore ineligible for the grace period.

To challenge this, Andrea raised a mandatory reconsideration, which essentially asked the DWP to review its decision. The DWP responded that its calculations were correct, as these were based on monthly earnings, and stated that a calculation based on four-weekly earnings was not possible. At that point, Andrea adopted a two-pronged approach. She appealed to the First-tier Tribunal on two issues, the unlawful application of the benefit cap and the DWP's negligence in not applying the nine-month grace period. She also sought further legal advice, resulting in the case being taken on for judicial review. The tribunal proceedings were then paused to await the outcome of the judicial review.

Barrier to participation

Eventually, Andrea managed to get the DWP to overturn the grace period and pay Ms Pantellerisco a lump sum for the money she was due. 'Unfortunately', Andrea said, 'because she had an overpayment of tax credits previously, they deducted all of that from her straight away.' Although Andrea acknowledged that the overpayment needed to be paid back, rather than taking the deduction all at once, Ms Pantellerisco could have paid it back at £20 a month, which, Andrea said, would have been acceptable. Andrea explained that Ms Pantellerisco was struggling, receiving help not only from the food bank but also relying on support for fuel and school uniforms for her children. Andrea ventured that 'they [the DWP] do it all the time with everybody, so they don't look at the fact that people might have rent arrears or mortgage arrears because of their actions in the first place'.

So, while there was no disagreement with regards to paying back the overpaid tax credits, there could have been some consideration on the part of DWP to not take a lump sum, but arrange a gradual repayment scheme. This example demonstrates that these processes are not participatory for rights holders and often fail to consider fundamental human dignity. The burden of DWP decisions is most acutely felt by the individual who is not given any opportunity to participate in processes that have a direct and significant impact. As Andrea pointed out, rights holders often end up in even more precarious financial situations as a result of benefit mistakes that then take a very long time to resolve.

The notion of participation was also raised in relation to the judicial review. We asked Andrea to what extent Ms Pantellerisco was able to engage with the legal proceedings and she responded: 'Sharon did start off with it, but she couldn't understand it, so I think again that was because it was all legal jargon.' Roland, the KC we interviewed, echoed the sentiment that by the time litigation reaches the level of judicial review, there is not much engagement with rights holders themselves. He said that 'at the level at which I get involved in advocacy on these sort of points of laws or issues, the answer is not very much, to be honest, I mean, it does become a conversation between lawyers or the judge'. He acknowledged that 'there's a lot of awareness about the need for claimants to be involved', but that if he were identifying a problem regarding participation, it would be at the local level rather than in the appellate system. The barriers around participation and access to advice will be examined in greater detail in Chapter 4 (the access to justice journey).

The benefit cap: work incentivization

All the practitioners agreed that on the face of it, the issue seemed almost absurd. The mere fact that someone who is paid on a four-weekly basis is subject to the benefit cap, while a person working the same number of hours, at the same pay rate but paid monthly would not be subject to the benefit cap seems rather senseless. The *Pantellerisco* judicial review came on the back of another benefit cap case, which was unsuccessful in May earlier that year (2019).[33] Claire, the solicitor who took on the case, explained:

> It was May last year we had lost the benefit cap case, the Supreme Court one, the one challenging it in relation to lone parents generally ... and then in June I pick up Sharon's case, and it doesn't matter that we've just lost the benefit cap case this is perverse, purely because of the way her employer pays her ... she's benefit capped. That was never the intention of the benefit cap. The benefit cap is all about work incentivization, even though they still apply it during the middle of a pandemic, but we know that's a side issue ... this is about incentivising you to work with an employer who pays monthly rather than four-weekly.

In addition to pointing out the flawed reasoning regarding the application of the benefit cap to Ms Pantellerisco, Claire also referred to the broader purpose of the benefit cap as an incentivization measure to encourage people to work. She pointed out that, aside from the challenge raised on Ms Pantellerisco's behalf, there are wider concerns regarding the fairness

---

[33] *R (DA and Others) v SSWP* [2019] UKSC 21, concerning lone parents subject to the benefit cap. Despite the policy, intended to incentivize work, having a disproportionate and damaging impact on the claimants and their children, the court held (by a 5–2 majority) that the discrimination was objectively justified and not manifestly without reasonable foundation.

of the legislation itself. A total of 70 per cent of those being affected by the benefit cap, before the COVID-19 pandemic, were lone parents, she said, and she questioned the validity of a work incentivization measure that disproportionately ringfences lone parents for such punitive treatment. Moreover, she continued, the benefit cap is inadequate in terms of level of subsistence benefit and it was recognized that it pushes families well below the poverty line (indeed, this point was accepted by the Supreme Court),[34] underscoring broader concerns about its inadequacy and the lack of accessibility to meaningful benefits.

This key point is indicative of the legal vacuum in terms of minimum thresholds and normative standards in SR protection. This legal vacuum can be seen in cases where lawyers are relying on ECHR arguments when it is not a treaty that recognizes the full breadth of human rights, and so practitioners cannot rely on the substantive standards or content of other treaties such as the International Covenant on Economic, Social and Cultural Rights (ICESCR). In other words, the inadequacy of the SR provision was not the subject of the case as there is no standalone right to an adequate standard of living (Article 11 ICESCR) or a right to social security (Article 9 ICESCR). Rather, the focus of the case was on whether applying the cap could be justified based on work incentivization, despite its discriminatory impact on lone parents whose right to private and family life was engaged. This frustration was apparent across our case studies where practitioners acknowledged the frustration of trying to make arguments for SR by using other legal vehicles that do not adequately capture the SR issue or facilitate an examination of the appropriate evidence.

Automation and algorithms

We now return to the calculations of Ms Pantellerisco's hours and wages that ultimately resulted in an unfair outcome and violation of her right to social security. Ms Pantellerisco's employer was a 'RealTime Information' employer, meaning that information about its employees is passed from the employer to HMRC and from them to the DWP. As such, it is an automated process that reports earnings directly from HMRC to the DWP. Tobias, the barrister involved, said 'it's rather a sophisticated operation', in the sense that the way in which Ms Pantellerisco's wages were calculated wrongly was due to an algorithm, which did not consider the frequency of her income, which was not because that information was not available to the DWP, but because it was not made use of. He continued:

---

[34] Ibid, [35]–[37].

> Say a person is paid every 4 weeks, how do we know that they're actually being paid every 4 weeks, other than it's not just that they happen to only do 28 days' work in that 31-day period? Well, the answer is because their own PAYE [pay as you earn] system tells them ... it's just that they [the DWP] couldn't be bothered to plug that into the system. They collect all the data that they need to be able to see that this is a person who is working the specified amount, but they then have an ... ultra-simplified approach to deciding what a person is earning, which fails to make use of that data.

The challenge is that the government has invested in a computer program, which is now proven to be unfit for purpose, but is extremely reluctant to change it. Key evidence from HMRC in the case demonstrated that the DWP was in receipt of all the information it required as part of the RTI provided by HMRC. It was this latter point that proved fatal to the SSWP's case in the initial judgment when Justice Darnham concluded:

> [T]he importance of ensuring that the payment system can be automated is clear and not in dispute. During the hearing, much of the most powerful consideration in favour of maintaining the status quo was the suggested difficulty in collecting and deploying the data necessary to enable the calculation of earned income in relevant assessment periods to be carried out automatically when payment had been made on a four-weekly basis. But that difficulty substantially disappeared when the further evidence was obtained from Ms Hargreaves and Ms Krahé. There was little evidence that the SSWP ever focused on the lunar month problem, as opposed to the general benefit of a universally applicable monthly assessment period, and nothing to suggest the possibility of solving that problem was ever considered and rejected. In those circumstances, it seems to me that the outcome of the balance is obvious and irresistible. I cannot see how any reasonable Secretary of State could have struck the balance in the way the SSWP has done in this case.[35]

The practitioner perspective of Tobias noted the importance of this evidence to the outcome of the case:

> I think the judge refers to the witness, the evidence of a woman called Helen Hargreaves ... who provided CPAG [Child Poverty

---

[35] *R (Pantellerisco and Others) v SSWP* [2021] EWCA Civ 1454 [80]–[81].

Action Group] with evidence about pay cycles, how common it was to be paid monthly, how common it was to be paid fortnightly, what HMRC were told by employers as a matter of routine, and one of the pieces of evidence that she was able to produce in response partly to what the DWP said at the hearing was the information that the nature of a pay cycle was automatically referred by the employer to HMRC. So, in other words, HMRC could know … whether you were paid monthly, fortnightly, or weekly or whatever. And once you've got there then it became very unreal for the Department to say, well, we just couldn't design a computer system to deal with it. They had the information. And they got the information without any extra hassle, it was being automatically supplied to them and all they had to do was apply it properly that was quite important, because otherwise you're back in the judge being very resistant to the idea that you could tell the DWP how to spend hundreds of millions of pounds designing a computer system, however odd the result. If you read the judgment, I mean one of the things to watch is that information about what HMRC were being told. I think the judge refers to it at the end, that's one of the things that did make a difference. I mean, you know, at the end of the hearing I was a bit bothered the judge had been persuaded by the DWP that the problems with computerization were so big that we ought to lose, but we did in the end crack that with the material from Helen Hargreaves.

The absurdity of refusing to use information being supplied as a matter of routine became all the more indefensible when balanced with the competing suggestion that Ms Pantellerisco should seek to change the way in which she is paid. As noted by Tobias:

We had pretty good evidence again from Helen Hargreaves, but also from Sharon herself about how impossible that was. I mean … at that level, the Department's case is pretty unconvincing really, because I mean the truth is that Sharon was being paid as a carer by a local authority whose own payment cycle would be four-weekly. They couldn't change it unless they changed their whole payment system to a monthly basis, which would muck up all sorts of other contracts. So, it was a pretty impractical suggestion that she go to the employer and ask them to change the payment cycle and the judge wasn't particularly attracted by it. So, in terms of holding decision makers to account, I suppose that's what it comes down to when we're talking about whether or not to hold DWP to account for changing their algorithms and changing their program.

A call for greater parliamentary scrutiny

One way to avoid such costly errors is to increase prelegislative scrutiny. Tobias said that 'if I could pass a law, it would be to require much greater parliamentary scrutiny of the detail of law ... it shouldn't be the case that when lawyers come to a situation, it emerges that we're the first people to think about it'. Particularly with regard to social security legislation, he cautioned:

> The amount of time people spend thinking about it and their practical opportunities to change it are very limited ... if you look at how long the subcommittee that addresses social security legislation has spent looking at an instrument that effectively affects millions of people and the government billions of pounds of public expenditure, you're not going to say, well, it's like an hour and a half or something.

In other words, a crucial component for achieving more just and fair outcomes is to allocate greater time for parliamentary scrutiny and the ability to amend regulations. More extensive prelegislative scrutiny is a way to achieve better decision making. 'We have millions and billions of pounds of public expenditure designed to protect the welfare of lots of very, very, very vulnerable people', Tobias said, 'and that's a huge public concern.' Effectively, the recognition that a policy is flawed should occur before reaching court.

We now return to the outcome of the case. By a judgment handed down on 20 July 2020, Garnham J had found in Ms Pantelleriso's favour, declaring that:

> The calculation required by regulation 82 (1) (a) read together with regulation 54 of the Universal Credit Regulations 2013 *is irrational and unlawful* insofar as employees who are paid on a 4-weekly basis (as opposed to a calendar monthly basis) are treated as having earned income of only 28 days' earnings in 11 out of 12 assessment periods a year.[36]

Despite an initial positive outcome, it did not immediately provide an effective remedy for Ms Pantellerisco, as the SSWP put in an application to the Court of Appeal, which meant more waiting. Claire said:

> The Court of Appeal is notoriously slow because it's understaffed, overworked, and COVID-19 has just exacerbated that situation even more. So even though permission to appeal the application went in

---

[36] *Pantellerisco* (n 2) (emphasis added).

sometime in July after the judgment and refused permission to appeal by the High Court itself, we're still waiting for a decision on whether they're going to be granted permission.

So, when the interviews were concluded, there had not yet been any progress with respect to a potential appeal and no materialization of any potential remedy for Ms Pantellerisco.

Pantellerisco *on appeal: a failure to provide a remedy*

In a disappointing outcome, Ms Pantellerisco lost in the Court of Appeal on 8 October 2021, when it overturned the judgment of Garnham J.[37] The Court, relying on the *SC*[38] case (which was issued in the intervening period), stated that intensity of review on the grounds of irrationality (unreasonableness) should be restricted in cases concerning economic and social policy, meaning that such cases are not open to challenge on the grounds of irrationality 'short of the extremes of bad faith, improper motive or manifest absurdity'.[39] This is an extremely high threshold, and demonstrates a reluctance of the court to interfere on economic and social policy areas despite violations of SR.[40] On this basis, the Court of Appeal took a deferential approach in *Pantellerisco*, relying on evidence provided by the DWP that the Department operates a 'test-and-learn philosophy' suggesting that steps to correct the legislative scheme could be taken as part of the test-and-learn approach – in other words, that a remedy via executive or legislative avenues would be more appropriate.[41]

Lord Underhill in delivering the judgment concluded that it is not the role of the court to judge the extraordinary complexity of a system that involves a range of practical and political assessments, even when 'some features of such a system produce hard, even very hard results, in some individual cases'.[42] He further clarifies:

---

[37] *Pantellerisco* (n 2).
[38] *R (SC) v SSWP* [2021] UKSC 26.
[39] *Pantellerisco* (n 2), [58], referring to Lord Reed in *R (SC) v Secretary of State for Work and Pensions* [2021] UKSC 26, who cites Lord Bridge in *R v Secretary of State for the Environment ex p Hammersmith and Fulham London Borough Council* [1991] 1 AC 521.
[40] It should be noted that Lord Underhill in an earlier case noted that: 'The threshold for establishing irrationality is very high, but it is not insuperable. This case is, in my judgment, one of the rare instances where the SSWP's refusal to put in place a solution to this very specific problem is so irrational that I have concluded that the threshold is met because no reasonable SSWP would have struck the balance in that way.' *Johnson* (n 33), [107].
[41] *Pantellerisco* (n 2), [90].
[42] *Pantellerisco* (n 2), [59].

I would add that the very complexity and difficulty of the exercise is bound to mean that following the implementation of the scheme it may become clear with the benefit of experience that some choices could have been made better. But it does not follow that the legislation was in the respect in question irrational as made, or that it would be irrational not to correct the imperfections once identified: the court cannot judge the lawfulness of such schemes by the standard of perfection.[43]

When Claire made her statement regarding the delay related to the appeal at the time of the interview in December 2020, five months had already passed since the judgment. Andrea, the welfare benefits advisor, had shared that she first began working with Ms Pantellerisco in February 2019. This means that when the appeal judgment was handed down in October 2021, Ms Pantellerisco's fight for social justice had taken more than two and a half years and, ultimately, she received no effective remedy.

The outcome of the case is a loss, not only for Ms Pantellerisco, but also for every other person who is paid regularly but not monthly, and thereby subjected to capping of their welfare benefits. The court accepted that the DWP operates a 'test-and-learn philosophy',[44] but the qualitative data suggest that there is no evidence of 'test-and-learn' being implemented in practice. As Claire, the practitioner involved in the case, identified:

> The government said, in response to the Work and Pensions Select Committee, they did say that they were looking into it. But, you know, they said they were looking into it when I first took on Sharon's case and that was well over a year ago, and they've done nothing about it. But it's set up a system that depends on or has so much of its real-time information feed and not being prepared to make adjustments in relation to that.

Claire's final comment underlines that there has been no effective remedy available through legislative, executive or judicial pathways. The England case study drew our attention to processes of automation and the deployment of algorithms in decision making. Furthermore, it raised our awareness about the difficulties in engaging in the access to justice journey in terms of resilience and participation. As further analysis will show, these dynamics are not unique to the English context. As of July 2024, there has still been no change to the system. During his visit to the UK in 2018, Philip Alston, previous UN Special Rapporteur on Extreme Poverty, noted that 'test and

---

[43] *Pantellerisco* (n 2).
[44] Ibid, [90].

learn' cannot be a decade-long excuse for failing to properly design a system that is meant to guarantee the social security of so many.[45]

Wales: closer to government, but with variable impact

It became clear early on in the study that the Welsh context was unique due to increased limitations of devolved powers compared to the other UK jurisdictions, particularly in relation to social security and justice policy. Unlike Scotland and NI, Wales forms part of a single legal jurisdiction with England. Although Wales has a separate devolved legal framework to England, the area of justice is reserved and so the administrative legal system, the courts and tribunals, and the types of remedies available for violations of rights fall under the jurisdiction of Westminster. Early fieldwork suggested that Wales does not have as distinct a litigation culture compared to the other UK jurisdictions. We therefore adapted our approach to consider the general context for SR and access to justice in Wales rather than focusing on one specific legal case.

Challenges for social rights protections relating to the devolution settlement for Wales

With the exception of one participant, the practitioners interviewed raised various challenges related to the devolution settlement for Wales (see Table 3.3 for the Welsh case study participants). In this section we will broadly map out the various aspects relating to devolution that impact on the framework for SR protections, service provisions, processes of implementation and available pathways for challenging SR violations. There are complexities in terms of the powers and responsibilities the Welsh government has and how it interacts with decision-making processes in England, which means that it is not always easy to determine which government is doing what (Seth).

For the purposes of this discussion, it is important to distinguish the relevant SR arenas where Wales has been granted more devolved powers, which include health and social services (and social care), education and housing. Nationality, immigration and asylum remain reserved, but this pertains to all of the UK jurisdictions. The three areas that are not devolved in Wales, and most pertinent to understanding the local context for SR are social security, justice and policing.

---

[45] Statement on Visit to the United Kingdom, by Professor Philip Alston, United Nations Special Rapporteur on extreme poverty and human rights, 16 November 2018, https://www.ohchr.org/en/statements/2018/11/statement-visit-united-kingdom-professor-philip-alston-united-nations-special

Table 3.3: Wales case study participants

Name	Role
Matthew	Solicitor, private law firm
Seth	Researcher, think tank (social rights)
Sam	Policy developer, NGO for children and youth
Eva	Development Manager, NGO to combat child poverty
David	Researcher, NGO to battle inequality
Kim	Programme Manager, NGO to combat food poverty
Rose	Welfare rights advisor, local county

Limited powers to address poverty and funding

One practitioner, Sam, notes that challenges around devolution have one of the biggest impacts on his work. He thinks that the fact that there are a number of policy areas that are not devolved to Wales results in complexities in terms of the powers and responsibilities that the Welsh government has, as well as how that interacts with decision-making processes in England. This is particularly significant in relation to the poverty agenda, he goes on to say, because the Welsh government has very limited powers in terms of welfare benefits and no powers around social security. This means that, in his words: 'The power [the Welsh government] have to make a real difference to low-income family situations in Wales is fairly limited.' He recognizes that the Welsh government do have a strategy and laws around child poverty, which extends to other areas relating to a number of protected characteristics groups. Sam states that his organization works with the Welsh government to keep it to task, but recognizes that 'lots of big complex issues sit outside the power of Wales'.

Kim, another practitioner working in the arena of the right to food, notes that the Welsh government relies significantly on central government for its funding and has no capacity to borrow money: 'we have nearly a third of children in Wales living in poverty, and we have a government that relies predominantly on central government for its funding and doesn't really have particular powers in terms of borrowing money either so we're kind of at the mercy of central government'.

In response to the interviewer's question to elaborate on tensions between the legal framework in England and Wales, another concern regarding funding was raised by Sam in relation to Brexit:

> You may well know that Wales is a net beneficiary of EU structural funds ... and of course we could well lose a significant amount of funding in Wales that we've had from Brussels over a number of years.

And, of course, all the decision-making processes around continuation funding under a new scheme has all been taking place elsewhere. So whilst the Welsh government have, and I guess the other devolved nations have been round the table where they've been able to put in their case, the decisions are all resting in Westminster in terms of that and, I guess, that links to the powers around human rights and the risk to some of the rights that children and young people currently enjoy from protections in Europe. There's still a great deal of uncertainty around those.

Different laws, limitations to law making and delays in adoption and implementation

Another area that received significant attention across the data is Wales's limitations in terms of making laws, as well as differences in laws between England and Wales. Sam, whose work focuses on children and families, notes that slightly different laws between England and Wales cause complexities, for instance, in relation to shared parenting arrangements, where courts sometimes have to take into account different pieces of legislation across England and Wales. This also leads to completely different outcomes, depending on the jurisdiction.

In Wales there is greater emphasis on children's rights compared to other parts of the UK (with the recent exception of Scotland). Matthew, a solicitor, attributed this difference to 'the incorporation of the rights of the child from the UN convention, that's enshrined in Welsh law, but that's not necessarily in England so those are key differences which we're starting to use now'. Having fully incorporated international human rights law can make a significant difference not only in terms of how the law can be used, but also to increase accountability. It is important to note that although the Rights of Children and Young Persons (Wales) Measure 2011 integrates the United Nations Convention on the Rights of the Child into the devolved legislative process in Wales and helps with policy implementation, the duty that is placed on ministers is one of 'due regard'. This is not sufficient to meet the threshold of legal incorporation because ultimately there is no remedy for a violation of the treaty and so no accountability for a failure to comply. What the duty does is to encourage compliance rather than make it a mandatory legal requirement. Nonetheless, the terminology 'incorporation' is used by practitioners when discussing the integration of the treaty under the devolved legislation.

One additional challenge raised regarding working across two different frameworks involves significant delays in passing and implementing laws. One example comes from Seth, who works for a think tank focused on SR issues. He shared that the Renting Homes (Wales) Act 2016, which introduces a number of changes to tenancy laws, including increased tenant protections by banning retaliatory evictions, was delayed coming into force and had still not been enacted at the time of the interview in late 2020. He explained that this delay was, in part, due to engagement with the Ministry of Justice. So, despite being a piece of legislation related to housing, which is mostly devolved, its interaction with justice policy lengthened the process for implementation. He further notes that 'you've got lots of really good well-meaning kind of legislation. The proof will be when it actually is implemented, and people are actually able to use it to protect their rights', iterating that efficient policy processes that foster swift implementation are key to upholding people's rights.[46]

Again, this relates back to the earlier point concerning implementation through weaker duties such as 'due regard' rather than full incorporation with legal remedies for violations. The duty to have due regard creates a procedural obligation to consider the treaty as part of decision-making processes, whereas a duty to comply would require substantive compliance. There is an important distinction to be made between procedural and substantive obligations, and how well-meaning legislation can ultimately fail to result in any substantive change.

Seth highlighted that Wales is more focused on tenants' rights than England, not because Wales changed the law, but because England moved away from a tenant-focused model while Wales moved towards it. This is one example of divergence in jurisdictions with regard to SR as a result of devolution. Referring to legislation for children's rights, Sam also referred to delays with the Children (Abolition of Defence of Reasonable Punishment) (Wales) Act 2020, saying:

> That took about 10 years legal wrangling and working out whether we had the powers to do that or not. So, that's why there was an intention from our government about 10, 15 years ago to introduce that and it's taken that long, lawyers in Wales to work with the lawyers in Westminster to work out whether it sits within social care or criminality. Eventually it fell to us, so we could implement the Act.

This example highlights the complexities and perhaps competing priorities from ministers in Wales and England.

---

[46] This sentiment was echoed in NI. Esther said: 'It's easy to get those public appearances and public declarations of support. It's extremely difficult to see actual change and movement. So, how do you translate that kind of public expressions or like informal expressions, like unanimously pass motions and to bring about any actual change, you know' (NI | Esther | Housing activist, NGO for human rights).

Challenges were also raised for the refugee sector due to having no powers around immigration. Sam stated that strategies for assisting asylum seekers and refugees are therefore targeted predominantly at services like education, health and housing, those areas where Wales has some power to make changes. This iterates tensions between housing and immigration policy, which were also particularly tangible in the Scotland case study.

The most detailed account of tensions between the Welsh and English legal frameworks came from a practitioner who works as one of the few public law solicitors in Wales. A piece of Welsh legislation that features prominently across the data, the Well-being of Future Generations Act 2015, focuses on sustainable development and wellbeing goals for Wales. We asked Matthew whether he could describe the interactions between broader UK legislation and Welsh laws, and whether he could identify any particular conflicts when there is engagement with two different frameworks. In his response, Matthew described the tensions that arose when the Wellbeing of Future Generations Act was used in a test case in 2019.[47] He said that on a practical level, the biggest problem in Wales is that it has some unique Welsh laws which are based on Welsh policies:

> [And] a direction of travel, if you like, of Welsh government, but then what happens is, when you run a case on to test that out, the Judge who comes in has parachuted in from England … is a High Court Judge from England, who just turns up … probably a former commercial QC [Queen's Counsel, now KC] … who lives in London and he won't have a clue about where this case is, where this policy has come from and the classic example is, we have something in Wales called the Well-Being of Future Generations Act … It's the only case that's raised that Welsh law and we tried it; Judge comes wafting in from England, he was a very nice chap but he just said, this Act is wholly aspirational, has no application to individuals, doesn't apply. So, then you say to yourself, what is the point of this Act? You know, what is an old QC on record … saying the Act is pointless right … that's an example … but I wonder if we'd have had a Welsh Judge, a Welsh-speaking, you know, a Judge from Wales who had heard all about the genesis of this Act and everything and was rooted in knowing about communities up the Welsh Valleys, I wonder if there would have been a difference. But that's a real problem we've got, that Judges come in and they just don't know what's going on because they don't know the context of some of this legislation and I think that's a real problem for Wales.

---

[47] *R (Williams) v Caerphilly County Borough Council* [2019] EWHC Admin 1618.

Matthew's example goes to show how a mere word, 'aspirational', uttered by someone in a position of power – a High Court judge from England – has the capacity to completely undermine a unique piece of Welsh legislation that has important meaning for the people of Wales. Matthew's comments suggest that the English judge is perceived as an outsider to the local community, lacking local (cultural) knowledge and authenticity. In other words, the 'parachuted' judge wields enormous power in a jurisdiction in which they are not fully embedded in the legal context or framework of devolution. This highlights how differences in legislation and cultures across jurisdictions can have significant consequences and a direct material impact on how particular legislation is understood.

Identified groups most impacted and (made) marginalized

We asked each participant if they could identify any patterns or particular challenges for certain groups of people related to issues concerning social security, housing and access to food and fuel. The answers from practitioners included the following: disability (Matthew, Seth, Sam, Eva, David and Rose), physical and mental challenges, learning challenges (David and Rose), neurodevelopmental difficulties, including autism (David), addictions (Rose) – particularly families with disabled children or another disabled family member (Eva).

Seth remarks that the increased risk factors due to disability may include (potential) reduced ability to work, additional living costs (perhaps needing an additional bedroom for a carer), increased transportation cost due to requirements to travel by taxi rather than public transport, as well as a lack of adaptable housing. He estimates that there are approximately 700,000 people in poverty in Wales, which is about a quarter of the population. About half of them, he states, live in families where one person has a disability.

Matthew, who is a solicitor, reflects on how groups are marginalized when schools and libraries, for instance, are closed or moved. He states that 'for them [disadvantaged groups], I think, the biggest problem often is access, and so when something changes, their access ability changes, and then often that's maybe not understood by the decision makers as well as it should be'.

Mental health challenges appear to be particularly difficult, especially because of stigma and difficulties for people to provide evidence of the impact of mental illness on their daily lives. Rose estimates that approximately 80 per cent of people she represents at tribunal have mental health problems that 'it is the reality that the people who kind of most fall foul, if you like, or most get negative decisions, are often people with mental health problems. Also, some people with learning disabilities, or a combination of both, and lots of people with addiction problems'. Rose said that over the years, she had seen a big increase in addictions, particularly heroin use in her area of South Wales. Long-term users, she said, develop quite serious physical and mental health problems as a result of these addictions. She stated that, as a result, it is difficult for them to access support services, are often hard to reach and sometimes difficult to work with for various reasons related to negative experiences, distrust and paranoia.

Children from disadvantaged backgrounds

According to Sam, children are also particularly disadvantaged if they also have additional protected characteristics, such as children in low-income families, asylum-seeking children, children in the care system, young carers and disabled children. David stated that another group at higher risk are children and young people who have additional educational needs, with people often describing a sense of 'having to battle or fight to access services'. Sam stated that Wales has a high number of children coming into the care system, more than most other parts of the UK. However, he thinks that this is a positive response in terms of people raising concerns and issues around safeguarding and child protection.

Minority ethnic background

Although based on limited data, Seth stated that the data they do have show that those from a minority ethnic background are more at risk of living in poverty and are at risk of living in overcrowded housing and bad-quality housing. However, he points out that the highest number of families living in poverty are White working families.

Refugees/asylum seekers and others with no recourse to public funds

Pointing out the difficulties experiences by asylum seekers, David remarks:

> It really draws into sharp focus, while the current social safety nets are I would argue inadequate, and you can see that in the number of people who claim welfare benefits who are still in poverty, but if you look at those who've got much more restricted entitlements to welfare benefits like asylum seekers, refugees, those denied recourse to public funds, it really puts [it] in sharp relief.

Kim notes that those with no recourse to public funds include 2,500 children.
Other groups that are at higher risk of poverty are lone parents (Eva and Kim), families on means-tested benefits (Eva), people working in

the low-paid manufacturing sector or on zero-hours contracts (Kim) and people with low skills/qualifications (David). However, it is recognized that there is intersectionality between these broad categories, as well as gender and educational dimensions, and that those with overlapping protected characteristics will be at further increased risk. The limitations of devolved powers in Wales have a direct impact on service provision and delivery, service implementation and the routes available for challenging problems when they arise.

Fragmentation of services

Social security is not devolved in Wales and in order to counteract the impact of austerity and inadequate social security support from the UK government, the Welsh government has allocated significant funding to mitigate the impact under specific areas of devolved policy such as food, housing or health. Seth estimated that this amounts to approximately £400 million, which to put it into context, he said, is the same amount that the DWP spends on Job Seeker's Allowance and Universal Credit in Wales combined. He recognizes this is 'a huge amount of money', relatively speaking, but 'it's not working for enough people'. One reason for this, he thinks, is that the system lacks a single point of access. This point is iterated by other practitioners as well. Eva states that unlike Scotland, which has essentially devolved quite significant parts of its social security system, 'Wales is just in this weird halfway place'. Earlier in the conversation, Eva referred to the Welsh benefits system as 'nebulous', which she then explained as follows: 'what has really *characterized* the system I think is the fact that it's just been so incremental and ... a lot of it is just *reactive* kind of [small laugh] and that's what I mean about being incoherent in terms of, you know ... it's just little bits and pieces'.

Specific services, such as council tax reduction schemes, are provided in different ways by local authorities, so there is no uniformity across Wales for the provision of various types of services. Eva stated that although there is a legal obligation to provide free school meals and eligibility criteria are set at a national level, how the provision is administered, including the value of the meal, is usually decided at the local authority level. This means that in one local authority, a child may have a daily allowance of £2.35 and in another authority it is £2.90. The frameworks around the provision of free breakfast in primary schools also allow discretion to individual schools to decide whether or not to offer it.

In response to the interviewer's question on the accessibility of services and whether or not people know where to go to get help, Sam responded that quite a lot of advice in Wales is fragmented:

> [But] in a positive way ... we don't have like a one-stop shop service as advice in Wales which in some ways, that would be good if there was one point of call, but sometimes, it's giving families and children the flexibility to engage with different services. So, I think there's a great deal of promotion that goes on, in terms of those services.

Sam feels that precisely because of limitations of powers in Wales, a lot of attention is directed at building awareness and signposting to services to ensure families know there is help and support available to them. He describes the support and services as 'kind of mitigation services' with a strong element of prevention, particularly in relation to early years and preventing problems escalating. However, when financial issues and fuel poverty are linked to lack of income, the powers of Welsh government are significantly reduced in terms of addressing that. Although there's lots of support and interventions for families, Sam says, 'it does not lift them out of low income'.

Sam also recognizes that there are geographical differences in terms of being able to access support, as it is more difficult to scale up services in rural areas: 'you hope there isn't a postcode-lottery to services but we know that there is, but that's not necessarily rural-urban, but I get the nature is there's more service face to face in urban settings'.

Lack of recognition in services on the interrelationship of rights

Another way in which the notion of fragmentation came to the fore in the interviews is through a lack of recognition of the interrelationship of rights, not from the individual practitioners we spoke to, but the welfare system more generally. The interviewer asked Seth regarding some of the main challenges people had with respect to accessing their right to social security. He responded that current responses can be quite siloed in their approach:

> If you've got a crisis, be that with housing, for example, you're in rent arrears, the first port of call tends to be to your social landlords. By the time you come to get advice centrally, your housing situation has entirely been sorted, because your social landlord, they're a housing organization, they know every last bit of housing welfare support you're entitled to. What doesn't happen very well, at the moment though, is that we're not very good then at transferring that person to make sure that they then also get free school meals if they've got children, so, it's really quite siloed, and that's something that's a big barrier. If we could shift some of that that could, you know, have a big impact.

The notion of siloed approaches was also echoed by Kim, as she reflected on challenges within her own work focused on the right to food. She said that one of the big challenges is having a very global food system, with more than 50 per cent of the food in Wales coming from 'across the water', and that those processes are influenced by a small number of powerful institutions:

> That is very challenging ... when you're trying to make change in one little part of the world [laughs] so I guess that's one challenge at a macro level, and then at a micro-level trying to get people to come out of their silos is very, very difficult you know, so working with government, how do you get people who are doing, you know, agricultural policy talking to people who are doing food manufacturing policy talking to people in, you know, welfare team and in the health team. So, trying to get those different strategies linked up is really challenging and government are not good at doing it.

Kim explains that the food poverty issue is challenging because nobody wants to talk about it, it is not being measured sufficiently well in Wales and 'it's very difficult to find the right space to have the conversations that are actually going to make a difference'. She highlights the intersections with manufacturing and retail sectors, which often do not pay a living wage, leading to food poverty and the need for staff to access food banks. The food industry 'absolutely has a part to play in these discussions', she says, and she thinks that one of the challenges is to make the food poverty business everybody's business.

One of the themes that resonates across the Welsh data is that although Wales has a wide variety of programmes and services to address people's needs, it is constrained in its delivery and implementation mechanisms by a lack of coordination across local authorities. In addition, the ways in which local authorities implement services differently creates additional difficulties for rights holders to know where to turn for advice and the processes involved in terms of challenging a problem when required. We return to this topic throughout our discussions and analysis.

Closer to government

One advantage Wales has due to its small size as a devolved nation is a sense of being closer to government. Many practitioners felt that in Wales, people feel more able to engage their government over issues they face, using their local councils as a source of information and solutions. We asked Sam, whose work closely engages with children, youth and families, to what extent information is taken up at a higher level. In other words, does the two-way communication result in change? Sam's answer acknowledged that it is difficult to assess whether the government has taken on board suggested changes after 'they've had a couple of conversations', but that sometimes the impact is visible. He recounted an event that took place just a few months earlier:

> We convened a group of young people to meet with our First Minister just before Christmas, at his request. I mean, it came out quite late in the day, but we managed to get a good group of young people together and they raised a number of issues around mental health, schools returning. And we did see – you know, he did refer to that and his education minister referred to engagement he'd had with young people fairly recently, in terms of informing his decisions around COVID. Young people also then raised, at that meeting, that they weren't getting sufficient information around COVID in a child-friendly manner. Within a week, we had a meeting of senior comms leads across Welsh government officials. So, one concrete example of how things can get changed, and we are influencing, and I think that's when we go to these large meetings at a government level, there's a good attendance rate because people will attend, because they know that we will have ministers on the call, senior officials. It's not all great, I won't pretend, it isn't, because it's all about individuals, isn't it, at the end of the day … if you can work well with a couple officials, you can make some inroads.

Eva also describes the conventional ways for engaging with government, such as writing consultation responses to committees or attempting to speak to individual politicians. Several times a year, her organization is able to communicate with civil servants through the anti-poverty coalition, where concerns can be raised and government can respond. She also echoes Sam's concerns that if the Welsh government doesn't want to listen to the committees and engage with 'very sensible evidence-based recommendations', progress is halted.

Sam's example shows an alternative route[48] to justice outside of legal processes – that when individuals who are directly impacted by SR issues participate in consultation processes, there can be positive outcomes. However, Sam and Eva also recognize that there are limitations, as implementation and progress are dependent on individuals being responsive to change and taking action.

---

[48] We adopt the term 'routes to justice' to mean pathways/avenues to access justice, including pathways to secure an effective remedy.

Legal routes to a remedy

We asked each of the interview participants how people can assert their rights when violations occur, and whether there are legal means for doing so. The shared perspective from practitioners was an apprehension for going down a legal court route for solving problems related to poverty, in large part because such an approach is hindered by limited powers under devolution, a lack of knowledge from rights holders about their rights and the means to challenge a problem, a lack of legal expertise, as well as limitations to funding for legal processes. Several participants expressed that there is simply no appetite for it. Kim said: 'I'm just not sure that we've got the-, whether it's the appetite or the teeth for the legal thing'. Sam reiterates this sentiment and links it to the complexities of the justice system:

> I would say there's not an appetite for it, I guess, in government at the moment and I guess it may well be because of trying to get pieces of legislation through where there has to be engagement with England on, as with the defence and reasonable punishment, our social services Act took a number of years to go through. Where there's other pieces of legislation that go through a lot quicker, where almost everything is devolved to Wales ... you know we can make changes a lot quicker, where we have the powers, where we have to try and engage with England, it just slows down the process.

Limited powers under devolution

Although there are efforts in Wales to adopt a more human rights-based approach, there are no redress mechanisms to challenge decisions for children, Sam says that 'we have rights legislation in Wales, currently, for children, but there's no opportunities for redress mechanism, linked to that, and opportunities for children, or professionals on behalf of children, to challenge decisions that have been made at a government level around children's rights more broadly'. He goes on to say that the Welsh government took the 'due regard' approach because the 'redress' approach links into the court system and the complexities surrounding it. He says that there are continued calls for legislation akin to what's being done in Scotland, but that this explains why laws are as they currently are. In his opinion, 'Ministers are very much looking at what's within their powers and what sits outside their powers'.

David also recognizes that access to legal routes for challenging a problem varies depending on the issue in question. He points to a legal framework in relation to refugees and organizations, such as the Welsh Refugee Council, that will provide legal advice to help people to assert their rights, albeit 'a very fraught and complex field', he admits.

In addition, David said, there is significant legislation in relation to special educational needs and more recourse to legal remedies than there is in other areas. 'It feels in other areas, but I'm not an expert', he said, 'that there is less recourse to it. I mean, I suppose it depends on how clear the legal rights are.' He explains that there are legal duties in relation to the provision of alternative education, and that local authorities can be challenged if it is deemed that provisions are inadequate and the legal obligations are not being met:

> So there are obviously areas where there are legal rights that can be asserted, particularly around education, but less so in relation to poverty. And I guess there's a legal framework in terms of what your rights are in relation to universal credit but the perception is that it feels, but I'm not an expert on this area and I'm sure others would have views on it, that [the] DWP has much more discretion about who gets support and who doesn't, what you can be sanctioned for and so on and-, you know, it's not an area I've looked at, but I don't hear as much about legal cases being brought to challenge those decisions.

David's point about 'how clear the legal rights are' is particularly significant with respect to enforcement. In order to uphold rights, they must be clearly defined, which offers an important counterdiscourse to the critique that SR are not justiciable due to being vague. The indeterminacy critique can be counteracted by recognizing the role different epistemic communities play in their interpretation. It is the responsibility of the legislature to ensure that rights are clearly defined, and equally, courts should not abdicate their role in giving meaning and content to rights.[49]

Lack of knowledge in seeking a remedy and limited legal expertise

Kim points out that another reason why legal remedies are not accessible is due to a lack of knowledge, both on the part of rights holders and those offering advice, relating to the legal consciousness barrier (the first barrier in the access to justice journey discussed in Chapter 4). Rights holders often do not recognize that they have rights, nor do they possess the knowledge about where to turn to challenge a problem. She said that 'the general feeling is that

---

[49] Frank Michelman, 'Socioeconomic Rights in Constitutional Law: Explaining America Away' (2008) 6(3–4) *International Journal of Comparative Constitutional Law*, pp 663–686, p 683; Kathrine G. Young, *Constituting Economic and Social Rights* (Oxford: Oxford University Press, 2012), p 30; Colm O'Cinneide, 'The Constitutionalisation of Economic and Social Rights' in Helena Alviar Garcia, Karl Klare and Lucy A. Williams (eds), *Social and Economic Rights in Theory and Practice, Critical Inquiries* (Abingdon: Routledge, 2015), p 274; Boyle (n 28), p 14.

people don't tend to challenge their rights because they don't know how to and, you know, actually you need somebody there with a lawyer's hat on to help you do that, and I'm not sure that we've necessarily got that expertise in Wales, I don't know'. She also wondered whether it might be because in Wales they are 'a bit closer to the political process and a bit closer to having conversations with people' or if it is a matter of being too polite. Perhaps, she said, 'people just do not know that they have those rights or that there are not enough activism type organizations that are supporting that push'.

Rose, who has worked in the advice sector for nearly 25 years and now works solely to assist people with challenging benefits decisions, also pointed out that the provision of specialist advice is inadequate to meet the demands of clients, especially since this demand has increased. She said that there are more organizations that will help people at initial stages, although she recognizes that these services are also underresourced, with demand vastly outstripping supply.

With regard to housing rights, Seth identified a lack of knowledge and awareness on where to turn for help. Referring to the Renting Homes (Wales) Act 2016, he noted that once in force, it should improve the situation for tenants, but, he said, there will still be a reliability on people going to court to enforce their rights, and he wondered whether people actually know that this sort of recourse is available to them. He suspected that in most cases, rights holders would need to seek out support from agencies to begin the process of resolving their problem and getting a remedy. Seth thought that when landlords are not challenged for behaving in ways that violate a person's right to adequate housing, they will likely get away with it and problems will continue, and that adequate and accessible mechanisms for challenging problems are thus imperative to making rogue landlords accountable.

Lack of funding for legal advice and representation

Access to legal funding is a significant barrier raised across the data for all jurisdictions and will be explored in greater detail later on. This section will briefly outline the challenges raised specifically within the Welsh context. Rose recalls that approximately ten years ago, there was a change in community legal service, where funding for solicitors to represent clients at benefit tribunals was pulled, which, she said, had a big impact resulting in significantly reduced access to funding. As Rose works for the local authority, her clients do not have to pay for legal advice and tribunal representation, but, she says, only some decisions within social security have a legal right to challenge; a host of other decisions do not have a right to appeal. Rose said those are ones where 'you need to speak to somebody, in that department, and persuade them that they're not applying the policy correctly, or that they've made a mistake. You know sometimes it's just they've made mistakes or something was a mistake on a form'.

Sam raised access to legal aid as 'a huge concern for people in Wales as well as England' and as a barrier to legal mechanisms for upholding SR. Kim reiterated this when she said that: 'If you do have a challenge around your rights, usually you're economically challenged, so then how do you go about getting that support to deal with it?'

In England and Wales, legal aid has historically functioned as a pillar of the welfare state.[50] The Legal Aid, Sentencing and Punishment of Offenders Act 2012 (LASPO) has effectively ended legal aid provision for legal problems encountered in relation to debt, welfare benefits, employment, education, most housing disputes, private family law, non-asylum immigration, clinical negligence, consumer or contract disputes and criminal injury.[51] While exceptional case funding is available on the grounds of a breach of human rights, the definition of human rights is restricted to those falling within the ambit of the ECHR or retained EU law, excluding most economic and SR by extension.[52] LASPO does not impede a case being taken on these grounds, but the practical effect is that people who cannot afford to access justice will be prevented from doing so.[53] In other words, LASPO is the manifestation of a 'conscious decision to substantially withdraw public funding for the support of the justice system and for promoting access to justice'.[54] One of the key calls in the literature is to address the legal aid crisis.[55] The dismantling of legal aid has led to 'a court system facing collapse, a legal system facing disordered change, and litigants left to steer through the rough waters of legal dispute without the guidance of legal advice and assistance'.[56]

In his work as a solicitor, Matthew and his colleagues have found that legal aid was not being made available for any COVID-19 challenge cases.

---

[50] The original conception of the early legal aid scheme was seen as 'one of the great pillars of the post-welfare state'. Sarah Moore and Alex Newbury, *Legal Aid in Crisis, Assessing the Impact of Reform* (Bristol: Bristol University Press. 2017), p 17, Lord Beecham, HL Debate, 19 May 2011, col 1535.

[51] For a full list of scope changes, see schedule 1 to LASPO and the practical 'bible on legal aid', *Legal Aid Handbook 2024/25*. Vicky Ling and Sue James, *Legal Aid Handbook* (Legal Action Group 2024/25).

[52] LASPO 2012, s 10(3)(a).

[53] Moore and Newbury (n 51), p 13: 'The cuts to legal aid don't thwart litigiousness: they simply mean that some people are disallowed access to the law when pursuing justice.'

[54] LASPO led to a conscious decision to substantially withdraw public funding for the support of the justice system and for promoting access to justice. Hazel Genn, 'When Law Is Good for Your Health: Mitigating the Social Determinants of Health through Access to Justice' (2019) 72(1) *Current Legal Problems*, pp 159–202, p 171.

[55] Moore and Newbury (n 50).

[56] Ibid, p 76.

When the interviewer asked why that was the case, Matthew answered 'well, because who's in charge of the Legal Aid Agency? It's the government, isn't it? [half laughs] so the government giving people money to sue the government, so no'.

Clearly, when people do not have the means to bear these kinds of legal costs themselves, they are barred from securing a legal remedy. But Matthew recognizes that this also causes other potential problems. People may use strategies of crowdfunding or attempt to raise money privately, but these approaches also risk undermining the legal aid system, as Matthew reckons that the response from legal aid will be: 'Why do we need to have legal aid if people can crowdfund all the time?' In this sense, the COVID-19 crisis has exposed another problem in legal funding.

In addition, Matthew iterates the perception expressed by other practitioners that people do not know that they can exercise their right in the legal context, and that they may not realize that legal aid is still available, 'even though it can be hard work to get it, people just don't know these things'. He thinks it is important to get awareness out to people and notes that when particularly disadvantaged groups engage with local authority agencies, they are often dissuaded from seeking legal help. He said, 'they'll say, you don't want to bother with a *lawyer*'.

Likewise, Matthew questions whether the third sector are well informed to guide people to seek legal advice. He refers to Shelter as an example of an organization doing valuable work in regard to homelessness, but states that he had spoken with other people working for charity organizations who were less informed about legal rights and remedies:

> They don't even know anything about judicial review or they don't know about legal aid, they just don't know. Obviously, people are coming to them with their issues and they might say to them, 'oh well, we'll try and write a letter to the local authority or something'. They never give them the legal option because they're not aware of it, you know, and that's part of the problem.

The right to food and free school meals provision

Although the research team did not set out to focus attention on one particular issue, many of the practitioners in the Welsh case study worked in areas addressing children's rights and food poverty, and, as such, access to these rights were discussed quite intensively. We will briefly describe the response of the Welsh government at the onset of the COVID-19 pandemic with regard to the provision of free school meals for eligible families.

Kim thought that the Welsh government was 'very proactive' in the first COVID-19 lockdown in the spring of 2020 to continue its support of families who receive free school meal provision over the Easter holiday. She stated that funding and guidance were made available for local authorities to provide those meals in one of three ways: vouchers, cash or meal delivery. Some local authorities opted for cash payments and others adopted a mixed approach. The Welsh government then made the commitment very quickly to provide that support all the way through to the Easter holidays in 2021, but, she continued, 'this was before the Marcus Rashford thing kicked off' (referring to the Marcus Rashford campaign, urging the UK government to reverse a decision not to provide free school meals during the summer holidays in 2020).

The programme has provided some protection for children who are receiving school meals, but there are large numbers of children still going hungry. Kim quotes figures that show that there are 70,000 children in Wales who are living in poverty, but who are not eligible for free school meals. Those children are not getting free school meals at school or over the holidays. The big concern, Kim says, was that at that time, Brexit was coming down the line, along with a potential 18 per cent increase in food prices, and it was 'going to cause *massive* problems for those families'. The reason for this is that the cut-off criteria for being eligible for free school meals is family earnings of less than £7,400 a year. Based on the forthcoming statistics from the Cost of the School Day project, Wales is definitely the worst-performing country among the four nations, she says. She calls for a four nations' appraisal to assess how much money per child is being invested by the governments and how much protection is actually being provided. At the moment, she says, it feels like they are providing a section of families 'with fairly good support and then another subsection with absolutely no support whatsoever', indicating unequal access to food for some families. Kim's example also highlights issues in identifying need and the shifting context created by Brexit.

One other aspect of the provision of school meals that is worth noting is related to the delivery of services and whether local authorities choose to provide vouchers, cash payments or food parcels. Organizations, such as the one Eva works for campaign for a 'cash first' approach to alleviating food poverty, which is what people on the receiving end generally prefer. Eva states:

> We want to see the direct value being transferred to families so that they can maximize the amount available and buy their own food and this is something that the people we've done research with have overwhelmingly said that's what they prefer and it works best. So, although people are happy with food parcels, vouchers and things on the whole, there's always quite a significant minority whose needs

aren't met by those schemes of support. So, you know, we really want to see cash first.

Eva describes significant resistance from some local authorities to provide cash support and great difficulty in changing mindsets.

The Welsh context has raised significant challenges related to devolution, with unique impacts on Wales in terms of meeting SR. Wales also shows how alternative pathways can sometimes lead to positive change – these routes appear to be explored more consistently in Wales due to a general shared feeling of being 'closer to government'. However, another dynamic expressed through interviews with practitioners was the notion of fragmentation on various levels, a point to which we will return in greater detail in Chapter 5.

Northern Ireland: terminal illness criteria impede access to benefits

The practitioner interviews within the NI case study loosely focused on the *Cox*[57] legal case, which challenged Regulation 2 and Schedule 9, paragraph 1 of the Universal Credit Regulations (Northern Ireland) 2016 made under the Welfare Reform (Northern Ireland) Order 2015 that in order to automatically and immediately qualify for Universal Credit and PIP on the ground of terminal illness, an applicant has to demonstrate that their death could reasonably be expected within six months.

In addition, the practitioner interviews illuminate the specific context for SR in NI, impacted by the aftermath of conflict, power sharing following the1998 peace agreement and political instability due to the suspension of the National Assembly. These factors are identified as closely linked to a particularly dire housing situation in NI, which will be discussed later on in this case study.

We interviewed six practitioners, half of whom had a connection to *Cox*, including a solicitor and two welfare rights advisors. We also interviewed an activist with a human rights NGO, the chief executive of an NGO for housing and a volunteer assisting those in need. (See Table 3.4.)

In late 2018, Lorraine Cox was diagnosed with motor neurone disease, a progressive neurological condition for which there is no effective treatment or cure. She was given an estimated life expectancy of two to five years and advised that as her illness progressed, her loss of motor function would become more severe and her care and mobility needs would increase. Ms Cox applied for Universal Credit and PIP. If a medical practitioner had certified that she could reasonably be expected to die within six months,

---

[57] *Cox* (n 3).

Table 3.4: Northern Ireland case study participants

Name	Role
Josie	Chief Executive, NGO for housing
Chloe	Volunteer
Oliver	Solicitor, NGO for legal services
Rowan	Welfare rights advisor, NGO for cancer patients
Kamilla	Welfare rights advisor, local community NGO
Esther	Housing activist, NGO for human rights

the 'special rules on terminal illness' would have applied and she would have been immediately entitled to Universal Credit and to PIP at the enhanced rate for help with daily living and the standard rate for mobility. However, because her life expectancy exceeded six months, there was a qualifying period of six months, and she had to undergo assessments to prove the existence of functional impairment. Therefore, it was not until mid-2019 that she established her entitlement to the benefits.

At the time of making her application for PIP in March 2018, Ms Cox's symptoms were less severe than they would be a year later when it was determined that she was entitled to the benefit. Kamilla was the welfare rights advisor who met Ms Cox when she requested help in raising a mandatory reconsideration after her initial application for PIP was denied. The mandatory reconsideration awarded her 8 points, which gave her the standard Daily Living Allowance of approximately £8 per week. She decided to appeal and when she received her appeal application form, she returned to Kamilla for assistance and representation at the tribunal.

Kamilla recalled that the evidence showed that her illness mostly affected the left side of her body. Because the criteria for PIP are so strict, Kamilla said, decisions are not based on the type of illness or condition a person has, but how it impacts them:

> So they [the Department for Communities] made the decision because she could drive, because she could do things, albeit slowly, and she had the use of her other hand, this was all … they were basing the decision on that, she could only get 8 points. And the consultant that she was under, he said in all his letters how progressive her type of motor neurone was … I've met Lorraine in person, I think it was probably August–September time 2018 and then I would have met her a couple of times in between that, coming for an appeal prep and every time I met her, I could see a deterioration in her. And because PIP is so strict, any deterioration after the date of decision won't be considered.

This is a crucial point, because for degenerative illnesses, such as motor neurone disease, the full extent of the illness is not considered. Kamilla explained that Ms Cox made her claim in March 2018 and received a decision in July that year. However, her appeal was not heard until April the following year, more than a year after she had made her initial claim. On recalling the event, Kamilla said:

> We went to the appeal and I remember going into the panel and speaking to them before Lorraine came in and I said to them, you know, I said like is there no way round this? You know, obviously she has motor neurone, it's a progressive disease. Of course, there's going to be a deterioration in 12 months and I remember the legal member saying to me ... I don't call them by their first name and they don't call me by my first name, and I remember him just looking at me and he shook his head and he says, Kamilla, I was up half the night last night going through this case and going through it and going through it again and he says, our hands are tied. He says, they are tied, and, this girl, you know, obviously she's going to be getting worse and worse and worse and it's awful and I could see the empathy in him. And he would be a hard nut panel member, you know, but that day, you could see that he had wracked his mind, you know, he had really thought and he said, if I could give her anymore, he says, 'I'd give her the whole thing', but we're bound by the law of the benefit'.

The six-month waiting period linked to the definition of terminal illness had been raised as a point of concern by other practitioners some time before *Cox* was identified as a potential opportunity to address problems with access to PIP.

Defining 'terminally ill'

Rowan, who works as a benefits advisor at a cancer hospital, had flagged up a problem with the policy's determining criteria for who is considered 'terminally ill' and thought it should be evaluated. He said that 'part of our job is to escalate things ... what we would do then is to escalate it to the Law Centre to say "right, you know, there's an issue here with how the social security system's working, it doesn't seem fair or logical and you know, is there a legal recourse to try and get that changed"?'.

However, Rowan said that prior to taking the issue to the law centre, he had participated in a quarterly meeting at the Department for Communities with representatives of PIP to raise the issue. This occurred shortly after the results were published of an independent review on how the PIP assessment was working in NI (also referred to as the Walter Rader report).[58] Rowan

---

[58] 'Independent Review of the PIP Assessment Process in Northern Ireland – Report and Response' (Department for Communities, 20 November 2018),

recalled that most of the points raised in the assessment were accepted by the Department for Communities, but 'what they said was that the one that recommended that the terminal illness six-month definition [be] removed and done on a clinical assessment, they said that they couldn't. They said it was interesting but they couldn't make a decision on it because there was no Minister' (the Northern Ireland Assembly was suspended during that period). At that point, Rowan approached Oliver, who was a solicitor at the law centre.

Oliver recalled when Rowan came to him regarding the six-month rule, stating how unfair it was and asking whether there was merit for a legal challenge. Oliver agreed that there was, but needed a client to take the case forward. At the same time, according to Oliver, Ms Cox herself had been campaigning on the issue and had provided input to the All-Party Parliamentary Group for Terminal Illness, raising awareness of issues relating to terminal illness in Parliament.[59] Oliver became aware of Ms Cox when he heard her speaking to the BBC with the frontline organization supporting her about what happened to her in the PIP case. 'We identified her as a client', he said, 'and we made contact and said we might be able to take a case here', and as such there were multiple organizations involved in the case before it went to the High Court. According to Rowan, the welfare benefits advisor who raised the issue with the law centre, there had been consideration of using a cancer patient for the case, but it was determined that terminal cancer prognoses are fairly straightforward. The degenerative nature of motor neurone disease, on the other hand, clearly illustrated why the current decision-making criteria were not fit for purpose, as non-cancer conditions, such as motor neurone disease, have unpredictable trajectories that make accurate prognoses and timescales difficult to assess.

On 7 July 2020, in *Cox*, the High Court found that Regulations made under the NI (Welfare Reform) Act 2015 resulted in an outcome that was 'manifestly without reasonable foundation'.[60] The Court found that there had been a violation of Article 14, Article 8 and Article 1 of Protocol 1 ECHR. It invited the parties to take time to digest the contents of the judgment and invite them to jointly present it with an agreed draft final order dealing with the questions of the appropriate remedies and costs.[61]

---

https://www.communities-ni.gov.uk/publications/independent-review-pip-assessment-process-northern-ireland-report-and-response

[59] 'Inquiry into Legal Definition of Terminal Illness' (Marie Curie, 2022), https://www.mariecurie.org.uk/globalassets/media/documents/policy/briefings-consultations/marie-curie-submission-appg-inquiry-into-legal-definition-of-terminal-illness.pdf

[60] *Cox* (n 3), [104].

[61] Ibid, [109].

In Oliver's own words, the High Court ruled there was discrimination in the case. He said:

> There's the group of people who have a diagnosis that they're likely to die within six months, but subsequently live beyond those six months and continue to receive the benefit, and then the group who are terminally ill but aren't diagnosed that they're likely to die within six months, so the different treatment was found by the court to be discriminatory.

At this time, Ms Cox was also awarded more points, gaining access to a more appropriate amount of PIP. However, it took two years to receive this outcome. Following the judgment, the NI Assembly considered the case and passed a motion that the six-month criterion for terminal illness be removed from the Regulations (although this made no immediate change to the application of the existing Regulations).[62]

The Department for Communities appealed the judgment of the High Court and on 3 August 2021 the Court of Appeal gave judgment in favour of the Department,[63] meaning that Ms Cox ultimately lost the case. The Court of Appeal recognized that her circumstances fell within the ambit of Article 14, but concluded that the difference in treatment between Ms Cox and a person suffering from a progressive illness whose death was reasonably expected within months was justified. The reasoning of the court is summarized as follows:

- Ms Cox's case is about whether and where to draw the line within the welfare system.
- Parliamentary consideration was given to the definition of 'terminally ill' in 1990 and 2010. Evidence indicated that the system operated well in practice until recently.
- There is no dispute that some special provision is necessary for those who might die as a result of a progressive illness in the course of the application process for benefits.
- Extension of the SRTI [Special Rules on Terminal Illness] to those with a progressive illness as a consequence of which death can reasonably be expected would change the basis of the award from needs-based to determination by diagnosis.

---

[62] Official Report, (Hansard), Tuesday 6 October 2020, vol. 131, No. 4, https://data.niassembly.gov.uk/HansardXml/plenary-06-10-2020.pdf

[63] *Department for Communities and DWP v Lorraine Cox* [2021] NICA 46.

- There is an element of clinical judgement involved in the determination of prognosis and this is an adequate and acceptable tool in the circumstances.
- One of the options open to policy makers is to have a test based wholly on clinical judgement. The court is not, however, in a position to consider factors, such as the robustness of compliance with a needs-based approach, the risk of diagnostic variability and impact on budget, which would be required to alter the current policy.[64]

Lord Chief Justice Morgan concluded that:

[T]he legislature has been involved in a detailed consideration of where to draw the line in this welfare benefit in 1990 and 2010. There has been continuing review of that decision since 2018. The Minister intends to submit a further proposed amendment to the Northern Ireland Assembly which will provide an opportunity for debate and reflection by the legislature. This is an area where considerable weight should be given to the views of the primary decision maker. These choices are for the political process and not for the courts.[65]

In June 2021, shortly before the judgment was issued, the Communities Minister Deirdre Hargey outlined her plans to extend the terminal illness provision to 12 months.[66] The Court of Appeal noted this ministerial intervention in its judgment.[67]

The Social Security (Terminal Illness) Act (Northern Ireland) 2022, which came into force in April 2022, adopts a 12-month rule for terminal illness. The wider 12-month definition aligns more with that used by the health service in NI and the General Medical Council for end-of-life care.[68] However, the Bill stops short of the Walter Rader's assessment process recommendation in his independent review of 2018 that the clinical judgment of a medical practitioner, indicating that the claimant has a terminal illness, should be sufficient to allow special rules to apply, which is the approach adopted in Scotland. Speaking on behalf of the Committee of Communities, Kellie Armstrong, Member of the Legislative Assembly

---

[64] For a discussion of the history of the case law and associated ministerial announcements, see https://www.lawcentreni.org/ni-court-of-appeal-upholds-terminal-illness-rules/
[65] *Cox* (n 3), [73].
[66] 'Communities Minister Hargey to Extend Terminal Illness Provision in Social Security Benefits', Department for Communities, 30 June 2021, https://www.northernireland.gov.uk/news/communities-minister-hargey-extend-terminal-illness-provision-social-security-benefits
[67] *Cox* (n 3), [32].
[68] Social Security (Terminal Illness) Bill: Second Stage (mySociety, 7 December 2021), https://www.theyworkforyou.com/ni/?id=2021-12-07.2.31

and Chair of the Assembly All-Party Group on Disability, commented that 'although the Committee fully supports the Minister in bringing forward this very important legislation as a very welcome first step, I hope that it will not be too long before we see the Department gather the data that it needs in order to look further at a clinical judgement model. We welcome the Minister's comment that the legislation is a staging post'.[69]

It is thus hoped that further legislative reform will take place in future to align the approach in NI with the Social Security Scotland model. While extending the six-month criterion to 12 months will benefit some people, it will undoubtedly still exclude others facing terminal illness with a predicted life expectancy beyond 12 months. This is a particularly salient point, given that Ms Cox was given two to five years to live and would still have been excluded from the extended provision. In addition to the barriers faced by her in relation to securing the appropriate level of PIP support, it is clear that the process to do so took far too long, a challenge that will be taken up in our analysis of what constitutes an effective remedy in Chapter 4.

Sufficiency of the individual remedy granted by the High Court

We asked Kamilla, who had worked closely with Lorraine Cox, whether being awarded the higher PIP benefit was a sufficient remedy. Was it a good enough outcome? Kamilla strongly felt that the remedy was ineffective:

> Well, it's good that she's got the higher rate, but no I think from the beginning she should have got the special rules. She shouldn't have had to fight this for two years, like she's wasted two years of her life on the benefits system and it just doesn't make sense, it doesn't make sense that a young woman, and with three children who she's bringing up on her own, [she] should have been using those two years productively with her children, has been focused on the system. And nobody can ever give her, or those two children, those two years back. They're gone.

We asked Rowan the same question and he answered that he believed that the court case was a first step, but did not think it would make any difference to her:

> It's helping people going forward, he said, and it really just depends on the outcome of the work that's being done by the Minister in

---

[69] Social Security (Terminal Illness) Bill: Second Stage, Assembly Business – Executive Committee Business – in the Northern Ireland Assembly at 11:00 am on 7 December 2021 (mySociety, 7 December 2021) https://www.theyworkforyou.com/ni/?id=2021-12-07.2.15

the Department. You know, if they come back and say yes, anybody who is viewed as being a terminally ill patient by their consultant or a specialist nurse, then absolutely, but you just never know ... they've all unintended consequences. If that is the case, then, you know, does the government then review the benefits system and how they deal with- you know, because at the moment if someone's viewed as terminally ill and has less than six months, they pull out all the stops and everything's done straight away for them. Will they continue to do that if there's ... you know, a lot more people ... meeting that definition?

Rowan recognizes that Ms Cox herself will receive little benefit from the challenge she took on, as she is not likely to live long enough to see the process come to a satisfactory conclusion that prevents others from facing the same difficulties. He also raises an important concern about whether changing the definition in legislation will ultimately prompt changes to the benefits system if it is perceived that too many people will then qualify under the special rules.

Resilience: fighting for a collective remedy

Cox also demonstrates another aspect crucial to undertaking a legal case such as this, where it is clear from the start that the fight is going to provide minimal personal gain. The cost for Lorraine Cox has been extremely high, given she spent two years of her very limited timespan in legal proceedings. Not every individual has the strength and capacity to undertake such an endeavour, but Kamilla said that there was no stopping Ms Cox, describing her as 'headstrong' and unwilling to drop the case, despite the fact she was unlikely to receive a satisfactory remedy. 'She's like a dog with a bone', Kamilla said laughingly, 'and she's just not letting it go.' It is thus an important point to consider the burden on an individual level and the associated difficulty in finding someone who is able and willing to see the entire process through.

Despite the forthcoming partial successful legislative outcome of a prolonged legal process, questions remain as to the effectiveness of this remedial approach for Ms Cox, insofar as her route to justice did not resolve the violation, nor did it result in substantive change for those impacted by the legislation either through executive, legislative or judicial pathways (her particular circumstances would not be covered by the new Social Security (Terminal Illness) Act (Northern Ireland) 2022 that extends the six-month threshold to 12 months). The remedial gap in this case is particularly pertinent, given the length of time exhausted by the applicant who only had a limited time to live due to her terminal illness.

Postscript

Sadly, Lorraine Cox lost her battle against motor neurone disease in July 2022, but her bravery and tenacity in seeking justice has led to a change in the law that will help to guarantee SR provisions to make a crucial difference for some in the UK suffering from a terminal illness for a longer period as an essential support for their end-of-life decline.[70]

The right to adequate housing in Northern Ireland

We now turn to the challenges expressed by practitioners in NI regarding access to adequate housing, drawing attention to problems with respect to the availability of social housing, low housing standards, particularly in the private rental sector, tenants' rights, as well as the historic legacy of the unfair distribution of housing between nationalist and unionist communities (with the former still disproportionately impacted).

We asked Esther, who works as a housing activist with a human rights NGO, what she perceived to be some of the most difficult issues to address. She said:

> Housing is a huge one, especially in Northern Ireland because it's so intertwined with so many other issues, you know. We're not just talking about gentrification or people being priced out of areas or land banking, all those kind of things and the lack of social housing that all cities are dealing with. We're also dealing with, you know, the legacy of the Troubles and the fact that still today there's huge discrimination in housing in Belfast in the north, that's been called out by the UN by the European Council for Human Rights, but it's very hard to actually kind of really tackle head on in Northern Ireland. So, just for example, like in an area of Belfast where the Build Homes Now campaign was started, you have an area of the city which is kind of a mosaic of majority kind of unionist Protestant communities and nationalist Catholic communities. So, it's a street-by-street almost kind of thing, but 94 per cent of the housing need in North Belfast is for Catholic families, minority Catholic and minority families.

These local tensions were foregrounded by all the practitioners we interviewed. Josie, head of a housing NGO, echoed concerns about the long waiting lists for social housing, which are exacerbated in particular

---

[70] Law Centre Northern Ireland, 'Lorraine Cox: An Inspiration', 26 July 2022, https://www.lawcentreni.org/news/lorraine-cox-an-inspiration-whose-courage-helped-to-sec ure-fundamental-change-to-the-law-on-terminal-illness/

areas. She said that the waiting list for social housing was just under 40,000 but was also on an upward trend and still growing. She estimated that approximately 1,500 new social houses are built per year, all undertaken by housing associations. However, 'to seriously tackle the waiting list', she said, 'they need to be doing at least double that'. In line with Esther's comments about the difficulties related to sectarian tensions, Josie explained:

> Even if you could build a hundred extra homes tomorrow, you've got to be able to build them in the right place for them to relieve that [pressure] do you understand what I'm saying? You need this, but sometimes the land, available land, isn't where the pressure for housing is the greatest, and it's not as easy as saying … just move to the other side of Belfast because that's where the land is and we'll build houses … because it's just not as easy as that.

Josie went on to say that the three groups whose access to social housing is disproportionately impacted are young people (under the age of 35) on low incomes, people from Black and Asian minority ethnic communities, and lone parents. Some of them are excluded from the social housing list because they are not eligible, she says, but mostly it is because they do not attract sufficient points to qualify for social housing and are therefore pushed into the private rental sector. And this is where Josie believes there are even greater difficulties to access what she would consider a secure and decent home, because in that sector, she said, are the poorer standards and poorer regulations.

Despite the fact that many more households are living in the private rented sector than in the social rented sector, the sector lacks a regulatory framework and tenants have virtually no protection. The interviewer asked Josie why the private rental sector is so unregulated and she answered that 'we have a lot of private landlords who also sit in our Assembly … ideologically there's a view that it's the private sector and the government shouldn't intervene, you know. So, there's all those, and then put on top of that the disruptions to the policy and legislative making processes'. The latter point is also closely linked to extremely low and outdated housing standards in NI.

Outdated fitness standards in the private rental sector

Josie explains that fitness standards are extremely low compared to the rest of the UK and there is no security of tenure. The current fitness standards, Josie said, date back to the early 1990s, meaning that the condition of a home which meets these standards is actually very poor. For example: '[O]ne socket in a room is considered to be an adequate provision of heating, you know. So, one socket in a room that would allow you presumably to plug in an electric heater or something is considered to be adequate heating. Now if you happened to need that socket for anything else ... that's pretty basic, isn't it, I think in this era?'

Josie expressed frustration that the outdated standards are tied, at least in part, to the fact that due to political dispute, the Northern Irish Assembly did not sit for years at a time, impacting on processes to advance political change. She said that 'it's like we've been talking about these things for years, and literally, *literally* there's about to be a change and then suddenly you have no assembly for four years and nothing happens, nothing happens, it just all goes into limbo'.

Furthermore, in terms of access to justice and opportunities to challenge SR violations within the private sector, Josie highlights that things are 'significantly worse' for private tenants than those in social housing. Even with mechanisms in place to protect social housing tenants, access to justice is not guaranteed, she says. Josie lauds that within the social rented sector there are quite well-established kinds of frameworks for redress, and she says:

> Both *internally*, within the social landlords themselves, but then even outside of that, because there's obviously the ombudsman and also there's access to the courts, so you know, if landlords are trying to bring possession claims against social tenants, that has to go to the court, so therefore there is an opportunity to defend the action and there's also the opportunity to appeal. There's you know, access.

However, she quickly points out that it is not necessarily a level playing field, because inevitably the landlord will be represented by probably quite a professional, highly paid legal team, whereas on many occasions the tenants may not even turn up. And if they do, Josie says, it is unlikely they will be represented. In fact, she says, 'most of them don't even turn up because we find that they're encouraged by the landlord *not to turn up*, you know, because the landlord kind of indicates to them that it's not really worth their while, because this is a fait accompli'. It is clear from Josie's comments that simply having mechanisms in place to access court proceedings is not enough when there is a complete absence of equality of arms.

This lack of equality of arms was also noted in the Scottish case study in relation to housing and eviction cases. Freya said:

> We sometimes forget, or there's sometimes a perception that these are eviction cases that are just about nonpayment of rent and all that is required is negotiation of repayment arrangements, when these are actually legal proceedings with lawyers acting for the landlords and rarely lawyers acting for the tenants. So, the statistics on people who are accessing lawyers to represent them are stark. Yet when you have

> a lawyer in who is looking at the paperwork and who is identifying whether things are done properly, i.e. when equality of arms are there, it makes a stark difference to somebody, as I say, keeping their house or not. Or at least, how their case is dealt with.

This would appear to represent a cross-jurisdictional issue with regard to unmet legal needs in terms of access to appropriate legal support in relation to the right to adequate housing.

Another barrier identified in NI is that many private landlords are now refusing to accept tenants who rely on social security benefits, driven by changes in the housing allowance under Universal Credit, which is less generous than the housing benefit it replaces. The 'no DSS' approach (no Department of Social Security), as it is referred to, operates covertly, as landlords will not openly admit to this, but Josie knows that it is happening, constituting a significant barrier to adequate housing based on the source of a person's income.

The limits placed upon legal and political progress in NI are intertwined with ongoing tensions relating to sectarianism, creating additional challenges for accessing justice for SR in NI. This case study highlighted how narratives about the conditionality of rights led to unfit, dehumanizing practices and limited access to effective remedies. These dynamics mirror challenges faced by various groups of rights holders across jurisdictions.

Conclusions

The case studies we have presented here have each provided glimpses of wider issues across the social welfare landscape. Each of them illustrated examples of processes and mechanisms that work together to constitute the jurisdictional frameworks for SR and the systemic gaps in the access to justice journey. Some thematic areas emerge across our case studies, including SR (provision and accountability) gaps when public functions are privatized, poorly planned and executed digitization of welfare provision, the complexities of multiple levels of governance and the fragmentation of services, as well as deprioritization, defunding and withdrawal of key services, including legal aid, advice and legal representation. We see that the burden of challenging the system rests with those who also carry the burden of widespread system failures, shortcomings or poor decision-making processes. The siloed nature of legal issues into distinct fragmented issues from street-level provision all the way up to departmental policy means that the indivisible nature of rights, and the clustered nature of violations, goes unnoticed and unaddressed by the justice system. For example, the cost of rent, the provision of social security, the rise of cost of living and the inability to pay for food, goods and energy are not dealt with as interrelated policy issues. The proliferation of 'banks' for those facing destitution reflect this fragmentation – there are food banks, white goods banks, baby banks, bed banks and so on. The research strongly suggests that more money, rather than vouchers, or fragmented 'banks' is the most appropriate and reliable way to lift people out of destitution and meet their particular needs. There are also, particularly within the devolved context, significant difficulties associated with clarity of competency over different areas of law when reserved and devolved issues collide, such as in relation to social security, housing and immigration.

Fragmentation, complexity and the automation of decision making as well as the accumulation of dehumanizing policy (such as in the case of asylum seekers) can manifest into a system that practitioners identify as 'cruel' and 'absurd'. Our analysis suggests that more interdisciplinary research is required to delve deeper into the decision-making sphere around cultures of denial and disbelief in the provision of care to those in need.[71] At times, the research suggests that policy fragmentation was specifically designed to worsen the conditions of those impacted and this was not always under the guise of 'incentivization', such as in the problematic cases of lone parents, the benefit cap and the disproportionate impact on women and children. Other examples draw on discriminatory discourses that dehumanize groups, such as asylum seekers whose needs are determined by their immigration status rather than as human beings, suggesting there is deeper injustice at play. The environment in which both immigration and social security provision is administered is more than 'hostile' – it can be cruel, dehumanizing, absurd, irrational and violent. This violence becomes embodied injustice for those who bear the brunt of SR violations.

The case studies reveal that courts are often reluctant to engage in matters of economic and social policy reserved to the executive/the legislature. In both the *Cox* and *Pantellerisco* cases, we saw an initial decision that upheld the rights of the individual and in both cases the upper courts took a more deferential position on appeal. These cases draw on discourses that prioritize the role of the legislature and the executive in resolving issues relating to resource allocation on matters of social policy. In the *Cox* case, we saw multi-institutional dialogue between the executive, judiciary and the legislature on the very difficult circumstances faced by those with a terminal illness, and ultimately the NI Assembly passed legislation which attempted to strike a fairer balance in response to Lorraine Cox's case, even though it would not have improved her situation. In the *Pantellerisco* case, we saw a similar

---

[71] See James Souter, 'A Culture of Disbelief or Denial? Critiquing Refugee Status Determination in the United Kingdom' (2011) 1(1) *Oxford Monitor of Forced Migration*, pp 48–59; and Simon Halliday, 'Administrative Justice and Street-Level Emotions: Cultures of Denial in Entitlement Decision-Making' [2021] *Public Law*, pp 727–746.

dialogue emerge, where the DWP acknowledged shortcomings in the social security system and indicated that internal processes to 'test and learn' should remedy any such shortcomings. And yet, there is still no change to the system. The lack of sufficient parliamentary scrutiny of welfare-related legislation was flagged by our practitioners, who appealed for more effort from Parliament to properly interrogate the implications of government policy on social security outcomes. As Tobias claimed, 'it shouldn't be the case that when lawyers come to a situation, it emerges that we're the first people to think about it'. Likewise, government decision makers, he argued, should 'spend time thinking about the implication of laws that affect hundreds of thousands if not millions of people in quite some detail'. Tobias was, he told us, 'astonished' that this often does not happen. Worryingly, in the NI evidence we heard, there was simply no functioning legislature or executive; rather than inertia, it was a governance void.

It is of concern that there is a reluctance of the court to engage in circumstances like that in NI, where there was an absence of a functioning government. Our evidence suggests that courts must be more proactive in circumstances where (a) there is a governance void, (b) where there are legislative blindspots, or (c) where there are examples of legislative and/or executive inertia. Indeed, as we will explore further in the next chapter, it is exactly in these types of circumstances that courts need to interrogate further, and to hold decision makers to account, in justifying their approach. At the very least, this would enable multi-institutional accountability where the court can draw attention to shortcomings, if not issue remedies that directly address them. Finally, and in a similar vein, our practitioners' stories highlighted that because SR are not incorporated as legal rights, all of our decision making, appeals processes and jurisprudence occur without the backdrop of human rights (short of limited ECHR claims). And this is where the greatest added value of social rights as legal rights can be understood. The absence of normative standards according to international human rights obligations (as outlined in Chapter 2) cascades into a litany of violations in people's daily lives. These violations are deeply embedded in the system, and marginalize groups through processes of structural injustice that operate without checks and balances. An important part of making these injustices visible is to render them open to scrutiny. Social rights as legal rights provide a means to do this.

We now delve into our analysis to examine more closely the various elements that constitute the access to justice journey (and the barriers people face) using the normative international human right to an effective remedy as our conceptual framework for justice.

4

The Access to Justice Journey: From Violation to Remedy

Access to justice has often been understood in a narrow sense, relating to the most fundamental barriers people face in having a chance to access a legal process such as access to advice, access to legal representation and access to legal aid. While overcoming these barriers is key to enabling people to access justice, the research also revealed that the access to justice journey requires us to take a step back and view it from a much broader perspective. There are significant gaps that require to be addressed across this journey to enable change.

The easiest way of explaining the gap between the narrow and broad understanding of access to justice is to think of the journey as crossing a large mountain range. To reach the first summit, those at the start of the journey must contend with the immediate barriers they face. These initial barriers may be the only ones that are visible. However, once the first peak is reached, more and more peaks come into view. This briefing explains how to broaden our conception of access to justice beyond those initial barriers towards a conceptualization of access to justice that results in an effective remedy for a violation.

Awareness and legal consciousness

The first barrier identified relates to what is referred to as 'legal consciousness' or an awareness of rights and legal processes. In other words, how can anyone claim their rights if they do not know that the rights exist? The research suggested that people are in the dark and without more human rights knowledge, education, information and awareness raising they could not be expected to know their rights, much less claim them:

People don't understand what their rights are, that they do have these fundamental social rights, you know, they've been undermined. Since, between civil and political rights and social rights, social rights are definitely the poor cousin but I think it has just become a point where it's desperate. Yet politicians I don't think are being held to account for it, you know, you don't see it on the news enough. Poverty is not reported on.' (NI, Chloe,[1] Volunteer)

People need to know about their rights and the processes available to claim those rights before the access to justice journey can begin. Our research suggested that practitioners are concerned that:

(1) people do not know that the rights to housing, food, fuel or social security exist:

So for example, when we went into Leith and we chatted to people about their right to housing and they were like 'right to housing? What are you talking about?', you know, 'what do you mean we've got a right to housing?!' They didn't know that that was there and they thought that it was all about lawyers taking human rights cases. So the narrative about human rights wasn't very clear, that this could be in practice for people. (Scotland, Carole, Consultant and activist, NGO for human rights)

(2) or how to challenge a violation of their rights because they don't know about the processes available to do so, or where to go for help:

The general feeling is that people don't tend to challenge their rights because they don't know how to and actually you need somebody there with a lawyer's hat on or whatever to help you do that. (Wales, Kim, Programme Manager, NGO to combat food poverty)

This means that we do not know the full extent to which people remain 'in the dark' about their rights and how to claim them: 'We often talk about this in work when we have cases, you know, people coming to us with issues. We often think how many more people experience this issue but didn't know where to go to' (NI, Josie, Chief Executive, NGO for housing).

---

[1] In order to ensure the protection of our participants' identities, all individual names used in the book are pseudonyms.

This can mean people who are facing SR violations can be further stigmatized and marginalized because the system is not designed to protect their SR:

> I think a lot of people just don't know where to turn ... I think services often struggle to be there when people need them because people typically get to a place of crisis, so they're living in vulnerable circumstances and they're dealing day to day with multiple extremely stressful life events that are pushing them to that point, where they are at risk of destitution. And if they're not engaged with agencies, and we're seeing this a lot in the pandemic, these aren't people who are problems, you know, to society, so, they don't have a social worker, they might not be working or getting any help from mental health service providers and so on. You have to be quite ill to meet the threshold to be allowed to even kind of get support from those teams, so lots of people just aren't on the radar and people, because of the stigma and the social kind of pressures, of not admitting that you need help. Poverty's highly stigmatized in our society and people don't reach out for help. Well, they don't even know where to turn. (Wales, Eva, Development Manager, NGO to combat child poverty)

Emotional, financial and legal resources

People need legal and financial resources to support them on their journey to finding a remedy for a legal problem. This can sometimes be referred to as 'legal capability'. However, the research also demonstrated the need for additional resources over and above purely legal ones, including emotional resilience, stamina, strength and overcoming fear.

Financial resources

There are significant barriers in ensuring access to justice because of a lack of appropriate funding. Prohibitive costs for pursuing legal cases are a significant barrier in ensuring access to justice. Legal aid acts as an important pillar of the justice system and provide a form of protection so that people can pursue important cases in order to resolve SR violations:

> Any risk of having to pay the government's cost just totally outweighs anything that they would personally gain from the case. So although we would do stuff pro bono, we would do it – not charging, the real problem is the costs risk of them having to pay the Secretary of State's costs if they were unsuccessful, so legal aid provides costs protection.

It means that if a case is unsuccessful, essentially it's the legal aid agency who steps into the client's shoes and one bit of government pays the other bit of government, you know. It's all a bit of emperor's new clothes type thing. But legal aid provides clients cost protection, and that's what I want. (England, Claire, Solicitor related to the *Pantellerisco* case)

As discussed in Chapter 3, LASPO has effectively ended legal aid provision for legal problems encountered in relation to debt, welfare benefits, employment, education, most housing disputes, private family law, non-asylum immigration, clinical negligence, consumer or contract disputes and criminal injury.[2] While exceptional case funding is available on the grounds of a breach of human rights, the definition of human rights is restricted to those falling within the ambit of the ECHR or retained EU law, excluding most economic rights and SR by extension.[3] The removal of legal aid for social welfare issues has had a chilling effect:

The operation of the benefit tribunal is quite different, say, from the employment tribunal or the immigration tribunal. I think it's a far less formal context. It's a context in which legal aid isn't available for people to be represented by a solicitor and so I do think it's more informal. I think that errors in law can far easier go unnoticed. It's perhaps an issue that is silenced because people don't necessarily know that they've missed out on the basis of an unlawful decision. (Scotland, Freya, Solicitor, NGO for housing)

While there are different legal aid regimes in Scotland and NI, similar problems are faced in terms of access to appropriate and sustainable funding for advice services and legal representation. This can impact the type of advice and representation available to people. For example, legal aid funding does not cover all the costs of advice and representation, meaning that it becomes very difficult to support access in areas relating to SR in a sustainable way. This has inadvertently created potential barriers through the increasing likelihood of advice deserts both geographically and in terms of the sufficiency of the numbers of solicitors providing a particular service within a specialist field of law.[4] The reluctance of private

---

[2] Vicky Ling et al, *The Legal Aid Handbook 20/21* (London: Legal Action Group, 2020), ch 1.
[3] LASPO 2012, s 10(3)(a).
[4] Scottish Government Consultation, *Legal Aid Reform Consultation Analysis* (2020), https://www.gov.scot/publications/legal-aid-reform-scotland-consultation-response/

providers to engage in these fields may be caused by the complexity and unsustainability of this work as a field of private practice: 'You don't have many, if any, legal aid high street firms or legal aid firms doing housing and only housing. Because it is not sustainable. So I think that that in and of itself is a human rights issue' (Scotland, Freya, Solicitor, NGO for housing).

For example, some providers of civil legal assistance must subsidize their work via other private practice or grants, meaning that not every hour worked on legal aid cases is paid. Respondents to a Scottish government consultation on legal aid reform highlighted concerns that housing, debt, employment, domestic abuse, immigration and asylum were areas currently poorly served by private providers (meaning an overreliance on already stretched third sector organizations) and that gaps in funding exist across these areas, for example, in relation to reasonable adjustments for people with disabilities, or in responding to mental health issues that intersect with all of the areas of concern they raised.[5]

Legal advice and representation

Advice services operate across different tiers (frontline, advice centres, lawyers, advocates and barristers). Sometimes advice will be required at only one of these tiers or it may be required across all of them. There are various barriers faced in accessing appropriate advice. First, there may be insufficient funding for one or more of the tiers (see the preceding discussion):

> The big problem at the moment is the lack of advice following [legal aid cuts] it goes together with law centres being under enormous pressure and often having to close and similar pressures on the Citizens Advice Bureau, which are a crucial part of the structure. (England, Roland, KC)

> What used to happen before was you had a kind of 'legal aid light' at any stage in the social security system. So if you were seeking a mandatory reconsideration you could get legal aid for help with that, if you were doing a tribunal you could get legal aid for help with that. And the legal aid wasn't for representation, it wasn't a forced certificate where you like pay your lawyer an hourly rate for turning up in court, it was just a fixed fee that organizations could get. But it meant also that organizations could pay for reports using the state's money, so it kind of enabled claimants who got advice to have some sort of equality of arms in terms of obtaining evidence-, commissioning evidence. That

---

[5] Ibid.

went in 2012/2013 and the number of expert welfare rights advisors plummeted. (England, Miles, Welfare rights advisor, NGO to combat child poverty)

There can be an overreliance on one tier of advice. For example, sometimes specialist legal advice is required. The lack of appropriate funding in areas of social welfare law means that there are not enough lawyers specializing in these areas of expertise:

> So if it's about services that can provide advice and help people challenge and have their rights enforced, I'm worried. I obviously look at it through the lens of like legal advice and that's not to say all these cases, most housing issues and homeless issues … will be dealt with without a solicitor. But at the end of the day, in the context of homelessness for example, it's judicial review that's the remedy. Where you would need a solicitor, and in many of these eviction cases it is court proceedings, we're overly reliant-, not overly reliant, we are dependent on charities and you know, Citizens Advice Bureaus and all of these organizations are doing everything that they possibly can. We have to ask ourselves why is there not a body of social security lawyers there to tease out what are really complex areas of law. Social security – like immigration law – changes all of the time. (Scotland, Freya, Solicitor, NGO for housing)

Second, even if one tier is engaged, it may not be obvious or easy to access the next level. For example, there may be insufficient funding or legal aid to enable access to legal advice or it may not be clear to frontline advice services where to turn next for legal advice:

> I've spoken to people in charity sometimes and they don't even know anything about judicial review or they don't know about legal aid, they just don't know. Obviously people are coming to them with their issues and they might say to them, 'oh well, we'll try and write a letter to the local authority or something'. They never give them the legal option because they're not aware of it. (Wales, Matthew, Solicitor, private law firm)

People who access appropriate legal advice and representation do better than those who do not. This means that, even for access to justice avenues where lawyers are not a requirement of the process (such as ombudsman or tribunal services), there is a disconnect between those who are able to access legal advice and representation and those who are not:

> Statistics from the tribunal appeal service suggests that people that have advice and representation do better than those people that don't ... we know that because in the rest of the UK, but also here in Northern Ireland because of funding restrictions, I'm sure that the situation's the same in Scotland, advice services are so stretched, you know, their capacity at the best of times is low. (NI, Chloe, Volunteer)

This can result in an unlevel playing field, where those who do not receive legal advice and representation are ill-equipped to access justice and sometimes an unrepresented litigant on one side will face a legal team on the other, meaning that it raises an 'equality of arms' issue. For example, in NI, as we noted in Chapter 3, Josie told us:

> Now of course it's not necessarily a level playing field, you'll know that, because inevitably the landlord will be represented by probably quite a professional highly paid legal, whereas on many occasions the tenants may not even turn up ... they may not be represented, it's unlikely they'll be represented in fact. Most of them don't even turn up because we find that they're encouraged by the landlord not to turn up, because the landlord kind of indicates to them that it's not really worth their while because this is a fait accompli. (NI, Josie, Chief Executive, NGO for housing)

Similarly in Scotland, Freya explained:

> We sometimes forget, or there's sometimes a perception, that these are eviction cases that are just about nonpayment of rent and all that is required is negotiation of repayment arrangements, when these are actually legal proceedings with lawyers acting for the landlords and rarely lawyers acting for the tenants. So the statistics on people who are accessing lawyers to represent them are stark. Yet when you have a lawyer in who is looking at the paperwork and who is identifying whether things are done properly, i.e. when equality of arms are there, it makes a stark difference to somebody, as I say, keeping their house or not, or at least how their case is dealt with. (Scotland, Freya, Solicitor, NGO for housing)

Emotional resources

The research demonstrates that in order for the very few cases that make it all the way to accessing a formal legal process (and even fewer that reach a remedy at the end of the journey), each depends on the individual person taking on an immense emotional burden. It could also relate to the additional stress and burden of fighting an individual case on top of the reasons for bringing the complaint:

> And then when I'm going to the different agencies, like housing rights and they're saying, 'well you have to do X, Y and Z', they potentially don't have the capacity to help you to do that. And I know that [the client] doesn't have the capacity, she doesn't have the legal capabilities to like go through the three stage complaint process that she has to go through. (NI, Chloe, Volunteer)

For example, those in housing stress, facing financial difficulties, contending with mental or physical disabilities or other complex, intersectional problems may already have depleted physical and mental resilience before contending with a legal dispute. The legal justice system often siloes issues into standalone legal problems, whereas violations of SR are more likely to be 'clustered':

> They're not able to reach all those people that are going through these tribunal appeal processes by themselves. And if they are, they then find that the individual that they're helping has a cluster of problems that may be stretching to housing. So maybe they come with a social security issue, then they find out that they have a housing issue, then they maybe have a family issue, a family law issue … It's so difficult to like unravel a health issue, mental health issue, to unravel all of those separate issues. I was talking to an advisor on Friday and she was saying that at the minute during COVID they have 15-minute slots for people. (NI, Chloe, Volunteer)

In addition, SR violations often impact multiple people at the same time. In other words, they are systemic in nature and relate to a structural problem that is impacting many people. However, the legal system leans towards relying on individuals to challenge the system without the power of a collective challenge and this can place an unfair burden on an individual:

> There's definitely a role for individuals trying to get recourse as well. What there isn't is a strong enough structure in place to be able to enable to do that easily without breaking them down mentally, physically, emotionally, you know. If you're already marginalized and then you've got to fight the system which is completely stacked against you – you know what? You really don't have a lot of [hope] for success unless you've got resilience coming out your pores. (Scotland, Carole, Consultant and activist, NGO for human rights)

Fear of retribution

In addition, there is the fear of potential retribution for challenging a case, something that in practice can manifest as subtle or explicit worsening of circumstances for the person complaining. 'I have definitely found that since we have been advocating on [her] behalf, that she has definitely been gaining even more maltreatment from the housing executive.' (NI, Chloe, Volunteer).

In some cases, this fear may be placed on the potential backlash of raising a complaint or drawing attention to a vulnerable situation, '[They] might never approach the authority because they're worried that they're going to be deported or detained because they think they're illegal' (Scotland, Freya, Solicitor, NGO for housing).

This fear can become a reality, creating a significant and often invisible barrier for access to justice. A practitioner emphasized that fear of consequences when defending yourself in the face of rights violations was not entirely misplaced. They expressed dismay that they could not:

> Give people assurances that nothing bad will happen if they complain, because sometimes things do happen when people complain and they're the ones that deal with it, I don't deal with it. I dealt with one example that I always think about, of a woman during the evictions, like after Serco had made the evictions and we were working with a lot of lawyers to get people represented in court. Anyway, I had this woman ... the court had placed an interim interdict ... the interim interdict says that they can't move you until the Ali case had been decided ... she called us saying 'Serco have said that they're going to come and evict me today', so I called Serco and was like 'are you aware that there's an interim interdict on this property and you will be breaking the law if you move her?!' and they didn't know! And they were like 'oh thank you for telling us' like 'she won't be moved'. But then there's this system in place where if somebody doesn't move, either when they come to evict you or they come to move you to a different property, it's called a 'Failure to Travel', so if you refuse to get in the van and go, they issue a Failure to Travel message to the Home Office and then your asylum support stops. So even though they would have been breaking the law if they had moved her, they still issued the Failure to Travel notice so then her asylum support stopped. (Scotland, Abigail, Evictions caseworker, NGO for asylum seekers)

Complexity of the journey: getting 'stuck in administrative mud'

The complexity of the access to justice system is not easy to navigate. Often people may prefer or be required to resolve a dispute through an informal route to justice. This could be, for example, through a complaints process, appeal mechanism or alternative resolution process. Sometimes these processes result in positive results that deal with the SR issue:

> I did a Survey Monkey thing where I asked people 'Have you downloaded a letter, what happened?' Really high percentage, something like 86 per cent or something of people who said that they'd used the letters in one way or another, it had resolved the issue for their client … They send a pre-action letter, actually send it as a pre-action letter to the DWP. The DWP will say 'we do not accept your argument, you're completely wrong and judicial review is a remedy of last resort. However, in this instance a mandatory reconsideration decision has been made', which actually has resolved the issue for the client. So it's sort of an indirect success … when I'm training advisors and say 'never expect them to accept your arguments, never expect them to agree with you because they will always disagree, but what you're looking for is to see whether there is a consequential change'. If [DWP] say, 'we trust that no further proceedings will ensue because we've issued a mandatory reconsideration decision in your client's favour', that's a success. (England, Jane, Welfare rights advisor, NGO to combat child poverty)

The complexity of the system compounds the barriers people face in accessing justice and the most appropriate path to justice is not always clearly identifiable. Some routes to justice could be via a complaints mechanism or an internal appeal process, like mandatory reconsideration, or it could be via broader institutional avenues like directly appealing to Parliament or government, as was the case in Wales that we noted in Chapter 3:

> We convened a group of young people to meet with our First Minister just before Christmas, at his request. I mean, it came out quite late in the day but we managed to get a good group of young people together and they raised a number of issues around mental health, schools returning. And he did refer to that and his Education Minister referred to engagement he'd had with young people fairly recently, in terms of informing his decisions around COVID. Young people also then raised, at that meeting, that they weren't getting sufficient information around COVID in a child-friendly manner. Within a week, we had a meeting of senior comms leads across Welsh government officials. (Wales, Sam, Policy developer, NGO for children and youth)

However, these paths can be mired with difficulties. While they may sometimes result in positive outcomes, this is by no means guaranteed, and can prolong the violation and delay the remedy: 'They informed me that we would have to go through the whole of the housing executive's internal complaints procedure, which is going to take another-, I don't know how long it's going to take. I don't even want to look because, as I say, it's so time-consuming' (NI, Chloe, Volunteer).

These routes do not necessarily guarantee human rights compliant outcomes, nor do they ensure accountability for violations of rights when they occur: 'It's easy to get those public appearances and public declarations of support. It's extremely difficult to see actual change and movement. So, how do you translate that kind of public expressions or, like informal expressions, like unanimously pass motions and to bring about any actual change' (NI, Esther, Housing activist, NGO for human rights).

Formal legal processes also exist via tribunals, ombudsmen and courts. While there are many positives to encouraging resolution through alternative routes, there are also potential setbacks to the complexity of the pathways available and the danger that people can get mired 'in administrative mud'. Ultimately, many practitioners argued that courts must be available, at least as a means of last resort, to ensure a remedy:

> The courts are the best remedy because if you try and introduce some, kind of ombudsman or commissioner or something ... something that might not work really, I don't know ... I think the courts are the best safeguard, the best safety net, but the problem is access to funding and access to lawyers who know what they're doing, because there aren't that many. Again, in Wales there's literally two or three lawyers like me, so I think access to justice both in funding and knowing and lawyers is the problem. But I think ultimately it should be the courts who decide these things, because they're so important and I think if you try and add another type of ombudsman or something like that, it'll just get mired in *the administrative mud* actually. (Wales, Matthew, Solicitor, private law firm, emphasis added)

The system is so complex that even those who work in it on a day-to-day basis may not know the best route forward. It is not always clear what route to justice should be prioritized for an individual in the particular circumstances, and how they can reach a satisfactory and timely remedy: 'It's not clear to people. You can never know, I think, as an individual citizen or resident rather, of Wales, what steps you're supposed to take [laughs] and who's supposed to help you. And for even sort of fairly well-informed and experienced advisors this can be difficult' (Wales, Eva, Development Manager, NGO to combat child poverty).

Adequate and effective access to justice

For those cases that manage to proceed to a formal legal forum, there are a number of significant barriers to ensuring that a SR violation is addressed:

First, the UK's domestic legal system does not include statutory or constitutional SR, meaning that when cases are adjudicated, they are not with reference to substantive SR standards.

> That's probably our most typical kind of case, in terms of disrepair and fitness, would be this lack of heating, and then condensation, damp throughout the house, and then all the kind of potential health ramifications that come with that, particularly if you have young children. Now, you see, there's very, very, very little in law that we can do about that, because it's not actually breaking any- you know, that is complying with the standards, so it's very hard to do anything. I mean, that's never getting into any court because there's no challenge for it. And in those sort of cases you just have to work with environmental health officers, they will kind of serve notices on landlords to try to get them to take action, not install heating or not upgrade heating, but just to maybe take action on the symptoms rather than the cause, but it's not really a satisfactory solution. (NI, Josie, Chief Executive, NGO for housing)

In addition, courts are reluctant to get involved in economic and social policy matters that are deemed to fall within the sole remit of the legislature and the executive:

> There's a very strong feeling of reluctance in the English higher courts to start actually deciding on social and economic policy, to be honest … this is at the top of my mind in a way, because back in late October I was arguing a case about the two-child rule, which says that for child tax credits, which is one of the major means tested benefits, you can't get benefit for the third and subsequent children born after April 2016. But that feels to me like a pretty draconian rule, given that the benefit is a subsistence benefit. It's a benefit to provide for basic needs and so you're just not providing for the basic needs of the third and subsequent children. But the court is terribly reluctant to get into it at all. They just say that sort of judgment is essentially a political judgment. (England, Roland, KC)

This is a frustration for practitioners because it means they are often trying to make arguments by using less appropriate legal structures to protect SR or trying to fit a 'square peg in a round hole'. One route to challenging SR violations has been to make arguments that the decisions, policies or statutory framework fall short of a reasonable standard so much so that they can be deemed irrational and therefore unlawful. The reasonableness test in UK law relies on the *Wednesbury* reasonableness test.[6] The threshold for a finding of unreasonableness under this test is a very high one: an action (or omission) must be 'so outrageous and in defiance of logic ... that no sensible person who had applied his mind to the question ... could have arrived at it'.[7] In recent cases involving challenges to social security measures, the court has further raised the threshold for those cases involving economic and social policy, meaning that such cases are not open to challenge on the grounds of irrationality 'short of the extremes of bad faith, improper motive or manifest absurdity'.[8]

Compliance with economic and SR law requires a broader reasonableness test.[9] The types of questions asked in a broader reasonableness assessment include the extent to which the measures taken were deliberate, concrete and targeted towards the fulfilment of SR; whether discretion was exercised in a nondiscriminatory and non-arbitrary manner; whether resource allocation is in accordance with international human rights standards; whether the option adopted is the one that least restricts rights; whether the steps were taken in a reasonable timeframe; whether the precarious situation of disadvantaged and marginalized individuals or groups has been addressed; whether policies have prioritized grave situations or situations of risk; and whether decision making is transparent and participatory.[10]

One practitioner noted that the court, at the very least, may be willing to engage when it is clear that a decision has been made by the legislature or the executive and there has been insufficient weight given to the potential impact of a policy:

> What things boil down to is a political decision about two imperfect situations that have both been fully scoped out, but

---

[6] *Associated Provincial Picture Houses Ltd v Wednesbury Corporation* (1948) 1 KB 223.

[7] *Council of Civil Service Unions and Others v Minister for the Civil Service* [1985] AC 374.

[8] *R (Pantellerisco and Others) v SSWP* [2021] EWCA Civ 1454, para 58, referring to Lord Reed in *R (SC) v Secretary of State for Work and Pensions* [2021] UKSC 26, who cites Lord Bridge in *R v Secretary of State for the Environment ex p Hammersmith and Fulham London Borough Council* [1991] 1 AC 521.

[9] For a discussion on the 'proportionality-inflected' broader reasonableness review adopted by the UN CESCR, see Sandra Liebenberg, 'Between Sovereignty and Accountability: The Emerging Jurisprudence of the United Nations Committee on Economic, Social and Cultural Rights under the Optional Protocol' (2020) 48(1) *Human Rights Quarterly*, pp 48–84, p 72.

[10] Ibid. See also Katie Boyle, *Economic and Social Rights Law: Incorporation, Justiciability and Principles of Adjudication* (Abingdon: Routledge, 2020), pp 32–35.

> I often get the sensation ... the decision makers in government have just not confronted the true complexity of the decision that they were making ... It's right that people spend time thinking about the implication of laws that affect hundreds of thousands if not millions of people in quite some detail. And I sometimes find it astonishing that so much law is made without that sort of analysis how is it as a society we make provision for lots of clever people to spend lots of time thinking about the colour and shape of sweet wrappers, but when it comes to how we provide the basics of systems income for millions of households with children, it's just like, oh wow, this will probably do ... there's a bit of a disconnect there and as I say, I think a lot of the litigation that I do with [name of organization] is fundamentally an accusation that the state just hasn't thought about a problem perhaps. And you know when we succeed the court is very frequently accepting that the problem hasn't really been confronted. And when we fail, they tend to be saying, and quite rightly, it's not the courts' job to say – but they're often saying, well, they've done it, you know, they've grappled with this enough and so we're not going to intervene. (England, Tobias, Barrister)

Other avenues for seeking to protect SR include under the ECHR. The ECHR is incorporated into UK domestic law via the HRA 1998 and the devolved statutes, but the ECHR does not extend to economic or SR. The UK has agreed to be bound by international treaties that protect economic and SR, but has not incorporated (embedded) them into domestic law. This creates an accountability gap for the UK and makes it difficult for practitioners to use a treaty that is essentially unfit for purpose in terms of making economic and SR claims (because it is not designed to do so):

> Yeah well obviously they don't really stand on their own in the ECHR, they're not incorporated, so they're not part of domestic law. They can obviously illuminate the arguments that you might have about nationality or discrimination in domestic law or even buttress the argument with references to international obligations. My own experience, that's just been where I'm coming from recently, it's quite difficult to really gain much added value as an advocate for the international conventions to social and economic rights and you can't litigate them by themselves because [they're] not incorporated. (England, Roland, KC)

Incorporation of international law into domestic law means embedding legal standards as set out in international law and making them enforceable at the domestic level.¹¹ A broad definition of incorporation includes a domestication of treaty provisions in a way that is completely contextualized within the specific constitutional setting from which it springs. Compliance with international human rights treaties can occur through domestic internalization of international norms by way of a variety of means.¹² Ultimately, the most robust form of incorporation is to grant a direct or indirect form of domestic recognition to international human rights law that is enforceable and coupled with effective remedies.¹³ There are now advanced processes of incorporation in Scotland¹⁴ and similar proposals in Wales.¹⁵

The UN human rights monitoring bodies have advised that the fulfilment of human rights requires states to take action at the domestic level in order to create the necessary legal structures, processes and substantive outcomes for human rights protection. Several UN committees have recommended that the UK both incorporates international human rights law and ensures effective justiciable remedies are made available for noncompliance.¹⁶ For example, the Committee on the Rights of the Child suggests that fulfilment of international obligations should be secured through the incorporation of

---

[11] Boyle (n 10), p 181.

[12] Oona A. Hathaway, 'Do Human Rights Treaties Make a Difference?' (2002) 111 *Yale Law Journal*, pp 1935–2042.

[13] Katie Boyle, *Models of Incorporation and Justiciability of Economic, Social and Cultural Rights* (Edinburgh: Scottish Human Rights Commission, 2018), p 14. See also UN Committee on Economic, Social and Cultural Rights (CESCR), 'General Comment No. 19: The Right to Social Security' (Art. 9 of the Covenant), 4 February 2008, E/C.12/GC/19, [77]–[80]; UN General Assembly, Basic Principles and Guidelines on the Right to a Remedy and Reparation for Victims of Gross Violations of International Human Rights Law and Serious Violations of International Humanitarian Law: resolution / adopted by the General Assembly, 21 March 2006, A/RES/60/147. See also CESCR, 'General Comment No. 9: The Domestic Application of the Covenant' (1998) E/C.12/1998/24, [4].

[14] See *First Minister's Advisory Group on Human Rights Leadership* (2018), https://humanrightsleadership.scot/wp-content/uploads/2018/12/First-Ministers-Advisory-Group-on-Human-Rights-Leadership-Final-report-for-publication.pdf; and the *National Taskforce for Human Rights Leadership Report* (2021), https://www.gov.scot/publications/national-taskforce-human-rights-leadership-report/documents/

[15] Simon Hoffman, Sarah Nason, Rosie Beacock and Ele Hicks (with contributions from Rhian Croke), 'Strengthening and Advancing Equality and Human Rights in Wales' (2021) Welsh Government Social Research Number 54/2021.

[16] Treaty bodies recommending incorporation: CEDAW/C/UK/CO/6 (CEDAW, 2009) Committee on the Elimination of Discrimination against Women; CAT/C/GBR/CO/5 (CAT, 2013) Committee against Torture; CRC/C/GBR/CO/4 (CRC, 2008) Committee on the Rights of the Child. Treaty bodies recommending justiciable enforcement and effective remedies: CRC/C/GBR/CO/5 (CRC, 2016) Committee on the Rights of the Child; E/C.12/GBR/CO/5 (CESCR, 2009) Committee on Economic, Social and Cultural Rights; E/C.12/GBR/CO/6 (CESCR, 2016).

international obligations[17] and by ensuring that effective remedies, including justiciable remedies, are made available domestically.[18] The UN CESCR has called for justiciable remedies for violations of economic and SR.[19] The Committee also indicates that a blanket refusal to recognize the justiciable nature of SR is considered arbitrary and that, ideally, SR, as well as economic and cultural rights, should be protected in the same way as civil and political rights within the domestic legal order.[20]

The lack of legal incorporation of SR, whether that be explicit, implicit, direct, indirect, holistic or sectoral, means that practitioners are left without the appropriate legal routes to litigate SR on their own merits:

> The limitation is that because we haven't incorporated [the] international covenant and economic, social cultural rights, we are having to run cases about unfairness in the benefits system – the main way of challenging them, is through Article 14 discrimination claims under [the] ECHR. So, Article 14 in conjunction with A1P1 [Article 1 of Protocol 1] and then Article 8 potentially. And you know it's putting *a round peg into a square hole*, for example. So in relation to the main challenges of the benefit cap, 70 per cent of those being affected pre-COVID were lone parents. You've got a work incentivization measure which is singling out lone parents, so you have to justify what it is about lone parents that singles them out for such punitive treatment. But that's because of a variety of issues as to how we got up to the Supreme Court and the lack of full substantive arguments ... down below it was treated as a discrimination case, whether an exception should be made for lone parents. And well to me that wasn't the issue. We were challenging the benefit cap square on because if you take lone parents out as opposed to lone parents of under-fives and lone parents of under two, you've scuppered the whole benefit cap. But it was a contorted

---

[17] CESCR, 'General Comment No. 5: General Measures of Implementation for the Convention on the Rights of the Child' (2003) CRC/GC/2003/5, [20]; Concluding Observations of the United Nations Committee on the Rights of the Child on the United Kingdom (2002) CRC/C/15/Add.188, paras 8 and 9; and Concluding Observations of the United Nations Committee on the Rights of the Child on the United Kingdom (2008), CRC/C/GBR/CO/4, para 7; CAT/C/GBR/CO/5 (CAT, 2013) Committee against Torture, para 7; CEDAW/C/UK/CO/6 (CEDAW, 2009) Committee on the Elimination of Discrimination against Women; E/C.12/GBR/CO/5 (CESCR, 2009) Committee on Economic, Social and Cultural Rights, para 13.

[18] CESCR CRC/C/GBR/CO/5 (CRC, 2016) para 5; Committee on the Rights of the Child, para 7.

[19] CESCR (n 13), [10]; E/C.12/GBR/CO/5 (CESCR, 2009), para 13.

[20] CESCR (n 13).

argument having to fit it into an Article 14 claim, as opposed to, well actually you have provided in the benefit cap something that is inadequate in terms of [the] level of subsistence benefit. It was recognized that it pushed families well below the poverty line. So inadequacy and lack of accessibility to meaningful benefits ... if you look in terms of general comment language about accessibility, adequacy etc, and then if you look at the various letters that were sent out from the head of the Committee on Economic, Social and Cultural Rights in response to the 2008/ 2009 financial crisis and austerity and so, you know, regressive measures, austerity measures were all going to be temporary. Works weren't going to be discriminatory, they're meant to be participative, all of those criteria that's irrelevant in the UK courts, *and that's really frustrating because the benefit cap, yeah potentially, could just be litigated on its own terms* without the discrimination argument. (England, Claire, Solicitor related to the *Pantellerisco* case, emphasis added)

Reaching an effective remedy is not guaranteed

As a result of the lack of substantive standards for SR, the outcomes of cases can often fall short in terms of adequacy and effectiveness. In other words, remedies are not sufficiently 'accessible, affordable, timely and effective'.[21] For example, they can take a long time, such as in the case of a terminally ill applicant who ultimately lost her case, despite an earlier judgment in her favour:

> She's wasted two years of her life on the benefits system and it just doesn't make sense, it doesn't make sense, that a young woman, and with three children who she's bringing up on her own should have been using those two years productively with her children, has been focused on the system. And nobody can ever give her, or those two children, those two years back. They're gone. (NI, Kamilla, Welfare rights advisor, NGO local community)

People are so worn down by the system that they will often accept less than effective remedies as an outcome:

> You know, 'cause I think people just get weary. Like I know [name of client] just wants a new house now. So the housing executive in the next week offer her a new flat that meets what she wants in a home

---

[21] Ibid, [9].

and she can be safe there, she will take it. That will be her remedy. So she won't seek to get the eight weeks' rent that she has missed or, for example, have her arrears waived because of what she has gone through … I don't think she'll seek any other redress because she's so worn down by the whole thing. (NI, Esther, Housing activist, NGO for human rights)

People's desperation for a result can mean that their resilience in terms of taking a longer route to a more satisfactory remedy is outweighed by mere survival instincts:

Yeah and they would never, even if they get the asylum support back, there would never be any recognition of that fact that it was not their fault that that happened. You know, there would never be an apology. I wouldn't even think to ask for an apology! Even though that's what they should get. But also because you're just dealing with the survival aspects of it, just that they need the asylum support back in order to be able to pay for food. (Scotland, Abigail, Evictions caseworker, NGO for asylum seekers)

Justice equals access to an effective remedy

A broader lens on access to justice includes securing access to legal processes that result in effective outcomes. According to Shelton, remedies are the processes by which arguable claims are heard and decided, whether by courts, administrative agencies or other competent bodies, as well as the outcome of the proceedings and the relief afforded to the successful claimant (leading to results that are individually and socially just).[22]

In relation to SR, this requires a reconceptualization of access to justice that begins with the violation of a right and ends in an effective remedy for that violation. Such an approach requires renewed focus on what is meant both in terms of effective legal processes (international human rights law suggests that they need to be 'accessible, affordable, timely and effective')[23] as well as an effective outcome of those processes.[24] The international legal position asserts that 'where there is a right, there is a remedy' based on the

---

[22] Dinah Shelton, *Remedies in International Human Rights Law* (Oxford: Oxford University Press, 1999), p 7.
[23] CESCR (n 13), [9].
[24] Remedies should be effective 'in practice as well as in law': Council of Europe, 'Guide on Article 13 of the European Convention on Human Rights, Right to an Effective Remedy', European Court of Human Rights, 31 August 2024.

principle of *ubi ius ibi remedium*.[25] The Maastricht Guidelines on violations of economic, social and cultural rights further state that the right to an effective remedy is available to individuals and groups for violations of economic rights and SR (through judicial or other appropriate proceedings at both the international and national levels), as well as civil and political rights. States are under a duty to provide access to an effective remedy if there is a failure to meet the obligations imposed by international human rights law. This includes facilitating access to a legal remedy in court if necessary, implying the existence of both a substantive and procedural duty toward rights bearers on the part of state parties.[26]

The legal right to an effective remedy

A remedy for a rights violation comprises both substantive and procedural elements.[27] Procedurally, it refers to a process or series of processes by which SR violations claims are heard by courts, quasi-judicial bodies, administrative agencies and/or any other competent bodies.[28] Substantively, it refers to the outcome of the hearing and the relief granted to the claimant.

An *effective* remedy for the violation is one that can serve three functions.[29] The first is to place the applicant in, as far as possible, in the same position as they were prior to the occurrence of the alleged rights violation. The second is to ensure ongoing compliance with the rights obligations of

---

[25] The formulation of this principle was first established in 1928 by the Permanent Court of International Justice in the *Chorzów Factory* case, where the court held that reparations ought to 'wipe out all the consequences of the illegal act and re-establish the situation which would, in all probability, have existed if that act had not been committed.' *Chorzów Factory*, 1928 PCIJ (ser. A) No. 17, at 47. The International Law Commission's draft articles on state responsibility require states to make reparations for wrongful acts (G.A. Res. 56/83, Annex arts 30 and 31, UN Doc. A/RES/56/83/Annex (28 January 2002)) reflecting the principle first formulated in Chorzów. This area of law is concerned with state responsibility between states rather than between the state and the individual; however, it is increasingly applying to the area of international human rights regarding the relationship between the state and the individual, and to wrongful acts committed against the international community; Shelton (n 22), ch 2; see also International Commission of Jurists 'The Maastricht Guidelines on Violations of Economic, Social and Cultural Rights, Maastricht, January 22–26, 1997' (1998) 20 *Human Rights Quarterly*, pp 691–704, para 23.

[26] CESCR, 'General Comment No. 4: The Right to Adequate Housing (Art. 11(1) of the Covenant)' (1991) E/1992/23, [17]; Shelton (n 22).

[27] Dinah Shelton, *Remedies in International Human Rights Law*, 3rd ed, (Oxford, Oxford University Press, 2015).

[28] *Council of Civil Service Unions and Others* (n 7).

[29] Kent Roach, *Remedies for Human Rights Violations: A Two Track Approach to Supranational and National Law* (Cambridge: Cambridge University Press, 2021), pp 2–5.

duty bearers. The third is to try and ensure that future violations of the right in question do not occur through (a) deterrence, and (b) an attempt at addressing the feature(s) of a legal system that caused the violation in the first place.[30]

The concept of an effective legal remedy is derived from Article 8 UDHR, which states that 'everyone has the right to an effective remedy by the competent national tribunals for acts violating the fundamental rights granted him by the constitution or by law'.[31] Various iterations of the right to an effective remedy and the right to reparation can be found across multiple human rights treaties. For example, the ECHR and the American Convention on Human Rights contain separate provisions for the right to an effective remedy (Articles 25 and 13) and the right to reparation (Articles 63.1 and 41 respectively). However, the ICCPR addresses both the procedural and substantive elements of an effective remedy in Article 2(3), meaning that an effective process as well as an effective outcome are required to demonstrate an effective remedy has been met. The Human Rights Committee, responsible for the interpretation of the ICCPR, clarifies that 'without reparation … the obligation to provide an effective remedy is not discharged'.[32] In other words, the definition of an effective remedy includes both the efficacy of the remedial process, as well as the efficacy of the outcomes of those processes (the relief offered).[33]

In terms of appropriate relief, the UN Guiding Principles[34] provide further clarification on what constitutes an effective remedy in international law, which includes restitution, compensation, rehabilitation, satisfaction, effective measures to ensure cessation of the violation and guarantees of nonrepetition. Specific remedies beyond compensation include public apologies, public and administrative sanctions for wrongdoing, instructing that human rights education be undertaken, ensuring a transparent and accurate account of the violation, reviewing or disapplying incompatible laws or policies, use of delayed remedies to facilitate compliance, including rights holders as participants in development of remedies and supervising compliance postjudgment.

---

[30] Ibid.
[31] Universal Declaration of Human Rights, UN General Assembly Resolution 217(A) III, 10 December 1948. Article 13 is based on art 8 UDHR, and art 47 of the EU Charter of Fundamental Rights draws its inspiration from arts 6 and 13 ECHR and goes somewhat further than art 6 in its scope of protection.
[32] UN Human Rights Committee (HRC), 'General Comment No. 31 [80], The Nature of the General Legal Obligation Imposed on States Parties to the Covenant', 26 May 2004, CCPR/C/21/Rev.1/Add.13.
[33] Ibid, paras 16–17.
[34] UN General Assembly (n 13).

Practitioner perspectives on what constitutes an effective remedy

One of the key questions asked in the interviews was how practitioners conceptualized effective remedies. Their responses shows that practitioners often conflated the notion of 'an effective remedy' with 'access to justice', highlighting that these distinctions are not always clear-cut and easy to dissect. There are two important points to reflect on in this respect. On the one hand, some practitioners thought of remedies as routes or processes that *may* enable access to justice (procedural justice). Others conceptualized effective remedies as processes (procedural access) that lead to just outcomes (substantive justice), including effective reparations, relief and cessation of the violation/preventing recurrence. Their responses echoed the duality of procedural and substantive issues in international human rights law, and reflected the principles of accessibility, affordability and timeliness, as well as both procedural and substantive effectiveness.[35]

Accessibility

For some of the practitioners, access to an effective remedy meant access to adjudication processes, such as better appeal rights/ways to challenge a SR violation, strategic litigation and access to legal representation. Some practitioners advocated for direct access to tribunals, expressing a preference for taking an appeal to the Commissioner for Social Security (Northern Ireland) rather than the High Court. One of the Scottish case study practitioners stated: 'I think it's positive that you've got a right of appeal to the Social Security Tribunal that's not like a judicial review procedure, it's a specific right of appeal to a court that comes from that statute. So I think more of that is ... necessary' (Scotland, Erica, Solicitor, human rights public body).

Access to an effective remedy was also expressed as having awareness and access to frontline advice, both legal and nonlegal. Kelly responded that an effective remedy:

> Can be something as simple as information and it can go all the way up through to sometimes you need a case. So you need to have a well-resourced, specialist legal sector that are there ... to take these cases, so it can be simple as access to information – so people have informed consent – 'OK, I'll do that'. But it goes all the way up to being able to implement or enforce the rights that these individuals have and that could go as far as a judicial review or a strategic test case in order to

---

[35] Shelton (n 22), p 7, para 9.

change some of these systems. (Scotland, Kelly, Solicitor specializing in women/children/ immigration, NGO delivering legal services)

Practitioners also highlighted that an effective remedy cannot be accessed if there are no clear and simple pathways to challenge a violation, calling for 'a clearer route for people to access legal remedies for SR in particular', without needing to go through a complex and difficult bureaucratic claims process. Chloe said that for housing, social security, managing health and social care, and immigration, it is difficult to know what route to go down. This includes lawyers, Chloe said, 'particularly those lawyers that aren't well versed in social welfare issues' (NI, Chloe, Volunteer).

Affordability

The notion of affordability was raised specifically in relation to judicial review, which was not deemed to be an effective remedy due to cost and should be treated as a 'remedy of last resort' after other options such as lower courts and tribunals have been exhausted (Scotland, Erica, Solicitor, human rights public body). In addition to the financial barrier, Erica identified another cost entailed in judicial review proceedings – the emotional burden:

> I would say even in a relatively personally privileged position that I am in, I would very much think twice about, if something happened to me, say something to do with my daughter's education or ... if she was disabled or something and I wanted to challenge the support and stuff that was made available to her, I would really, really, really think hard about whether I would want to go down the route of a judicial review or something or a court case. So I feel like if I think that, in my position of being a lawyer, knowing about human rights, being relatively like financially okay and stuff like that ... what is that if ... people in my position think 'oh god I would never do that!' ... what does that say about that being an okay remedy as for the general population? (Scotland, Erica, Solicitor, human rights public body)

Erica emphasizes how the great financial and emotional strain of court proceedings poses a significant barrier to accessing justice.

Timeliness

We have already highlighted in Chapter 3 how the *Cox* case demonstrates the importance of accessing a remedy in a timely manner, given Lorraine Cox's terminal illness. Long timescales and delays act as a deterrent and a barrier to obtaining an effective remedy. There was broad consensus among practitioners that timeliness was of the utmost importance for a remedy to be considered effective, citing court of appeal delays as especially problematic. Even when a rights holder is successful at tribunal, receiving an individual remedy can be significantly delayed. Rose, a welfare rights advisor in Wales, said: 'It [getting a remedy] should be automatic, it should be unquestioned, but that can take quite a lot of time. And so, for me, from an administrative point of view, that takes a lot of – often phone calls, and letters, and things like that – to make sure that people do actually get [it] after successful tribunals' (Wales, Rose, Welfare rights advisor, local county).

Time was not only measured in terms of how long rights holders were left without a solution, but it also referred to the time commitment required to obtain a remedy due to the number of hoops a person must jump through and the toll it takes on them. These routes to 'justice' wear people down and lead them to accept unsatisfactory solutions.

Esther claimed that an effective remedy entails an immediate solution in response to a violation:

> If someone is homeless then their ... right to adequate housing, they're living in a hostel, then I mean, unless I'm being too obvious, the obvious remedy is that a house is secured for them to live in. Or if someone has damp and that damp is making their child sick, the obvious remedy to that, right to health, adequate housing, is that that damp is fixed or they're moved to an alternative safe accommodation. (NI, Esther, Housing activist, NGO for human rights)

Furthermore, she recognized that one can have local, national and international human rights legislation in place, but 'until that damp is actually fixed, that means nothing to that family'. It is through an effective solution that SR are realized.

Effectiveness

Practitioner judgments on the effectiveness of a remedy were influenced by a number of different factors related to damages/financial compensation, whether or not amendments were made to legislation, restitution, acknowledgement of liability/fault, apologies, accountability and enforcement, clear and simple pathways to challenge a violation, minimum core requirements, clear boundaries of entitlement and requirements for feedback.

Practitioners felt that as a minimum, an effective remedy would provide the amount of money rights holders 'lost out on', meaning that a successful outcome would backdate payments of social security benefits missed. In the case of a rat infestation, it would entail compensation for eight weeks rent paid while unable to remain in the accommodation. Ideally, compensation would be paid for undue stress caused, delays and any private monies spent on legal representation. But practitioners widely recognized that financial compensation is generally not enough. Julie said 'that's just a limitation in terms of how far law gets you [laughing] I suppose!' (Scotland, Julie, Solicitor specializing in asylum/immigration, NGO for legal service).

Erica recognized another important element of an effective remedy, stating that:

> You could get compensation, but another part of [an] effective remedy is like restitution … to the extent possible, you should be restored to the position that you were in had that rights violation not happened to you, but compensation won't necessarily do that, so you might need educational, counselling, health measures – like various other things to be put in place. (Scotland, Erica, Solicitor, human rights public body)

In addition, Erica and others raised the importance of an apology or acknowledgement of wrongdoing. She went on to say:

> To some people a finding of liability is important – a finding of fault and then comes with that the apology. And then obviously … human rights law has got stuff to say about what an apology should be as well. So I think that the important thing would be, and to a lot of people as well, that public aspect of it … of having that sort of 'day in court' is important for access to justice. (Scotland, Erica, Solicitor, human rights public body)

The acknowledgement of liability, of wrongdoing, is essential for fostering a new culture of responsibility and accountability that upholds human rights. This is also intimately tied to the enforcement of rights. Eva reflected on the framework for SR in Wales and commented:

> I mean with something like the socioeconomic duty there's no real kind of enforcement, you know. It's another one of these things, like we have lots of these frameworks in Wales, that don't actually give any power to- [laughs] there's no actions, you know. They can make recommendations. Lots of bodies and commissioners and things that can recommend things and even the ombudsman they can recommend that the council does – they don't have to do it. They can just ignore it if they want and so yeah you get to that point where it's like well who actually does enforce accountability … and the system that we've got at the moment, I mean there's so much <u>more</u> that needs to be done. And if you took a rights-based approach first and foremost

> I think that would really help, where everyone designing the system and administering the system for the people who are actually on the receiving end of these systems, you know what to expect [laughs] but also then be able to seek recourse when it doesn't work well. (Wales, Eva, Development Manager, NGO to combat child poverty)

Enforcement can only be mandated if SR are legally embedded in ways that enable effective remedies for violations. These legal protections also require the definition of minimum core thresholds and normative standards, in accordance with international human rights standards, to ensure that SR provisions are adequate. This relates to our discussion with Josie, Chief Executive with a housing NGO in NI, about low fitness standards (see the NI case study). She explained that due to outdated fitness standards, one socket in a room is considered adequate heating. Many people, particularly those with low incomes, rely on electric heaters for warmth, but a typical fitness issue is that when the house is freezing, it becomes damp, impacting on health and exacerbating the situation.

The absence of substantive standards was a recurring theme and its connection to establishing entitlement to support. For example, Eva explains that most of the support available in Wales is discretionary, so it is based on a subjective assessment of someone's circumstances, meaning it is heavily means tested. The process is very degrading for people and many people cannot apply because they are not able to provide the types of documentation that are required in the process:

> But it's very hard for people to know whether or not they've been turned down or their award is not what it should be if it's not clearly stated exactly what the boundaries of eligibility are. And that's because it is, you know, very much up to the person, and it's an obscure process … it's impossible to know whether your rights have been upheld or whether you are being unfairly treated because you don't know what it is, what it means to be fair. And so that first step of giving people the information about what their rights are, so that they can understand that their rights aren't being upheld, is missing. (Wales, Eva, Development Manager, NGO to combat child poverty)

Matthew and Erica raised concerns that remedies should be available in courts and that other less formal mechanisms can result in people becoming stuck in the system or stuck in 'administrative mud' (Wales, Matthew, Solicitor, private law firm). Erica explained that an ombudsman or regulatory kind of function might not properly deal with issues and might merely create an additional tier, further exacerbating concerns about the timeliness of remedies.

In terms of providing effective collective remedies, practitioners called for amendments to legislation. For instance, in the *Pantellerisco* case, legislation should be amended so that if a person is working 16 hours at the national living wage, their earnings are converted into a monthly amount to get over the benefit cap threshold or, alternatively, the threshold is amended (England, Claire, Solicitor related to the *Pantellerisco* case). Claire called not only for a collective remedy, but also for an individual remedy that would pay Sharon back payments for the time that the grace period was finished, but was still being affected by the benefit cap. In addition to her 'legal answer', Claire would have liked to see an apology from the DWP for the hardship caused to rights holders, such as 'the humiliation of being reduced to using a food bank'. She said that 'you'd never be able to ask the court here for that, but … how can a remedy go beyond, you know, purely what the court would order?' (England, Claire, Solicitor related to the *Pantellerisco* case).

Rowan, welfare rights advisor in NI, stated that an effective remedy in the *Cox* case would be a change to the definition and assessment criteria of terminal illness in NI. In relation to asylum support, Jonas said that the reform of provisions for asylum support would constitute an effective remedy:

> There's too low a level paid currently from my perspective, so without going into the particulars I would say that reform is always the highest and probably best way of achieving what we're seeking rather than through the courts necessarily … yeah I think reform, but that may be driven by legal action. (Scotland, Jonas, Solicitor related to the *Ali* case)

Finally, Rose responded to our question regarding her interpretation of an effective remedy, which entailed a discussion around apologies and whether she had experienced receiving apologies for wrongdoing in the course of her many years as a welfare rights advisor:

> There never is any apology and, as I say, more worrying than that is there isn't [any] feedback. So because they're not getting feedback, they're not getting the tribunal coming back to them and saying, 'look, we have overturned this decision because you failed to take account of this piece of evidence, or you misinterpreted this piece of evidence or you misinterpreted this bit of the law', there's never any of that feedback and that's a real issue … I'm not naive enough to think that that would turn everything around, but I think it could have some, in a small way, it could. You know, there might be some decision makers who could actually-, I think if it was drawn to their attention that they're always making a certain type of mistake, or they're always ignoring a certain piece of evidence or underestimating a certain aspect of a case, or something like that … we don't always, we don't get to know the

names of the individuals who have made the decisions, but I see lots of bad decisions – are they being made by a whole variety of people across the board, or is there actually a handful of people making bad decisions, and there are lots of them making good decisions. I don't know, because that's what I'm not privy to. So, that would be very interesting, if I could have confidence that the government department concerned was actually taking that side of things seriously, if they were prepared to be a bit more self-critical and analyse decisions and analyse results. And think, 'well actually, are we not training our staff well enough', you know. But there you go [laughs] I can but dream [laughs]. (Wales, Rose, Welfare rights advisor, local county)

Feedback loop

Access to justice needs to be an iterative process whereby the end of the access to journey feeds back into law, policy and decision-making processes as a matter of course. This is particularly important where it becomes clear that there is a flaw in the system that needs to be addressed. In other words, ideally there should be feedback mechanisms that help enable longer-term change for systemic issues. For example, at the tribunal level, if there is a repeated pattern of poor decision making or a repeated flaw in the decision-making process, case outcomes should be fed back into the decision-making process.

This means there should be improved communication to stop violations continuing to happen earlier on in the decision-making process. It is also an important way of ensuring that the system gets fixed for everyone and is not just a fire-fighting exercise of dealing with one individual problem at a time without fixing the overall systemic issue. In this sense, a feedback loop can help others avoid the arduous access to justice journey, enabling fast routes to remedies once a lead case has identified a recurring violation.

Rose's concern about a lack of feedback is reflected in data gathered from tribunal hearings. Miles also identified that while tribunals can help fix a problem, there is no feedback loop to fix systemic problems with decision making:

> I think the tribunals arrive at the right answer most of the time and the quality of their decision making is pretty good, but I don't think that there's any real mechanism for feeding back to decision makers what was wrong with their decision. Certainly, there's no mechanism at the individual decision maker level. Like the individual decision maker who made a decision in [Name] Benefits Service Centre will never know that that decision was overturned ultimately, unless they stumble across the case sometime later. (England, Miles, Welfare rights advisor, NGO to combat child poverty)

Tribunal data

A manifestation of the absence of a feedback loop is in repeated poor decision making reflected in the number of decisions overturned on appeal in relation to housing, social security and asylum cases.[36] In this section, we present statistical data regarding First-tier Tribunal decisions for social security and child payments (see Tables 4.1 and 4.2 and Figures 4.1 and 4.2, where the figures are the visualizations of the data in the tables). We also share a subset of the social security data showing appeals related to the PIP benefit (see Tables 4.3 and 4.4 and Figures 4.3 and 4.4). The social security statistics are presented subsequently in tables and figures showing total case numbers, as well as percentages. We also present data of first-tier immigration decisions allowed and dismissed. These statistics are expressed in percentages (see Table 4.5 and Figure 4.5).

All the statistics cover the financial years 2015/2016 to 2020/2021 and are drawn from published UK government (Ministry of Justice) statistics.[37]

Social security

The social security tribunal data, as seen in Tables 4.1 and 4.2 and Figures 4.1 and 4.2, show that in financial year 2020/2021, out of 91,809 appeal decisions made at First-tier Social Security Tribunals, 27,122 decisions were upheld for government, whereas 64,077 decisions were made in favour of the claimant. This means that 70 per cent of government decisions were overturned. From the financial years 2015/2016 to 2020/2021, these statistics show an increasing trend of poor decision making, with the number of decisions overturned and granted in favour of claimants steadily increasing, albeit with a small reduction in 2020/2021 compared to the previous year (2019/2020). However, even the latest figures show that the government only got its decisions right the first time 29 per cent of the time – an unsustainable decision-making model.

---

[36] We do not include housing statistics here, as we found the processes of challenging housing decisions to not be very transparent, leading to great difficulties in terms of finding representative tables and figures.

[37] We have not included the data for the year 2021/2022 due to the impacts of the COVID-19 pandemic on the ability to hear tribunal cases and consequent impacts on the data. In our view, the period chosen between 2015/2016 and 2020/2021 best demonstrated the impacts of the post-LASPO access to justice landscape in terms of tribunals data. The raw tribunal data are published by the Ministry of Justice (MoJ) and all tables are accurate as of 12 June 2024. See MoJ, 'Tribunal Statistics Quarterly: January to March 2023' (2023), https://www.gov.uk/government/statistics/tribunal-statistics-quarterly-january-to-march-2023

Table 4.1: Social security and child support (number of cases)

Financial year	Upheld government	In favour of claimant	Cleared at hearing
2015/2016	57,895	72,374	131,319
2016/2017	61,601	99,616	162,369
2017/2018	62,231	115,303	178,849
2018/2019	50,498	115,370	166,989
2019/2020	38,444	100,891	140,115
2020/2021	26,742	63,892	91,001
Total	**297,411**	**567,446**	**870,642**

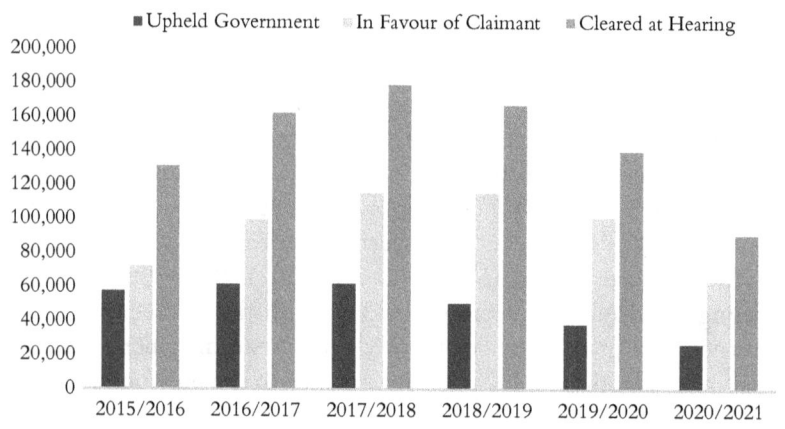

Figure 4.1: First-tier social security appeals (number of cases)

Table 4.2: Percentage of cases cleared at hearing upholding decision or finding in favour of the claimant

Financial year	Upheld government	In favour of claimant
2015/2016	44	55
2016/2017	38	61
2017/2018	35	64
2018/2019	30	69
2019/2020	27	72
2020/2021	29	70
Average (%)	**33.83**	**65.17**

Figure 4.2: First-tier social security appeals (%)

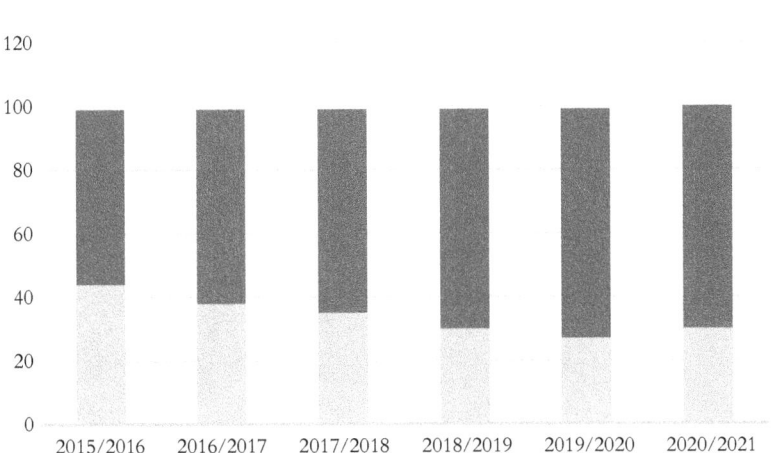

Table 4.3: Personal Independence Payment (number of cases)

Financial year	Cleared at hearing	Upheld government	In favour of claimant
2015/2016	49,742	19,112	30,236
2016/2017	70,329	24,074	45,697
2017/2018	83,886	26,289	56,971
2018/2019	83,954	21,984	61,476
2019/2020	77,156	17,711	59,090
2020/2021	55,006	13,171	41,751
Total	**420,073**	**122,341**	**295,221**

Given the contentious nature of medical assessment procedures for social security benefits, such as PIP, we have also included these statistics (Tables 4.3 and 4.4 and Figures 4.3 and 4.4).

The number of appeals upheld for government with respect to applications for PIP is dismal. There has been a steady increase (a slight 1 per cent decrease between 2020/2021 and 2019/2020) in decisions made in favour of claimants. With less than 25 per cent of decisions upheld for government, these statistics lend proof to our qualitative findings that decision-making processes, especially medical assessment procedures, are unfit for purpose. The impact of unjust decisions made in relation to initial applications results in a lengthy and arduous journey for rights holders with significant consequences. The processes and procedures for the evaluation of PIP

Figure 4.3: Personal Independence Payment (number of cases)

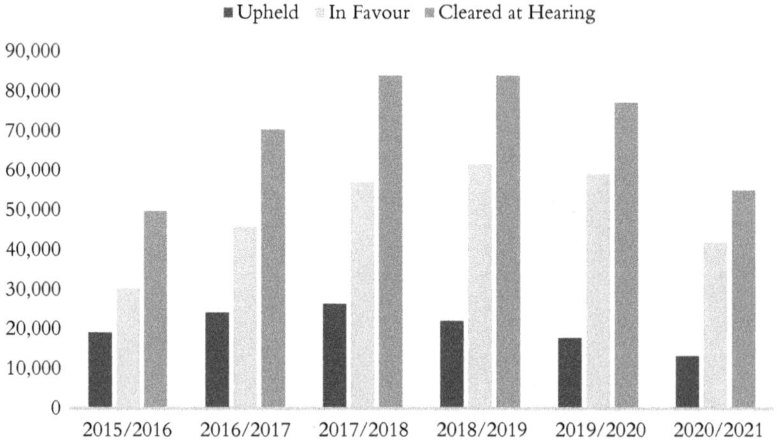

Table 4.4: Personal Independence Payment (%)

Financial year	Upheld government	In favour of claimant
2015/2016	38	61
2016/2017	34	65
2017/2018	31	68
2018/2019	26	73
2019/2020	23	77
2020/2021	24	76
Average (%)	**29.3**	**70**

applications require close scrutiny and review to produce fairer processes and outcomes. In response to claims that the PIP process is unfit for purpose, the DWP has said it supports 'millions of people a year' and 'the vast majority of PIP cases were not appealed'.[38] This defensive position runs contrary to the 'test and learn' philosophy claimed by the DWP as evidence of a responsive approach to 'setting it right' in the *Pantellerisco* case.

Immigration/asylum

We have also included the following statistics regarding immigration decisions at the First-tier Immigration Tribunal (see Table 4.5 and Figure 4.5 for further details).

---

[38] Alex Homer, 'Seven out of 10 Win Benefits Challenges at Tribunal', *BBC News*, 24 September 2021.

Figure 4.4: Personal Independence Payment (%)

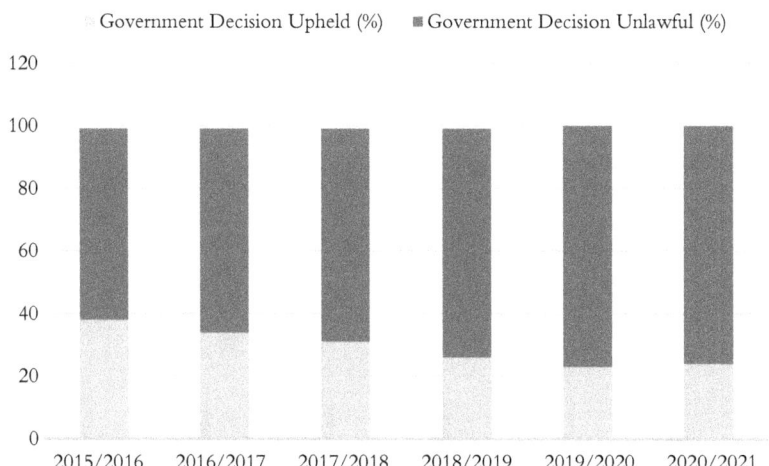

Table 4.5: First-tier immigration decisions allowed and dismissed (%)

Financial year	Allowed	Dismissed
2015/2016	39	61
2016/2017	43	57
2017/2018	49	51
2018/2019	52	48
2019/2020	50	50
2020/2021	49	51
Average (%)	**47**	**53**

Although the number of overturned decisions for immigration/asylum cases are not as extreme as those for social security cases, the trend from 2015/2016 to 2020/2021 shows that, on average, 47 per cent of decisions are in favour of the claimant. This is still nearly half of all decisions made in immigration cases, demonstrating flaws in decision-making processes for immigration and asylum too.

This approach undermines access to justice at a systemic level. As Erica explains:

> I mean I think the cynical part of me would say, you know, that these things are designed the way they are because they hope by rejecting more people then people just won't appeal it, they won't challenge it, so therefore if they are not having to pay x amount of money and

Figure 4.5: First-tier Tribunals (immigration and asylum): number of appeals determined at hearing or on paper (%)

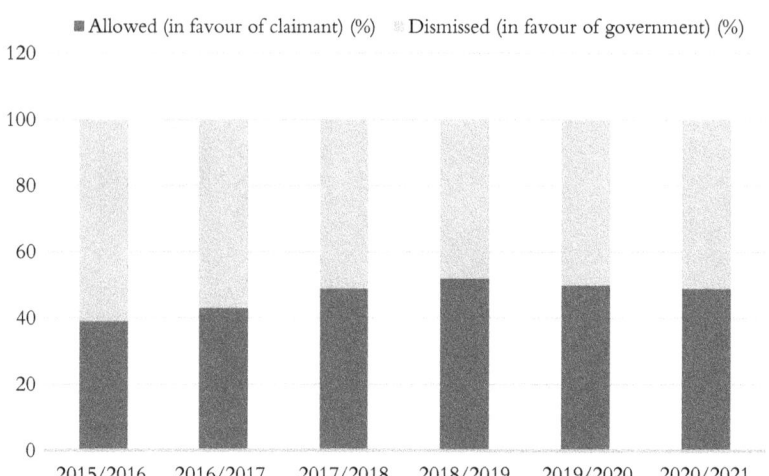

therefore they think they are saving money. But in reality if you have that many decisions overturned, that logic doesn't apply anymore, like the success on appeal rates are so high that basically a lot of the people with lived experience were like 'I expect to be denied what I'm entitled to at first and then I will get that-, chances are that [I] might get that on appeal'. But you have to have the mental and emotional capacity to do that. (Scotland, Erica, Solicitor, human rights public body)

Systemic injustice and structural responses: a missing component

Often cases involving SR violations can become systemic in nature. This means that the violation of an SR is often felt by many and ideally a case should stop the violation happening to anyone else. One of the key issues arising in the interviews demonstrated how difficult it is to navigate a legal avenue that enables access to justice beyond the individual to enable access to justice on a collective basis (for everyone impacted):

> Whereas there's many cases where you would really love to have the opportunity to get it into court to have the issues heard and aired because then it could be more helpful beyond the individual, that's not a decision that you can make on behalf of the person, you know, you just can't ... if you're in that situation and somebody said to you 'no OK, we will accept you're homeless', obviously you're going to say 'that's great, thanks very much', and that's what people do. They're not

going to say, 'well hold on, I want to make an important legal point here'. (NI, Josie, Chief Executive, NGO for housing)

There are various ways to seek collective justice, such as through strategic public interest litigation (a lead case that helps many) or through group proceedings or class actions (where multiple people collectively challenge a violation). International human rights and comparative law has seen the growth of remedies which are structural or collective in nature (this is discussed further later on) – in other words, they seek to address both individual relief and collective relief through guarantees of nonrepetition. Structural remedies are well suited to the UK system as they often involve a strong degree of dialogue, where the court facilitates a remedy with the participation of the rights holders and decision makers.[39] The power of collective challenges can help counteract the burden placed on an individual taking a case:

> I think in some individual cases there are great advocacy organizations in Scotland that are supporting that work. You know, look at Clan Childlaw [law centre] as well, who are doing strategic litigation work in terms of rights around children and education and trying to shift the system from that perspective, so individuals might get a bit of support and recourse there but that's not a strategic thing ... it's just a nightmare to go through in terms of supporting people to do that. There are organizations that will help people to do that, to try and get their rights addressed, but the issue is if you've been broken down by a system and completely marginalized, where are you going to go when [they] stop listening?
>
> The people in Leith, for example, the Council said 'we've not had complaints about this issue' – so the issue was around pigeon waste and rats, you know, vermin.
>
> 'We've not had complaints' ... Like if I was the tenant living in Leith and I'd complained about the same issue for five years – and in some cases for 20 years – and nothing had been done, why would I even, take that [leap]? It's so depressing and it's so disempowering. It is, but it also can be hopeful when you can get people together to realize that actually you still have the power. *And it's the power of the collective* which can be really helpful in engaging some of that ... and to realize that they're not alone, because that solidarity and power of the collective is

---

[39] For a full discussion of this, see Gaurav Mukherjee, 'Briefing: Effective Remedies & Structural Orders For Social Rights Violations', Nuffield Access to Justice for Social Rights, Addressing the Accountability Gap (2022).

actually really, really strong. (Scotland, Carole, Consultant and activist, NGO for human rights, emphasis added)

However these routes are, for various reasons, underexplored across the UK,[40] and more so in some parts compared to others. The following section considers the comparative practice of structural remedies as a response to systemic issues.

Comparative practice in structural relief

Remedies for SR violations usually take three broad forms: individual (they help address a violation for one person), programmatic (they address a systemic issue that impacts lots of people), and hybrid (they achieve a mixture of both individual and systemic relief). A singular focus on individual or programmatic relief could produce problems: courts that focus solely on individual cases may jeopardize relief for a broader class of petitioners while leaving intact a systemic feature of a legal system that may require attention, thereby being unable to ensure nonrepetition of the rights violation. Likewise, delivering only systemic relief may leave individual petitioners without access to a remedy.

Hybrid remedies of the kind referred to previously may also take the form of collective litigation in situations involving multiple complainants and multiple duty bearers. In such remedies, courts may also encourage the parties to engage in dialogue about the best way forward. Such 'dialogic' forms of judicial remedies are especially suited to claims involving SR. Courts may consider the meaning and content of rights, but defer back to the decision maker in relation to the remedy. The court can also play an important role in mitigating interinstitutional confrontation where there may be more than one department responsible (this can include dialogue and collaboration between executive departments at the national level or indeed disputes about obligations between the national level and the devolved level). Dialogic forms of judicial remedies can be innovative in nature in an exploration of how best to address systemic issues. In such kinds of remedies, courts can act as an intermediary between different rights holders and duty bearers to find an effective remedy that requires multiple duty bearers to respond as part of a structural interdict (a hybrid remedy that can offer individual and systemic relief potentially involving multiple applicants and multiple defendants).

---

[40] See, for example, the work of Michael Molavi, *Collective Access to Justice, Assessing the Potential of Class Actions in England and Wales* (Bristol: Bristol University Press, 2021).

In the field of SR, the development of a 'structural remedy' has formed an important part of jurisprudence in South Africa,[41] Kenya,[42] Colombia,[43] the US[44] and Canada.[45] Language around the use of structural remedies for systemic issues draws on different framings of individual versus collective/[46] systemic/[47]structural relief; specific versus general measures;[48] and simple versus complex remedies.[49] The use of the term 'structural orders' covers the broad field of remedial responses, including a complex aggregate of remedies (interim, delayed, declaratory and mandatory orders), and offers individual and systemic/structural relief involving both individual or collective cases where there may be multiple defendants and the court may perform a supervisory role postjudgment.[50]

The following section briefly considers some of the structural remedy litigation at the international and domestic levels, drawing out examples of individual cases that offer systemic relief as well as collective cases that offer systemic relief and on domestic examples from India, Canada, the US, South Africa and Colombia.

---

[41] *Equal Education and Others v Minister of Basic Education and Others* (22588/2020) [2020] ZAGPPHC 306; [2020] 4 All SA 102 (GP); 2021 (1) SA 198 (GP), 17 July 2020.

[42] Victoria Miyandazi, 'Setting the Record Straight on Socio-Economic Rights Adjudication: Kenya Supreme Court's Judgment in the Mitu-Bell Case', *Oxford Human Rights Hub*, 1 February 2021, https://ohrh.law.ox.ac.uk/setting-the-record-straight-on-socio-economic-rights-adjudication-kenya-supreme-courts-judgment-in-the-mitu-bell-case/

[43] Manuel José Cepeda Espinosa and David Landau, *Colombian Constitutional Law: Leading Cases* (Oxford: Oxford University Press, 2017), especially ch 6 on social rights.

[44] Katharine Young, 'A Typology of Economic and Social Rights Adjudication: Exploring the Catalytic Function of Judicial Review' (2010) 8(3) *International Journal of Constitutional Law*, pp 385–420.

[45] Kent Roach, *Constitutional Remedies in Canada*, 2nd edn (Toronto: Canada Law Book, 2013).

[46] Also in relation to class action, multi-party proceedings and group proceedings.

[47] Systemic and structural can be used interchangeably in the literature and in practice. See further Roach (n 29); and for national examples of interchangeable use of the term structural remedies, see the South African Constitutional Court and Kenyan Constitutional Court, which has issued 'structural remedies' that are framed in similar terms: *Mahlangu and Another v Minister of Labour and Others* [2020] ZACC 24; *Equal Education and Others v Minister of Basic Education and Others* (22588/2020) [2020] ZAGPPHC 306; and *Mitu-Bell Welfare Society v Kenya Airports Authority*, SC Petition 3 of 2018

[48] Roach (n 29), p 77.

[49] Ibid.

[50] Katie Boyle and Nicole Busby, 'Subnational Incorporation of Economic, Social and Cultural Rights: Can Devolution Become a Vehicle for Progressive Human Rights Reform?' (2023) 74(1) *Northern Ireland Legal Quarterly*, pp 63–94.

Structural remedies at the supranational level

The European Court of Human Rights, for example, now uses a pilot system to deal with systemic cases.[51] The central idea behind this procedure is to ensure that applicants obtain redress more speedily if an effective remedy is established in national law to address a systemic issue.[52] This allows the court to deal with its heavy caseload and limited resources by ensuring repetitive cases, and those cases that are urgent or raise questions of wider public importance can be adjudicated holistically and more speedily where the structural remedy addresses the systemic issue.[53]

The European Court of Human Rights has issued structural orders under the pilot system. A notable instance was its judgment in response to claims for compensatory land for property abandoned because of boundary changes following the Second World War in Poland. The Court held that the state should take measures that would afford a remedy to all those who faced a violation of Article 1 Protocol 1 ECHR. The Polish government then adopted a new law under which financial compensation was made available to all those impacted, meaning that an effective remedy had been made available at the national level.[54]

Other regional human rights systems adopt a similar approach. For example, the Inter-American Court of Human Rights issued a structural order to address the vulnerable situation of the Xákmok Kásek Indigenous Community in Paraguay who had been unable to take possession of their ancestral land and who were, in the meantime, left without access to adequate food, medicine and sanitation.[55] The Court ordered the return of the Xákmok Kásek Community's land, instructed a public act of acknowledgement of the wrongdoing by the state, and instructed the state to amend the domestic law to create an effective system for Indigenous peoples to reclaim ancestral lands at the domestic level. Further, it undertook supervision of compliance with the judgment.[56]

This approach is also evident as part of international complaints mechanisms. Similar approaches to preventing future violations from occurring have been

---

[51] These orders are granted under Rule 61 of the Rules of Court. For an explanation, see Janneke Gerards, 'Abstract and Concrete Reasonableness Review by the European Court of Human Rights' (2020) 1(2) *European Convention on Human Rights Law Review*, pp 218–247.

[52] European Court of Human Rights, Pilot Judgment Procedure, Information Note Issued by the Registrar, para 6.

[53] Ibid.

[54] *Broniowski v Poland* no. 31443/96, ECHR 2004-V. See also *Broniowski v Poland (friendly settlement)* no. 31443/96, ECHR 2005-IX 2 and *E. G. v Poland*, no. 50425/99 and other big river applications, decision of 23 September 2008.

[55] Inter-American Court Of Human Rights, *Case of the Xákmok Kásek Indigenous Community v Paraguay*, Judgment of 24 August 2010 (Merits, Reparations, and Costs), para 2.

[56] Ibid.

the subject of cases before the UN Human Rights Committee (on access to medical care),[57] the CEDAW (on domestic violence)[58] as well as the CESCR (on eviction orders).[59]

In the case of *Toussain*, a woman with precarious immigration status was denied healthcare constituting a breach of her right to life. The UN Human Rights Committee held that Ms Toussaint should receive compensation. In addition, it also held that Canada (the state party) was under an obligation to take steps to prevent similar violations in the future, including reviewing its national legislation to ensure that irregular migrants have access to essential healthcare to prevent a reasonably foreseeable risk that can result in loss of life.[60] Similarly, in the case of *Molina Thiessen v Guatemala*, the Inter-American Court of Human Rights produced a step-by-step guide[61] on how to ensure structural changes seeking to address the wider issue of access to justice and systemic impunity in Guatemala based on a violation in one incident. This guarantee of nonrepetition is again linked to the concept of an effective remedy, part of which requires cessation of the violation in the case at hand and for others that may be impacted.

As was noted earlier, supranational courts' exclusive focus on either individual or systemic relief carries risks. While individualized supranational remedies may fail to prevent future violations or remedy the feature of the legal system that caused the violation, systemic remedies may leave individual claimants without a remedy and also not address the intangible harms that rights holders have suffered. Twin-track supranational remedies that provide both are more capable of successfully negotiating the tensions between these categories of remedies. Some examples from international and regional human rights are provided later on.

In *IDG v Spain*,[62] the CESCR held that the individual complainant,[63] whose home was about to be subjected to foreclosure after she had

---

[57] *Toussaint v Canada*, United Nations Human Rights Committee, CCPR/C/123/D/2348/2014, 7 August 2018. See also *Mbongo Akwanga v Cameroon*, Merits, UN Doc. CCPR/C/101/D/1813/2008, IHRL 172 (UNHRC 2011), 22 March 2011, para 14 – the state was required to prevent such violations from occurring in the future.

[58] *X and Y v Georgia*, Communication No. 24/2009; UN Doc. CEDAW/C/61/D/24/2009, para 11(b)(ii).

[59] Communication submitted by: Rosario Gómez-Limón Pardo *Rosario Gómez-Limón Pardo v Spain*, E/C.12/67/D/52/2018.

[60] *Toussaint v Canada* (n 57), para 13.

[61] Order of the Inter-American Court of Human Rights, 16 November 2009, *Case of Molina-Theissen v Guatemala* (Monitoring Compliance with Judgment), para 32. For a discussion of this, see Lucrecia Molina Theissen, 'Until We Find Marco Antonio' (2020) 12 *Journal of Human Rights Practice*, pp 157–162.

[62] *IDG v Spain*, Merits, UN Doc. E/C.12/55/D/2/2014, IHRL 3882 (CESCR 2015).

[63] Note that Spain has signed the OP-ICESCR (Optional Protocol), which opens the door for individual complaints.

fallen behind on payments, could challenge the action due to procedural impropriety. While preventing the auction, it also added that 'in principle, the remedies recommended in the context of individual communications may include guarantees of non-repetition and recalls that the State party has an obligation to prevent similar violations in the future'. The case was hailed as an important step in ensuring access to justice for people who had bought homes on the cheap during the run-up to the burst of Spain's housing bubble.[64]

In a case[65] concerning the eviction of a Roma family from irregularly occupied government-owned land (later transferred to a private individual) near Sofia, Bulgaria, the European Court of Human Rights provided interim protection from eviction under a Rule 39 ruling.[66] Additionally, it also held that the 'general measures in execution of this judgment should include such amendments to the relevant domestic law and practice'. Such amendments would ensure that 'even in cases of unlawful occupation', rights under Article 8 ECHR would be subject to proportionality analysis and any removal order would only be justified if it responds to a 'pressing social need' and if it is 'proportionate to the legitimate aim pursued'.[67]

Structural relief in domestic adjudication

One of the first jurisdictions to use structural orders to address systemic issues was in India, when its Supreme Court heard petitions calling for government action on starvation deaths in the country. The Court started issuing interim, systemic orders that made discretionary government food distribution schemes justiciable, paving the way for a further set of judgments that would overhaul the country's public food programmes.[68] Other countries engaged with SR adjudication followed suit. Structural orders from domestic courts take several forms that depend on the features of the jurisdictions, some of which are discussed later on.

---

[64] Daniela Ikawa and Chris Grove, 'Historic Step towards Access to Justice for ESCR Violations at UN', *Open Democracy*, 1 December 2015, https://www.opendemocracy.net/en/openglobalrights-openpage/historic-step-towards-access-to-justice-for-escr-violatio/

[65] *Yordanova and Others v Bulgaria*, No. 25446/06.

[66] The ECtHR, under r 39 of its Rules of Court, grants interim measures that may be directed at any state party to the Convention.

[67] *Yordanova and Others v Bulgaria* (n 65), para 123.

[68] *People's Union for Civil Liberties v Union of India and Others Writ Petition* (Civil) No. 196 of 2001, (2002) (India).

Structural remedies through suspended declarations

A structural remedy of this nature comprises a declaration of constitutional incompatibility or invalidity on a government act or omission. Thereafter, such a declaration is suspended for a definite period, pending government action to correct the error that led to the situation. Suspended declarations of invalidity serve at least two important objectives: *first*, where courts are unsure of how to remedy a particular situation, these can provide governments with an opportunity to remedy the oversight/problem/concern within a period, thereby respecting courts' institutional incapacity as policy makers in most cases; and, *second*, it can prove to be a strain of a lesser degree on the separation of powers compared to other kinds of more invasive remedies. Two examples in particular of structural remedies done through suspended declarations of invalidity are instructive – healthcare litigation in Canada and school finance litigation in the US.

In *Chaoulli*, the Supreme Court of Canada struck down restrictions imposed by the province of Quebec on private health insurance due to the inordinately long waiting times for hip surgeries that were being observed.[69] The problem at hand was clearly polycentric, in that it involved and affected parties who were not before the court and whose actions would determine the outcome. The Court was also not sure whether more government spending on healthcare would reduce waiting times.[70] The way out was a systemic remedy wherein the Court held that the bar on private insurance purchase was unconstitutional. The remedy was operationalized through a suspended declaration of invalidity,[71] following which the province enacted legislation that permitted private insurance for knee, hip and cataract surgeries. While this may have constrained the availability of an individual remedy,[72] it allowed for the government to devise a remedy in response to the Court's strong normative declaration of invalidity.

The federal constitution of the US does not contain a set of justiciable SR, and any doctrinal innovations to that effect were closed off after the 1973 Supreme Court decision in *Rodriguez v San Antonio School Board*,[73] which found that education was not a fundamental interest protected under federal constitutional provisions. The Supreme Courts of Texas and Kentucky then became arenas for the contestation of education rights under their respective

---

[69] Roach (n 29), p 415.
[70] *Chaoulli v Quebec* [2005] 1 SCR 791, para 103.
[71] Roach (n 29), pp 416–417.
[72] Kent Roach, 'The Courts and Medicare: Too Much or Too Little Judicial Activism?' in Colleen Flood, Kent Roach and Lorne Sossin (eds), *Access to Care, Access to Justice* (Toronto: University of Toronto Press, 2005), p 200.
[73] *Rodriguez v San Antonio School Board*, 411 US 1 (1973).

state constitutions. The Texas Supreme Court held[74] that the unequal funding of school districts violated the state's constitution, while noting that 'we do not now instruct the Legislature as to the specifics of the legislation it should enact; nor do we order it to raise taxes. The Legislature has the primary responsibility to decide how best to achieve an efficient system'. According to the court, 'band-aid will not suffice; the system itself must be changed'. Following this, the state of Texas was given seven months to respond, after which its response too was held to be unconstitutional in subsequent litigation.[75] It was only after the adoption of more comprehensive reforms, a prominent feature of which was the tax cross-subsidy of poorer districts by wealthier ones, that the Court certified constitutional compliance.[76] Similarly, the Kentucky Supreme Court found that the existing funding system of public schools was unconstitutional in 1989.[77] The Court listed a set of learning outcomes that served as the normative undergirding of the subsequent set of reforms that were undertaken by the state following consultation with civil society groups[78]. Both of these cases illustrate the ways in which suspended declarations of invalidity can grant governments the time and space to respond to judicial opinions that can be respectful of the principle of the separation of powers, while also recognizing the harms that rights violations can cause.

Structural remedies through declarations and retention of jurisdiction

Courts can also issue structural remedies where they grant declaratory relief and retain jurisdiction over the matter, often because governments may not comply with the decision. The likelihood of government noncompliance is often a motivating factor for courts to design these kinds of orders. The likelihood of noncompliance is gauged by courts using the facts on record and the past conduct of the government on a given dispute. In cases where the likelihood of noncompliance is high, courts have held that declaratory relief may not be sufficient and may need to be backed up with the retention of jurisdiction over the matter in order to oversee the implementation of relief. These concerns become heightened in cases where the affected parties are especially vulnerable: examples include early childhood learners[79] and

---

[74] *Edgewood Independent School District v Kirby*, 777 S.W.2d 391 (Tex. 1989).
[75] Edgewood II, 804 S.W.2d 491 (Tex. 1991); Edgewood III, 826 S.W.2d 489 (Tex. 1992).
[76] Edgewood IV, 893 S.W.2d 450 (Tex. 1995).
[77] *Rose v Council for Better Education*, 790 S.W.2d 186 (Ky. 1989).
[78] Roach (n 29), p 418.
[79] *Equal Education and Others v Minister of Basic Education and Others* (22588/2020) [2020] ZAGPPHC 306; [2020] 4 All SA 102 (GP); 2021 (1) SA 198 at para 88.2: 'Children are categorically vulnerable, poor hungry children are exceptionally vulnerable. The degree of the violation of the constitutional rights are thus egregious.'

groups of individuals (which include children and the elderly) who may be rendered homeless as a result of government action.

In a South African case[80] concerning the availability of meals under the National School Nutrition Programme (NSNP) despite school closures during the COVID-19 pandemic, the North Gauteng High Court at Pretoria granted a structural interdict to oversee the rollout of the revised plan to ensure that the NSNP would continue uninterrupted. The Court noted that the provincial governments' responses to the filing of litigation that sought to resume the NSNP despite closures while restricting eligibility as being fragmented and without 'rhyme and reason', while being 'chaotic and unachievable'.[81] The remedy ensured relief for both the immediate class of claimants, while also ensuring that the NSNP, a federal programme, would be provided across the nine provinces which had been joined as parties to the case. This implies that courts' and claimants' awareness of the possible broader effect of a ruling to a wider range of affected parties can help navigate the tension between individual and structural relief.

Canada is a rich source of decisions where courts are able to engage with legislatures and the executive while retaining jurisdiction over cases. A series of minority school language cases, most notably *Doucet-Boudreau v Nova Scotia*,[82] provide a model for the ways in which courts were able to ensure that the issue of providing for minority language schools in the territory of Nova Scotia was addressed. The case had been complex and involved several parties and schools across locations. The lower court ordered a broadly worded remedy that required the government to make 'best efforts' to ensure compliance with constitutional rights and achieving homogenous Francophone education. The Supreme Court of Canada upheld the order despite its relative open-endedness, with Justices Iacobucci and Arbour stressing the 'need to respect general principles about the need for effective and responsive remedies, adherence to a flexible understanding of the separation of power and fairness towards the defendant'.[83]

Structural remedies through declarations of a state of unconstitutionality

The Constitutional Court of Colombia, after permitting the *tutela* mechanism to enforce individual SR, was flooded with complaints. Observers began

---

[80] *Equal Education and Others v Minister of Basic Education and Others* (22588/2020) [2020] ZAGPPHC 306; [2020] 4 All SA 102 (GP); 2021 (1) SA 198 (GP) (17 July 2020).
[81] *Equal Education and Others v Minister of Basic Education* (n 80), para 88.
[82] *Doucet-Boudreau v Nova Scotia* [2003] 3 SCR 3.
[83] Roach (n 29), p 392.

to note[84] how relief from the Court was being obtained by well-organized, well-funded repeat players, giving weight to the *pro-hegemonic* critique[85] of SR adjudication. The Court then engaged in a form of institutional self-correction. It did so by ensuring that its attention turned towards dialogic remedies where the court can set broad goals and standards according to which decisions left to the elected branches could be evaluated.[86] The apex of such a turn came in the structural judgment on the right to health,[87] which called for structural changes in the health system.[88] Some commentators[89] have argued that the 'state of unconstitutionality' which the Court declared with respect to the healthcare system allowed it to preserve its institutional capital by not naming the government department in question.

Structural orders through hybrid individual and systemic relief

Domestic courts that have an exclusive focus on either individual or systemic relief can run into certain difficulties. As discussed previously, individual remedies may fail to prevent future violations or remedy the feature of the domestic legal system that caused the violation. As a corollary, systemic remedies may leave individual claimants within the legal system without a remedy and also not address the intangible harms that rights holders have suffered.[90] Twin-track remedies that provide both are more capable of successfully negotiating the tensions between these categories of remedies.

The approach of the Constitutional Court of South Africa in a series of housing rights cases illustrates the benefits of a twin-track approach. In *Blue Moonlight*,[91] the eviction of several unauthorized occupants of a private property was halted pending the provision of alternate *temporary* accommodation that met constitutional requirements. To do so, the Court had to examine the constitutionality of the Ekhuthuleni Overnight/Decant

---

[84] David Landau, 'The Reality of Social Rights Enforcement' (2012) 53 *Harvard International Law Journal*, pp 190–247, p 225. Note the pushback against the pro-hegemonic critique: Mila Versteeg, 'Can Rights Combat Economic Inequality?' (2017) 133 *Harvard Law Review*, pp 2017–2060, p 2034: 'my own best reading of the official statistics is that both the poor and the middle classes benefited from the *tutela*'.

[85] Boyle (n 10), p 17.

[86] César Rodríguez-Garavito, 'Beyond the Courtroom: The Impact of Judicial Activism on Socioeconomic Rights in Latin America' (2011) 89 *Texas Law Review*, pp 1669–1698, p 1676.

[87] T-760/08 (Decision T-760/08 (2008) (Colombia).

[88] Alicia Ely Yamin (Decision T-760 (2008) (Colombia).

[89] David Landau, 'Political Institutions and Judicial Role in Comparative Constitutional Law' (2010) 51(2) *Harvard International Law Journal*, pp 319–378, pp 342–344.

[90] Roach (n 29), pp 14–15.

[91] *City of Johannesburg Metropolitan Municipality v Blue Moonlight Properties 39 (Pty) Ltd and Another* [2011] ZACC 33; 2012 (2) SA 104 (CC).

Shelter House Rules, which put in place a number of restrictive rules on curfews, gender segregation and onerous registration/signing requirements on beneficiaries of temporary accommodation. The Court held these restrictions to be unconstitutional and violative of the right to dignity, freedom and security of a person, as well as privacy. Here, we see that the Court provided relief to the class of petitioners (33 in total), while also ensuring that the city altered its rules on temporary alternate accommodation in order to be constitutionally compliant.

Nussberger and Landau highlight that structural approaches to economic, social and cultural rights are underexplored and may have potential that has not been fully realized in the comparative practice of enforcing ESC rights.[92] While not a panacea, research suggests that they can be particularly effective in enabling dialogue between impacted communities and decision makers,[93] as well as longer-term material change enabled through legislative reform that follows awareness raising of major systemic problems.[94] This aligns with the empirical data of the importance of rights claiming as a performative act in a participative and deliberative democracy.

Conclusions

This chapter frames access to justice as a journey. In so doing, it reconceptualizes the access to social justice journey as one that begins with a violation and ends with an effective remedy. The empirical data reflected the sheer frustrations which many of our practitioners felt in relation to the arduous nature of the journey and the danger of getting mired in 'administrative mud'. It was also clear from the research participants that the system, in its current format, is simply unfit for purpose. People do not have the resources to challenge the system, and the system is stacked against them. The law does not adequately protect SR. The routes to justice are complex. The end results are not effective in practice. Even when a remedy is forthcoming, it does not meet the standard of an effective remedy according to international human rights law. There is no mechanism to address systemic errors in decision making, with tribunal data showing up to 75 per cent of cases being overturned at the tribunal level. Other countries that have embedded SR in their legal framework provide examples of how justice systems can adapt to address systemic and collective violations in different ways. There is much greater scope across the UK to learn from these jurisdictions to address the gaps in the access to justice journey.

---

[92] Angelika Nussberger and David Landau, *The Justiciability of Economic, Social and Cultural Rights* (Cambridge: Intersentia, 2023).
[93] Ibid, pp 44–45.
[94] Ibid.

5

Challenging Discourses That Marginalize: Reclaiming the Narrative

This chapter returns to the data to discuss in greater detail the broader concerns and challenges that emerged relating to competing discourses that marginalize those who experience violations of SR, thus pushing them further towards the margins and further away from social justice. We do this by drawing attention to various mechanisms, made visible through discourse, that we believe sustain the current framework and often facilitate injustice. We take inspiration from the work of Elana Shohamy[1] and Nikolas Rose,[2] who, each in their own way, provide ways of thinking and practical tools for empirically investigating the production and legitimation of knowledge and evaluating how laws and policy materialize in practice. Our discursive approach to policy includes a conceptual frame that directs attention to the social construction of knowledge.

This chapter identifies various dynamics across our data that interconnect with laws, policy and public services that create the daily realities of policy in action 'on the ground'. It examines how policy mechanisms are situated between legal frameworks and broader ideologies in the public space and practice. Ideologies are expressed as wider circulating discourses, include myths, propaganda, coercion and stigma. Our data show how ideology and policy mechanisms transect with limitations of the legal framework for upholding SR. In combination, these different factors work together to sustain a highly complex and fragmented system, resulting in barriers to

---

[1] Elana Shohamy, *Language Policy: Hidden Agendas and New Approaches* (Abingdon: Routledge, 2006).
[2] Nikolas Rose, *Powers of Freedom: Reframing Political Thought* (Cambridge: Cambridge University Press, 1999).

accessing justice for SR by preventing full participation and access to an effective remedy. This chapter returns to the data to examine moments of tension where different logics and discourses intersect, making competing mechanisms visible and demonstrating how discourses that marginalize need to be challenged in order to reclaim the discourse.

The case studies in Chapter 3 provided 'snapshots' of wider issues across the social welfare landscape. Each of the case studies provides examples of processes and mechanisms that work together to constitute the current legal SR framework. We interpret these workings of governance for the provision of SR as the mechanics of a complex system with many interrelated components: humans, technologies, institutions, governments, NGOs and charities, as well as discursive and ideological currents embedded within a broader sociopolitical context.

As has been brought to the fore in the case studies, different constitutional arrangements under devolution result in different legal frameworks, contributing to an already fragmented system for the provision of social welfare. Laws and policies governing this arena are also influenced by broader ideological currents. The case studies we presented highlighted various contentious issues with respect to specific policies/legal cases in each of the jurisdictions, with evidence of poorly reasoned policies. We also identified challenges with respect to legal processes related to the inadequacy of complaints mechanisms, the adjudication of rights and limited funding. In contrast to neoliberal rationalities that underpin many of the workings of the operational welfare system, normative frameworks for international human rights are rooted in the protection and realization of rights, emphasizing the principles of equality and nondiscrimination, participation and inclusion. This means that every person has the right to participate in and access information relating to the decision-making processes that affect their lives and well-being.

In order for rights holders to access their SR and participate in the (legal) frameworks governing public services and social welfare, they need awareness, information, advice and advocacy. The data show that the services provided by practitioners, including welfare rights advisors, charities, legal practitioners, volunteers and activists, are absolutely essential. Unfortunately, the capacity of the third sector has been severely impacted by austerity measures, resulting in funding cuts and closures of advice centres and law centres. By way of an example, in the midst of the COVID-19 pandemic, five Citizens Advice Bureau (CAB) centres in Glasgow faced closure. Although they appear to have been saved from that fate, the centres faced significant funding cuts.[3] The COVID-19 pandemic has highlighted some

---

[3] Ruth Suter, 'Five Glasgow Citizens Advice Bureaux Saved from Closure', *Glasgow Times*, 17 September 2020, https://www.glasgowtimes.co.uk/news/18728745.five-glasgow-citizens-advice-bureaux-saved-closure/

of the challenges facing not only the third sector but also the realization of SR more broadly.[4]

Nikolas Rose's work,[5] expanding Foucault's notion of governmentality, empirically investigates how different types of knowledge and expertise articulate with practical techniques in constructing 'governable subjects'. Rose directs attention to how diverse elements, such as authorities, technologies and strategies, work together to create specific realities and particular subjectivities.[6] In brief, these elements urge us to ask questions about who gets to define certain phenomena to be problems and to determine the criteria of proof required. Which kinds of tools are used to make judgements? Are there conflicts between different claims to authority? What kind of subjectivities are promoted and what kind of strategies are adopted? As we show in our analysis, tensions across the data alert us to relationships between various dynamics that articulate together in the current framework for the protection of SR.

Similarly, Elana Shohamy urges us to pay attention to different mechanisms that intersect with stated policy and impact on practice, creating and perpetuating 'de facto' policies. These overt and covert mechanisms are used mostly, but not exclusively, by those in authority, and the effects and consequences of these mechanisms, she says, often lead to violations of democratic processes and rights.[7] Examples of such mechanisms might be strict rules and regulations or means of assessment and testing. Funding allocations can also serve as a policy mechanism that counteracts stated policies.[8]

Considering the influence of policy mechanisms and techniques helps us to recognize and identify the interrelated factors that impact on the day-to-day experiences of rights holders. Thus, examining how policy mechanisms intersect with legal provisions and practice helps us to better understand how policy is 'both text and action, words and deeds, it is what is enacted as well as what is intended'.[9]

---

[4] Barry Black, Paul Pearson and Jo Ferrie, 'Human Rights in Health and Social Care in Scotland: Where We've Been and the Journey Ahead', *The ALLIANCE*, 2023, https://www.alliance-scotland.org.uk/policy-and-research/wp-content/uploads/2023/02/The-opportunity-is-now-human-rights-in-health-and-social-care.pdf

[5] Rose (n 2).

[6] Ibid.

[7] Shohamy (n 1).

[8] Diana Camps, 'Restraining English instruction for refugee adults in the United States' in E. M. Feuerherm and V. Ramanathan (eds), *Refugee Resettlement in the United States: Language, Policy, Pedagogy* (Multilingual Matters 2016), p 67.

[9] Stephen Ball, *Education Reform: A Critical and Post-structuralist Approach* (Buckingham: Open University Press, 1994), p 10.

Competing discourses: immigration and Scottish housing

One of the clearest examples of how fragmentation of the (legal) framework for SR intersects with practice is the lock-change eviction policy in Glasgow (see the Scotland case study in Chapter 3). The notion of fragmentation is constituted not only in conflict between reserved and devolved law, but also in the outsourcing of public services. These mechanisms are also intimately linked to ideological conceptions, which become salient through discourse. The following analysis identifies different discourses that are foregrounded in the data.

The lock-change eviction policy resulted in a clash between Scottish housing policy and UK immigration policy, creating tensions that became visible in the competing dynamics and logics produced through discourse. Practitioners in Scotland advocating on behalf of asylum seekers challenged the policy on the basis that it contravened housing law in Scotland by failing to obtain a court order to authorize the evictions and failed to comply with human rights law. On a practical level, practitioners expressed that immigration policy curbed the powers of the Scottish government by preventing Scotland from acting in a way that adhered to its principles of 'making things better', which contrasts sharply with the racialized 'hostile environment' policy embedded by the UK government's Home Office.

Constructing 'failed' asylum seekers

The tensions identified here make visible competing dynamics rooted in different rationalities and ideologies. The sentiment of making things better referred to commitments in Scotland to uphold human rights. This alignment with principles of human rights, as embedded in international human rights law, can be interpreted as a 'human rights discourse'. We demonstrate in our analysis how the human rights discourse is promoted in other parts of the data, but first we discuss how it intersects in the Scottish case study with another dominant discourse that comes to the fore through a single idiom: 'failed asylum seeker'.

We explain by drawing attention to the first line of the *Ali* judgment of the Inner House, Court of Session, which states: 'The appellant is a failed asylum seeker.'[10] Although this has become the default terminology used by the UK Home Office for describing individuals who have exhausted their appeal rights, it is by no means a neutral term. The practitioners we spoke to preferred not to use the term, favouring the designation 'appeal rights

---

[10] *Ali (Iraq) v Serco Ltd* [2019] CSIH 54.

exhausted asylum seekers' or '(potential) refugee'. Julie, an immigration solicitor in Scotland, said 'you would hear me say "this is a refugee" or "this is potentially a refugee" because in law that is true ... what we're seeing at the end of the process is they're recognized as a refugee'.

Also, describing those seeking asylum as 'a person seeking asylum' foregrounds the humanity of the person rather than their status. Although a person may be denied asylum, they may also submit a new case and be granted asylum in the future, meaning that the label of 'failed asylum seeker' is neither an objective nor a permanent category. Designations such as refugee, migrant and (failed) asylum seeker are merely determinations of status, granted by the authorities, which allow or restrict access to particular resources. These labels are generally not used in uniform ways, particularly in the media, often conflating terms and confusing meanings.[11]

Bridget Anderson reminds us that immigration and citizenship are 'not simply about legal status, but fundamentally about status in the sense of worth and honour – that is, membership of the community of value. The debates around immigration are about the contours of the community of value as much as they are about trade-offs and economic impacts'.[12] In relation to the realization of SR, it is important to acknowledge the importance of legal designations, as these political framings play a significant role in constructing the contours of who is included and who is excluded in collective imaginations of entitlement to justice.[13] Our interest is in the (mis)framings that impede access to justice, both in terms of the constitutional framing of SR and of the framing of particular groups of rights holders and the consequential impact on the access to justice journey. On the latter point, those seeking asylum in the UK can be considered one such category of people whose 'representation'[14] delimits their ability to claim SR as they are consistently marginalized by the system.

Asylum-seeking processes themselves are difficult and highly contested procedures. For instance, there is a significant body of critical sociolinguistic research examining how discriminatory practices of using asylum seekers'

---

[11] It is beyond the scope of this chapter to discuss the legacy of legal distinctions between (types of) migrants and citizens. Moreover, challenges around legal status, labelling and framings are not unique to the UK context. See, for instance, Emily Feuerherm and Vaidehi Ramanathan, *Refugee Resettlement in the United States: Language, Policies and Pedagogies* (Bristol: Multilingual Matters, 2016).

[12] Bridget Anderson, *Us & Them: The Dangerous Politics of Immigration Control* (Oxford: Oxford University Press, 2013).

[13] Nancy Fraser, *Scales of Justice: Reimagining Political Space in a Globalizing World* (New York: Columbia University Press, 2009).

[14] Ibid.

linguistic background often limits access to refugee status.[15] The UK Home Office's 'hostile environment' ideology is visible in efforts currently underway to reform the immigration/asylum system by passing the highly contested Nationality and Borders Act 2022,[16] the Illegal Migration Act 2023,[17] and the previous Conservative government's plans to send asylum seekers to Rwanda for processing their asylum claims.[18] Numerous human rights organizations and immigration lawyers have raised serious concerns about undermining human rights and breaching international and domestic laws.[19] In November 2023, the UK Supreme Court found the Rwanda plan to be unlawful.[20] In April 2024 the UK government responded and the UK Parliament passed the Safety of Rwanda (Asylum and Immigration) Act 2024. The legislation asserts that Rwanda is a safe country in perpetuity for the purposes of the immigration removal instructing courts to comply with the statute notwithstanding human rights violations de facto and de jure.

Interestingly, it is the post-Brexit devolved framework in NI that is providing routes to remedy for human rights incompatible primary legislation via the Windsor Framework, whereby the UK has committed to ensure there is no diminution of rights in NI. In the case of *Dillon*[21] in February 2024, the High Court held that granting immunity from prosecution under the Northern Ireland Troubles (Legacy and Reconciliation) Act 2023 would constitute a diminution of rights (namely Article 2 ECHR procedural obligations) applying Article 2 of the Windsor Framework together with the section 7A of the EU (Withdrawal Act) 2018, both of which were engaged under the EU Victim's Directive. Under the incompatible legislation, state actors would have been able to apply for immunity without the ECHR required backstop of amnesty operating alongside posthumous procedural protections (Articles 2, 3 and 6 ECHR and Articles 3, 4 and 7 of the EU

---

[15] See, for example, Jan Blommaert, 'Language, Asylum and the National Order' (2009) 50(4) *Current Anthropology*, pp 415–441. Diana Eades, 'Testing the Claims of Asylum Seekers: The Role of Language Analysis' (2009) 6(1) *Language Assessment Quarterly*, pp 30–40.
[16] 'Nationality and Borders Act 2022' (UK Parliament).
[17] 'Illegal Migration Act 2023' (UK Parliament).
[18] Agreement between the Government of the United Kingdom of Great Britain and Northern Ireland and the Government of the Republic of Rwanda for the provision of an asylum partnership to strengthen shared international commitments on the protection of refugees and migrants (UK-Rwanda) (signed 5 December 2023) CS No 1/2023; Safety of Rwanda (Asylum and Immigration) HC Bill (2023–24) [414].
[19] OHCHR, 'UK Illegal Migration Act: UN Refugee Agency and UN Human Rights Office Warn of Profound Impact on Human Rights and International Refugee System' (Geneva, 18 July 2023).
[20] *R (on the Application of AAA and Others) v Secretary of State for the Home Department* [2023] UKSC 42.
[21] *Dillon* [2024] NIKB 11.

Charter of Fundamental Rights). This 2024 case can be viewed as part of a longer trajectory in NI where the state has fallen short of human rights standards. Outstanding issues around incompatibility with Article 2 ECHR have been under enhanced supervision for over 20 years by the Committee of Minsters in the Council of Europe (as part of the Committee's role in supervising the execution of judgments) following *McKerr* (2001).[22]

In the recent judicial review brought by the NI Human Rights Commission, the Illegal Migration Act 2023 was deemed incompatible with Article 2 of the Windsor Framework, including access to an effective remedy (Article 47 of the EU Charter of Fundamental Rights). The statute's duty to disregard any claim of human rights breaches, refugee status, victimization through human trafficking or judicial review from any person who enters the UK without compliance with the requirements of immigration law was deemed a diminution of rights and therefore unlawful under the Windsor Framework (Article 2).[23]

As pointed out by Julie in the Scottish case study, the ability to make a successful claim to asylum is connected with access to advice, support and legal representation, a journey that is also fraught with difficulties. In fact, the high number of asylum cases overturned at the First-tier Immigration Tribunal (for further details, see the statistics in Chapter 4) suggests that, through its policies and procedures, the UK Home Office 'constructs' failed asylum seekers. It is a system of structural inequality. Persons suffer injustice as a result of structural inequality when 'their group social positioning means that the operation of diverse institutions and practices conspire to limit their opportunities to achieve wellbeing'.[24]

The term 'failed asylum seeker', in particular, strips individuals of any legitimacy and imbricates them in a semantic web of varying meanings, placing them in complex societal structures through their relationship to other (il)legitimate groups.[25] It is an ideological framing that is intimately linked to the UK Home Office's 'hostile environment' policy and invokes wider discourses of fears relating to illegal entry/immigration, 'bogus refugees',[26]

---

[22] The ECHR judgment in *McKerr and Others* in 2001 (*McKerr Group* [28883/95] and *McCaughey Group* [43098/09]) remains under supervision. See https://hudoc.exec.coe.int/eng

[23] *NIHRC and JR295's Applications for Judicial Review* [2024] NIKB 35.

[24] Iris Marion Young, 'Structural Injustice and the Politics of Difference' in Kwame Anthony Appiah, Seyla Benhabib, Iris Marion Young and Nancy Fraser (eds), *Justice, Governance, Cosmopolitanism and the Politics of Difference: Reconfigurations in a Transnational World* (Berlin: Humboldt-Universität zu Berlin, 2007), p 82.

[25] Feuerherm and Ramanathan (n 11).

[26] The term 'bogus refugee' is 'nonsensical', because the status of refugee is only conferred after completing a successful application; see Costas Gabrielatos and Paul Baker, 'Fleeing,

(un)belonging and national identity, costs to taxpayers and losses of UK jobs, among others. This in turn may invoke perceived associations and traits, such as criminality, fraudulence and dishonesty. In other words, the term 'failed asylum seeker' becomes synonymous with negative representations that instantly qualify someone as a specific type of person who, as we show through the data, is not 'deserving' of humane treatment. Operating on a logic of difference, we refer to this as a 'valuation discourse', constituted as a deserving and undeserving dichotomy.

We suggest that the 'failed asylum seeker' designation prevails with the UK Home Office because it fits the rhetoric and ideological framing of those seeking asylum in the UK and serves as a justification for not meeting people's basic social needs. This is further exacerbated by other mechanisms, such as the outsourcing of public services and elements of street-level bureaucracy in the form of routinized low paid work.

The 'hostile environment' policy is powerful in the sense that ideology becomes practice through rules and regulations that marginalize a large group of people on account of their immigration status. Bearing in mind that the tribunal data demonstrate the construction of 'failed asylum seekers' at the decision-making level, asylum seekers whose applications are refused are stripped of any support as they have no recourse to public funds (NRPF), including social security and homelessness support. Any section 4 asylum support via an Aspen card is further constrained by not allowing cash access (see the Scottish case study).[27] As evictions caseworker Abigail explained, asylum seeker possessions cannot exceed £1,000 in value. If the Home Office checks, asylum support is stopped. Of course, people may very well have possessions that exceed the designated limit due to generous donations, including electronics, but these items do not provide for the daily necessities of life.

Furthermore, those seeking asylum are closely monitored to ensure they do not leave their homes for more than a few days at a time. Abigail provided accounts of housing managers changing the locks on people's homes when they were away, on the pretext that the person had abandoned the property. She said it was difficult to explain to people that they could not go and stay with their friends for prolonged periods of time, especially if they were living in houses without any power or heating:

> Because if people don't have jobs [asylum seekers do not have legal permission to work] like they want [laughs] they want to fill their time!

Sneaking, Flooding: A Corpus Analysis of Discursive Constructions of Refugees in the UK Press, 1996–2005 (2008) 36(1) *Journal of English Linguistics*, pp 5–38, p 31.

[27] Immigration and Asylum Act (1999), s 4(11).

They just want to be normal people! Like they want to [laughs] feel good so they go and stay with their friends. And then you're having to be like ... 'please make sure you're going home' ... you shouldn't have to say to someone like 'you're not supposed to be away from your home for six days' because it's, what's the word, I don't know, well it's just so controlling. (Scotland, Abigail, Evictions caseworker, NGO for asylum seekers)

Abigail's comment about the controlling nature of Home Office policies reflect the type of surveillance and disciplinary practices of governmentality brought to the fore in Foucault's work. This is evident in the ideological valuation of those seeking asylum which has filtered into operational language used by housing providers, through use of the terms 'positive and negative moves-ons', correlating with a person's immigration status and related availability of support. Abigail explained that when the housing provider refers to 'positive moves-ons', this means that the person got a positive decision on their claim to asylum and are moving on. 'Negative move-ons', on the other hand, identify people who received a negative decision on their asylum claim. She went on to say:

With the 'positive moves-ons', it's like there's quite a clear path, even though there's lots of failings in that path as to what people will do once they've got status, but with the 'negative move-ons', it's kind of like, 'well they have to go and then, we don't know what'. Like, no one knows what! ... And so it's this sort of vagueness and I think it's really amplified by that language of 'negative move-on', it's ... sort of vague ... but at the same time operational. (Scotland, Abigail, Evictions caseworker, NGO for asylum seekers)

Abigail's examples illustrate the interdiscursive connections between the language of the UK Home Office and the operational language of housing providers. It exposes the more insidious side of the 'hostile environment' and valuation discourses, in the sense that the rules and regulations carried out in practice amount to the creation of particular subject positions and reflect operations of power at micro-levels of practice, including at the street level. Other scholars have drawn attention to how forms of expertise and disciplining activities function to construct particular ways of being, such as becoming employable workers[28] or productive

---

[28] Alfonso Del Percio, 'Engineering Commodifiable Workers: Language, Migration and the Governmentality of the Self' (2018) 17 *Language Policy*, pp 239–259; Mi-Cha Flubacher, Alexandre Duchêne and Renata Coray, *Language Investment and Employability: The Uneven Distribution of Resources in the Public Employment Service* (London: Palgrave Macmillan, 2018).

citizens.[29]

What has been highlighted in these examples is not merely a difference in authority and decision-making power, but a clash in ideology made salient through discourse. The 'hostile environment' discourse pervaded legal proceedings in the *Ali* case when the judgment opened with the line 'This is a failed asylum seeker' – acting as a precursor to a decision that marginalized human rights when housing was provided by a private actor. Dennis Klinck's writing makes it clear that the 'us' versus 'them' dynamic is not new, not even in the court of law. Klinck,[30] reflecting on the contribution of influential English jurist Lord Denning (1899–1999), provides numerous examples of similar value-laden interpretations conveyed in court proceedings and judgments over his long career. Discourses thus make visible the ideological workings that often run below the surface.

Valuation discourses feature prominently across the various UK jurisdictions, not only with respect to immigration status, but also related to low income, disability, mental health challenges, addictions and criminal records. We will return to these discourses throughout our analysis, discussing them as they intersect with other discourses that are foregrounded in the data.

Accountability gaps: outsourcing government functions

In this section, we raise important considerations in relation to the various ways in which a lack of accountability is constituted through different and intersecting policy mechanisms. We continue the conversation around the *Ali v Serco* case, drawing out different issues, and extend our conversation to other connections across the data related to the outsourcing of medical assessments and the private housing sector.

Privatization and outsourcing are hallmarks of neoliberal rationalities, and the entailed lack of oversight and accountability was the biggest problem identified by practitioners. This concern was raised by various practitioners regarding the lock-change evictions. It also revealed unjust practices relating to the provision of services to those seeking asylum, including provisions for housing and asylum support.

Abigail explained that there was a common practice of harassment, with housing managers turning up at people's homes and asking them to leave. Often, out of fear, people would leave, but they had nowhere to go. Due

---

[29] Alfonso Del Percio, 'The Governmentality of Migration: Intercultural Communication and the Politics of (Dis)Placement in Southern Europe' (2016) 51 *Language & Communication*, pp 87–98.

[30] Dennis Klinck, 'This Other Eden: Lord Denning's Pastoral Vision' (1994) 14(1) *Oxford Journal of Legal Studies*, pp 25–55.

to their immigration status, asylum seekers who have exhausted their appeal rights do not have access to homelessness services, and Glasgow only has one shelter for asylum seekers, with limited capacity and only catering to men.[31] Abigail also felt that the lack of oversight and accountability combined with low wages facilitated housing managers carrying out cruel decisions, such as evictions, in a routinized fashion without any empathy or concern for human dignity. Routines and standardized practices and operations are illustrative of the mechanics of street-level bureaucracy.

Another important point is that becoming homeless makes it almost impossible to carry on with an asylum claim, so Serco's eviction efforts not only undermined a person's safety by thrusting them into destitution and homelessness, but also potentially prevented them from completing the asylum-seeking process to obtain refugee status and their right to remain in the UK.

Privatization and human rights

A major element of the Scottish legal case revolved around the outsourcing of public services to the private provider. Serco was found not to be a public authority for human rights purposes, because the court's analysis prioritized Serco's motivation to make a profit as a private company rather than looking at the functions it was performing. As highlighted in the case study, the judgment raised concerns for the practitioners we interviewed because of the prevalence of outsourcing in the delivery of public services and concerns that it could result in a two-tier human rights system. It creates the potential of inequity in service provisions: if services are provided directly by the government, they must comply with human rights standards, whereas if they are provided by a private company, there is less clarity about their obligations and this leaves the door wide open for injustice.

We explained in the case study that the Serco verdict has had a material impact that extends far beyond the conclusion of the case. More broadly, the failure to hold Serco to account does not encourage and advance a human rights-based approach in line with international human rights standards. Instead it opens the door to future injustice by creating a space for private companies to potentially shirk their human rights responsibilities, rather than increasing the capacities of 'duty bearers' to meet their obligations. It is clear that contradicting logics advance neoliberal rationalities over principles of human rights.

---

[31] A smaller project catered to women, but did not have its own premises, so it entailed finding spaces in people's homes (Scotland, Abigail, Evictions caseworker, NGO for asylum seekers).

In this section, we take a closer look at Erica's comments regarding section 6 of the HRA 1998, where she explains that the application and interpretation of the principle has been problematic. We draw on the theoretical constructs of entextualization to explain how the perceived original 'intention of Parliament' is transformed into another legitimate interpretation. Erica states:

> Section 6 of the Human Rights Act says that all public authorities, so all public bodies, must act in compliance with the European Convention on Human Rights. So that's fine but then there's a provision of that which says that … private bodies, when they are performing functions of a public nature, are also caught by the Human Rights Act … that's to fulfil the principle that a state can't contract out of its human rights obligations and that the principle is really like when you're standing in the shoes of the state, then you also must comply with their human rights obligations. So I think that's a fine line and relatively uncontroversial, but *how that provision has been applied and interpreted over the years by the courts has been problematic* … everything in the intention of parliament at the time when the Human Rights Act was going through is that you should look at the function. So it doesn't matter if this company is a private company and if they're for-profit and they have shareholders and essentially they look very much like a private entity, if they're performing … a function, so in this case it would be the provision of accommodation and other support to asylum seekers, if that function is of a public nature then in exercising that function they are obliged to comply with the convention. (Scotland, Erica, Solicitor, human rights public body, emphasis added)

Although Erica believes that the intention of Parliament, at the time that the HRA was created, was to look at function, by means of the Serco legal proceedings, others have been able to produce meanings that recontextualize the 'original' text and allow for ideological repositioning. Processes of recontextualization transform discourses, thereby taking on new or different meanings. An ideology of fixed text – the perception that a text artefact is a stable, clear and precise semantic unit – underpins the construction of a space that allows different parties to produce legitimate entextualizations of the source text.[32]

There is close interaction between linguistic ideologies – the ideology of fixed text – and broader social and political ideologies.[33] Blommaert states

---

[32] Jan Blommaert, *Discourse: A Critical Introduction* (Cambridge: Cambridge University Press, 2005), p 187.
[33] Ibid, p 201.

that: 'Power resides in this interplay between an ideology of fixedness and practices of re-entextualisation, for it is precisely through this interplay that authority in the domain of interpretation of texts can be managed and channelled.'[34] The new interpretation of section 6 HRA in the Serco case receives legitimacy from the outcome of the legal process that upholds this meaning as valid. The entailed transformation in meaning had significant impact on the outcome of the Serco case. Although this interpretation may later be overturned or reinterpreted, legitimacy has been created for this application of section 6 HRA, which, as stated earlier, could facilitate future injustice.

These various tensions illustrate how mechanisms of law, policy, rules and procedures intersect with ideological conceptions of worthiness, expressed through 'hostile environment' and valuation discourses. The outsourcing of services and lack of oversight further exacerbated transgressions of human rights.

Prejudicial practices: privatized housing

Practitioners across the jurisdictions raised concerns regarding the private housing sector, particularly with respect to security of tenure and fitness standards. Our NI case study presents many of these challenges, so we will not reiterate them here. However, we would like to draw attention to the intersecting mechanisms in the privatized housing sector that the NI case study revealed. Concerns about the lack of a regulatory framework and inconsistent oversight and accountability for the private housing sector echo problems encountered by practitioners in the Scotland case study.

Josie, head of an NGO for housing in NI, expressed the increased vulnerability of people in the private rental sector, as there is no security of tenure. Even if someone has been a model tenant, she said, they can be asked to leave at any time under a 'no-fault eviction'. In addition, high levels of harassment and illegal evictions combined with inadequate mechanisms of redress create precarious circumstances for people. There are clear legal processes related to eviction that call for a 28-day notice period followed by due process through the courts. However, Josie said that 'a number of landlords for a variety of reasons choose not to operate that process and basically just illegally evict their tenants, so don't give them required notice or harass them to such an extent that they're forced to leave'.

There are legal protections against harassment and illegal eviction, but it is not enforced in practice, she said:

---

[34] Ibid, p 202.

Whilst there's an offence of harassment and illegal eviction that requires the environmental health staff of the local council to prosecute the landlord, I could count on two hands the number of prosecutions that have ever been brought. And those that have been brought, if you look at what happens to the landlords, it's pitiful and it's insulting. And the environmental health know that ... so they have a number of arguments for not taking action. One is that they don't have the resources and they have other priorities. Two is that actually they think that by prosecuting landlords and by landlords seen to be getting maybe a £200 fine or something it's actually not *discouraging* the practice ... Why would that put you off? ... I know quite a lot of staff who work in environmental health who are so frustrated by this. So in many cases they decide that it's probably in everybody's interests for them not to bring the prosecutions, because it's just highlighting how inept and how inadequate the fines are. (NI, Josie, Chief Executive, NGO for housing, emphasis added)

Josie's account illustrates how the absence of accountability and oversight facilitates unjust practices that violate people's right to adequate housing. Josie thought that a landlord licensing scheme, akin to the one utilized in Scotland, could improve the situation in NI by having means to punish landlords with more appropriate consequences, such as losing their licence. Legal protections and mechanisms for redress are only accessible and useful when there is a culture of accountability. As Josie said, not only are consequences for private landlords rarely enforced, but merely promoting their enforcement would not be enough, as the penalties themselves are not an adequate means to change behaviour. Threatening landlords with a mere £200 fine both upholds appalling practices and undermines a rights-based approach to the provision of SR.

Other alarming practices related to housing in NI included the 'no DSS (Department of Social Security) approach', denying housing to those whose main income consists of social security benefits, as well as landlords asking for rental deposits for social housing. In addition, Josie raised concerns regarding a new recommendation that is going to be implemented in relation to applicants for social housing. Although this provision relates to social housing and not the private rental sector, we will raise it here because the new measure will target a specific portion of the population and relates to broader discursive currents that circulate across jurisdictions.

Josie explained:

I've been talking to you about people who are actually coming through the statutory homeless route but this recommendation, this is a new proposal which the minister has given the go-ahead to, which is now going to come into the system, but I think needs probably new regulations ... and that is that if you're an applicant for social housing and ... you're assessed and you're on the waiting list waiting for your house, and you've x number of points and you're basically waiting for your turn to come, that if you're involved in any behaviour which, you know, is of a persistent nature which suggests, and I think this is really controversial [laughs], which suggests that you may not be a suitable tenant, then you can be deferred from the list. (NI, Josie, Chief Executive, NGO for housing)

As Josie suggests, the wording in the document is ambiguous; phrasings such as 'of a persistent nature' leave lots of room for recontextualization, meaning that different interpretations may result in different outcomes. Josie addressed this concern, saying the reason why the recommendation was controversial was because it lacked definition and clarity. She then gave her interpretation of the recommendation:

What they're obviously targeting is, well I can tell you because I kind of know the whole rationale behind it, they're talking about people mainly, this is what it says, people who are temporarily housed in hostels who exhibit antisocial behaviour ... their rationale is, these people are problematic, we don't want them as our tenants, get them off the list ... that's where it's coming from. But of course it doesn't explicitly say this is about, you know, people living in hostels and antisocial behaviour. So there is that whole issue about, how do you define ... what test has to be applied, what is the burden of proof, you know, is there no opportunity to kind of have it reviewed or revisited ... I think it's very controversial actually ... obviously we're saying you'd have to have comprehensive guidance on how this is going to be applied ... if you're going to leave this to individual decision makers to make such subjective decisions which have such enormous consequences for people's future. (NI, Josie, Chief Executive, NGO for housing)

The data make it clear that subjective and discretionary decision making generally results in poor decisions with enormous negative consequences for individuals. Furthermore, once again we see intersections between mechanisms of procedure, outsourcing of functions and ideological instantiations of the valuation discourse that categorize people according to their perceived worth – for instance, those who receive benefit income as not being worthy candidates for private housing.[35] This sentiment is perhaps

---

[35] The authors recognize that there is also a financial component to decision making due

even more salient in the potential new social housing policy that will penalize the perceived antisocial behaviour of those temporarily housed in hostels. Hostels are often the only housing option to those facing homelessness, including those seeking asylum, so this policy once again targets a portion of the population already at risk and reproduces racialized and marginalizing discourses. The lack of clarity in the proposed recommendation embeds various entextualizations that can be wielded in future by individual decision makers, fuelled by different ideological positionings. Combined with potentially limited oversight and accountability, as well as unclear routes for challenging decisions, this raises a red flag for possible rights violations in the future and barriers to effective remedies.

Assessments, automation and algorithms

An enduring theme across the practitioner interviews involved challenges related to the medical assessments required for benefits such as PIP and Employment and Support Allowance (ESA). We discuss here how assessments function as a technological tool used in the categorization and hierarchization of people, and are part and parcel of valuation processes. We argue that ideological conceptions and stigma of mental health result in systemic discrimination and difficulty in accessing benefits for certain rights holders. In addition, medical assessment services are contracted out to private entities, further fragmenting and obscuring the processes involved. Additionally, the data shows arbitrary and subjective decision making results in a high percentage of errors, as evidenced by the high number of PIP appeals that result in positive outcomes for clients (see statistical data in Chapter 4: around 75 per cent of PIP cases are overturned representing a high prevalence of unlawful decision making), raising further concerns about the adequacy of accountability structures and influences of ideological conceptions of mental health.

It is common practice that the medical assessment process is subcontracted to a private assessment provider, whose assessors carry out functional assessments to determine entitlement to benefits. Oliver, a solicitor, reported that an enquiry in NI found that the medical reports produced by the local contractor, Capita, was being audited and potential changes were made to reports without clients being made aware of them.[36] There was evidence that an auditor would assess a report, identify quality issues and then make recommendations for change. Oliver warned that it is an 'inequality of arms

---

to a reduced housing benefit under Universal Credit.
[36] Peter Coulter, 'PIP Disability Benefit: Concerns Raised over NI assessments', *BBC News*, 11 November 2017, https://www.bbc.co.uk/news/uk-northern-ireland-41918936

issue that people are unaware of this key piece of evidence being edited and it's important that they are made aware of that'. He explained that there are several levels of audit, one conducted internally, as well as a wider audit done by the Department for Communities (NI). The example provided referred to an internal audit by the assessment provider, assessing the quality of reports of new assessors, amounting to nearly 20 per cent of reports deemed to be of unsatisfactory quality. This figure is disconcerting, as these assessments serve as important evidence and perform a gatekeeping function to determine who can access sickness or disability related benefits. In 2021 the NI Public Services Ombudsman found that there was 'systemic maladministration' in terms of how the Department for Communities handled PIP claims.[37] By 2023, out of the 33 recommendations made by the Ombudsmen to improve practice, 10 have been fully met, 18 partly met and 5 not met.[38]

In addition, auditing practices, which Nikolas Rose and Peter Miller[39] call political technologies, are emblematic of neoliberal governmentality, reflecting practices aimed at identifying inefficiencies and improving quality, following market-type rationalities. It 'governs people through a relentless pursuit of economic efficiency, deregulation, outsourcing, and privatization; it involves marketization and the privileging of competition over cooperation, as well as increasing emphasis on calculative practices aimed at promoting individualisation and responsibilisation'.[40]

A common concern expressed by practitioners was that claimants' statements during their medical assessments are not always accurately represented in the final report. Some of the welfare rights advisors, who regularly accompany clients to their assessment appointments, experienced this themselves and reported that it was impossible to challenge the content of a medical report, as those appointments are not routinely recorded. This highlights a clear power imbalance in favour of the assessment provider, and by extension the DWP, because the textual output – the medical assessment report – cannot be challenged.

The absence of any recording means that a challenge to the contents of a report is reduced to the 'word' of the assessor versus the 'word' of the claimant, a dynamic that is highly unequal in power. The claimant is therefore unable to produce any 'legitimate' evidence to counter the 'truth'

---

[37] Northern Ireland Public Services Ombudsman, *Own Initiative Follow up: PIP and the Value of Further Evidence* (Belfast: NIPSO, 2023), https://www.nipso.org.uk/sites/default/files/2023-09/PIP-Follow-up-report.pdf

[38] Ibid.

[39] Nikolas Rose and Peter Miller, 'Political Power beyond the State: Problematics of Government' (1992) 43(2) *British Journal of Sociology*, pp 173–205.

[40] Alfonso Del Percio, 'Audit as Genre, Migration Industries, and Neoliberalism's Uptakes' in C Chun (ed.), *Applied Linguistics and Politics* (London: Bloomsbury, 2022).

entextualized in the report. The textual authority of the report is legitimated by bureaucratic processes that designate the assessment provider/DWP to be legitimate actors in the decision-making process, and this legitimacy grants them the power to control a (constructed) space of allowed interpretations.[41] The lack of transparency of medical assessments, combined with the power such an assessment assumes in written form, warrants close oversight and accountability to ensure fair and unbiased decision making.[42]

Privatization and the outsourcing of government functions thus create a legal accountability vacuum, meaning that individuals cannot access transparent processes to participate and challenge potentially unlawful or erroneous assessments. This lack of transparency and accountability is further impacted by the lack of legal normative human rights standards in the private space. In other words, the Serco decision potentially renders privatized public service provision beyond even the most basic human rights protections.

Disproportionate impacts on mental health

Rose, a welfare rights advisor in Wales, reflected on the appeals she undertakes with clients and reported that approximately 80 per cent of people she represents at tribunal have mental health problems (see the Welsh case study in Chapter 3). The majority of these appeals are benefit decisions, challenging a sickness/disability test result. She explains the problem like this:

> For me, there is some inherent discrimination against people with mental health problems within those tests, so trying to fit people with mental health problems into those tests is more difficult. It is often more straightforward if somebody has a physical disability to apply those rules to them. Now you know, the Government would say, 'oh no, no, no, we're not discriminating against people with mental health [issues]', but over the years I've done my job I have seen that the way that they assess them ... so the kind of evidence they require ... so if somebody has got arthritis, often they'll want to see x-rays, you know, they'll often want to say, is there a record that someone's had x-rays, and do the x-rays show that there is arthritis, yes or no ... and with diabetes, there might be records of what somebody's blood sugars are and things like that. So there'll be easier ways, if you like, to confirm a level of someone's functioning or disability. With mental health it is more difficult, to decide

---

[41] Blommaert (n 32), p 186.
[42] Recent developments suggest potential improvement following recommendations by the Work and Pensions Committee to record all medical assessments as standard: Work and Pensions Committee, *Health Assessments for Benefits* (HC 2022–23, 128).

whether that mental health really disrupts somebody's functioning and ability to do certain activities, but I do find that they're very loath to accept people's own evidence, which is what you need to do with mental health. (Wales, Rose, Welfare rights advisor, local county)

Rose highlights two separate issues: first, that the medical assessments themselves are not designed for evaluating psychiatric disorders, making it difficult to slot into the pre-established criteria for physical illnesses; and, second, that because mental health challenges are often invisible, it is important to listen to individuals being assessed, as they know best how their illness impacts on their daily functioning. An additional challenge identified by practitioners is the difficulty in obtaining the required medical evidence, due to a lack of capacity (and funding) of mental health services, with reported wait times for a mental health diagnosis exceeding two years (England, Andrea, Welfare benefits advisor related to the *Pantellerisco* case).

Arbitrary and discretionary decision making

Rose's comment about resistance to accepting people's own evidence reflects wider discourses of mistrust and stigma around mental health. This distrust also translates into practice and poor decision making, as evidenced by examples from the data. For instance, Andrea, a welfare benefits advisor, recalled the story of a client who had a severe sight impairment related to a brain tumour. She was required to undergo a reassessment for her PIP and was denied on the basis that she was wearing lipstick and her hair was neatly combed (she wore a wig). Not only did this assessment process violate a person's dignity, but the erroneous and subjective decision making resulted in an immediate halt of benefits, which led to rent arrears. The client was not able to use public transport and could no longer afford taxis. As a result, she became housebound, which affected her mental health. 'The whole thing just started to snowball completely … we got it overturned but it should never have happened in the first instance', Andrea noted (England, Andrea, Welfare benefits advisor related to the *Pantellerisco* case).

Other examples entailed a young man with severe mental illness whose application for ESA was turned down. This occurred because the General Practitioner (GP) mistakenly submitted medical evidence for another patient. Although it was blatantly obvious that the information received from the GP was a mistake (it referenced hip replacements the claimant had not undergone), the DWP ignored it and refused the application on the basis that the medical evidence did not support the claim. It took ten months, with the assistance of his welfare benefits advisor, for the young man to have his ESA benefits reinstated (England, Andrea, Welfare benefits advisor related to the *Pantellerisco* case).

Iterations of subjective decision making without merit are found across the data. Importantly, due to the interrelationship of rights, the infringement of one SR, such as access to social security, has a knock-on effect on other areas of a person's life and wellbeing. Moreover, the high number of overturned decisions at tribunal is an important indicator that decision-making processes and the entailed accountability structures are inadequate.

Current medical assessment tools are constructed as instruments that unfairly categorize physical and psychiatric conditions in a hierarchy that places physical illnesses at the top. These instruments are unfair, unfit for purpose and must be adapted to adequately assess all types of illness in order to interrupt systemic discrimination against those with mental health conditions and provide access to SR and justice for all.

Automation, digitization and algorithmic decision making

Automation and digitization are hallmark features of neoliberalism and a common approach to governing a bureaucratic system, as standardized systems often increase productivity and reduce cost. However, practitioners raised several concerns ranging from digital exclusion to significant errors in decision making.

Online application processes entail barriers for those who do not have digital access. It is often assumed that in our digital age, people can access online platforms, but for a significant portion of the population, this is not so easy due to data and Wi-Fi limitations or a lack of computers and mobile phones. In speaking about some library closure legal cases, solicitor Matthew said that 'people always think library cases are about books but they're absolutely not about books'. He fittingly described how libraries (and schools) still serve important functions for people to access public services, employment and schooling. Their closure, felt acutely during the COVID-19 lockdowns, impeded access to digital platforms. In addition, when it comes to applying for social security benefits online, people often do not grasp the importance of the task as an application process to a legal entitlement and, without independent advice, mistakes are often made that result in a denial of benefits or take a long time to resolve. The importance of access to independent information and advice is highlighted once again.

Algorithmic tools are another form of technology in the categorization and sorting of information and people. Identified problems regarding the use of algorithms entail concerns of discrimination and unfairness, information protection and (lack of) opacity and transparency.[43] The literature on

---

[43] Lilian Edwards and Michael Veale, 'Slave to the Algorithm? Why a "Right to an Explanation" Is Probably Not the Remedy You Are Looking for' (2017) 16 *Duke Law & Technology Review*, pp 18–84.

'algorithmic accountability' questions whether algorithms can be made more transparent and explainable in order to facilitate accountability when their use adversely affects human rights or causes other types of societal harms.[44] McGregor, Murray and Ng argue that international human rights law provides a suitable framework. Although not a panacea, a human rights-based approach to algorithmic accountability offers an organizational scheme to identify factors that states and businesses should consider in order to avoid undermining or violating human rights.[45]

A recent review attempted to address some of these concerns, but acknowledged the well-established risk that algorithmic systems can lead to biased decisions.[46] On the point of transparency in the public sector, the review recommends 'a mandatory transparency requirement on all public sector organisations using algorithms that have a *significant* influence on *significant* decisions affecting individuals'.[47]

Although this appears to be a sensible recommendation, the repeated word 'significant' is vague and ambiguous, leaving a large space for multiple entextualizations/interpretations of what would constitute 'significant influence' and how 'significant decisions' are to be defined. The review recognized precedent of failures in large-scale (although not all algorithmic) decision-making processes that had impacted on a large number of individuals, citing fitness-to-work assessments for disability benefits and immigration caseworking. The authors of the review cautioned about the significant impact decisions made at scale by public sector organizations can have if they go wrong, urging for the highest standards of transparency and accountability.

For Sharon Pantellerisco, algorithmic decision making resulted in errors and loss of income relating to the benefit cap policy, with no effective remedy at the conclusion of lengthy legal proceedings. Tobias, a barrister on the *Pantellerisco* case, expressed frustration that the DWP did not make use of all the information it had at its disposal to create a better, more nuanced, computer program. He recommended increased levels of parliamentary scrutiny, and welfare rights advisor Miles echoed suggestions for legal input and greater interaction between lawyers and programmers at the design stage to avoid built in bias:

---

[44] Lorna McGregor, Daragh Murray and Vivian Ng, 'International Human Rights Law as a Framework for Algorithmic Accountability' (2019) 68 *International & Comparative Law Quarterly*, pp 309–343.
[45] Ibid, at 313.
[46] *Review into Bias in Algorithmic Decision Making* (London: Centre for Data Ethics and Innovation, 2020).
[47] Ibid, ch 9 (emphasis added).

For certain categories of cases where you knew that the decision the computer was needing to make was probably one that would need human oversight ... you'd filter them out to an expert decision maker. And like none of those things *really* seem to happen ... I mean, it would be both design and also training ... you can see in the design of like their [DWP] flagship benefit Universal Credit that what's happened is, in the room at the stage they designed their computer system you've got some policy people and you've got some programmers, and the policy people have at some point talked to lawyers and think they've understood what's going on, but you haven't got any lawyers in the room when they're *actually* designing the system. And what you end up with is a system that's not compliant with the rule of law. Like it doesn't *do* the things that it would be required to do and it *can't* from the ground up do those things because you're sort of taking it back to the premise of design, it's not *designed* to actually do the things that it's supposed to do. (England, Miles, Welfare rights advisor, NGO to combat child poverty, emphasis added)

In *Pantellerisco*, the court, on appeal, accepted that the algorithm for calculating benefit entitlement was lawful, despite the algorithm discriminating between those paid monthly and those paid every four weeks. An important factor in the court's decision was that the DWP exercised what it termed a 'test and learn philosophy'.[48] Despite the High Court finding the operation of the flawed algorithm irrational, and therefore unlawful,[49] on appeal Lord Justice Underhill stated:

[W]here that happens, it does not in my view automatically follow the legislation was irrational ... it cannot be the case that whenever imperfections in a legislative scheme are corrected by amendment in the light of experience of the original version is to be characterized as irrational on the basis that it should have been got right first time round.[50]

The Court adopted a deferential approach, referring the matter back to the DWP so that the test and learn philosophy could operate in practice. The data overwhelmingly suggest that this philosophy provided by the DWP's witness statement is not something that operates well as a matter of practice. The Court of Appeal in *Pantellerisco* has left open the door for a finding of

---

[48] *Pantellerisco v SSWP* [2021] EWCA Civ 1454, 90 (Underhill LJ).
[49] *Pantellerisco v SSWP* [2020] EWHC 1944 (Admin) 88 (Graham J).
[50] *Pantellerisco* (n 48).

irrationality if the DWP does not take steps to resolve the problem now that it has been identified.[51] However, this approach leaves both Sharon Pantellerisco and all others impacted by the flawed algorithm facing a continued SR violation without an effective remedy to date, long after the issue first arose in July 2019.

Resource distribution: discourses of entitlement

We see recurring tensions across the data between the neoliberal concept of entitlements as commodities and human rights-based interpretations of rights. We saw in the case of asylum seekers in Glasgow that even basic food provisions were difficult to access due to restricted usage of the Aspen card and the disallowance of cash (see the Scottish case study in Chapter 3). An unwillingness to provide support in the form of cash was also raised in the Welsh case study in relation to the provision of food for children and young people. The conflict was particularly salient in a discussion with Eva around school meals and voucher programmes (Wales, Eva, Development Manager, NGO to combat child poverty).

Eva said that 'the reason that most people don't have enough food is not because there's a lack of food, it's because they have a lack of money. Even in the pandemic that was the key thing'. She explained that her organization campaigns for a cash-first approach to alleviating food poverty. They want to see the direct value being transferred to families so that they can maximize the amount available and buy their own food. She said that based on their research, people overwhelmingly said that's what they prefer and it works best:

> Although people are happy with food parcels, vouchers and things on the whole, there's always quite a significant minority whose needs aren't met by those schemes of support so we really want to see cash first and so the option has been available to local authorities to provide cash payments. (Wales, Eva, Development Manager, NGO to combat child poverty)

Eva explained that their consultations with hundreds of families provided numerous examples of why direct provision of food boxes or other schemes do not work well. She tried to feed that information back to local authorities and encourage them to consider making cash payments, but received significant resistance from them:

---

[51] Ibid.

> The lack of interest [laughs], to say the least, in what people on the receiving end of the services think about, it is really shocking to me, because ... I think that sort of mindset is like well, you know, beggars can't be choosers really ... we just need to do what's operationally best for us at the local authority, it doesn't matter if it's not meeting people's needs very well [laughs] ... it's not our top priority really and that's quite hard I think in terms of who's been wanting to hear ... as an anti-poverty solution cash is best, but trying to communicate that or trying to advocate on behalf of people who were having problems with the system is really challenging. (Wales, Eva, Development Manager, NGO to combat child poverty)

The researcher pressed Eva for her interpretation as to why local authorities are reluctant to provide cash. She said:

> For me it's rooted in the stigma, it's a discriminatory attitude towards people in poverty. It's rooted in a belief that people in poverty are poor because they are incapable of managing money and they may be negligent as parents. So the idea that if you give people money it will be spent on something other than what it's intended for. I've done research this year which absolutely disproves that ... there are *huge* amounts of evidence, national, internationally in developing countries and across the UK that when you give people money, particularly when you call that money, you know, 'child benefit' or 'child payment', it gets spent on children or if you call it 'free school meal money', they spend it on food. And that's what I found very much in the work I've done in the South Wales valleys. I asked parents what they used the cash payment they had for and they use it to buy food and then they were able to talk about how it had helped them budget more effectively with the remaining money that they had ... so they could actually afford to buy better-quality meals, fruit and vegetables, things like that, they could eat themselves, they could buy learning resources for their children. So you know, all these benefits that just a box of catering supplies just doesn't [laughs] provide at all. (Wales, Eva, Development Manager, NGO to combat child poverty, emphasis added)

Once again, we see intersections with ideological conceptions expressed as discourses of worthiness. The valuation discourse manifests here through the structuring of programmes that keep power and control with the government, as poor individuals are deemed incapable of making good decisions, handling money and parenting. These mechanisms work together to result in structural discrimination. Furthermore, Eva elaborated that she feels it is rooted in the design and administration of local welfare systems in Wales and at the local authority level. She continued:

> It really sticks with me going to a consultation event for Welsh government. They were doing a review of their child poverty plan and it was kind of a stakeholder event just before the pandemic where we had a group of roundtables, people talking about what the welfare system for Wales should look like. And the amount of people who were really obsessed with fraud, they were really obsessed with making sure ... there was no opportunity for people who didn't really deserve it to get it ... they were like [we] 'must eliminate dependencies', all these kinds of real myths not grounded in empirical evidence [laughs] not grounded at all in what it's actually like and really discriminatory against people on low incomes, *really* stigmatizing attitudes towards families affected by poverty and *really* poor understanding of what the needs of those families are. But these were people, some of them quite senior, just talking in terms that actually I find quite offensive about casting aspersions on the kind of trustworthiness of people. And talking about how you need to *design* welfare systems to exclude or punish or control or coerce people [laughs] so that they stop being undesirable, you know, rather than seeing a kind of rights-based approach ... we all have an entitlement and we need to work now to get it to as many people as possible. So that's kind of a contrary thing but it's just I'm really *conscious* of those stigmatising attitudes because it's what we work against with the children and young people in our project the thing that makes their life *so hard* is that judgement on them and their parents. (Wales, Eva, Development Manager, NGO to combat child poverty, emphasis added)

In Eva's narrative, the valuation discourse is expressed as distrust, a fear of people fraudulently making a claim on the welfare system. We can see clear interdiscursive links with the comments made by the former DWP Secretary Iain Duncan Smith regarding the benefit cap policy. Resistance to cash payments appears to be rooted chiefly in discrimination and misguided conceptions of welfare and welfare recipients. Furthermore, some policy makers present at the meeting felt the need to design welfare systems with punitive measures, focussed on exclusion, control and coercion. Once again, we see glimpses of social control tactics and discriminatory attitudes that stand in stark contrast to rights-based approaches that frame entitlements as rights for everyone, rather than commodities for some, at the behest of personal discretion.

Our intention here is not to say that all discretionary systems of resource distribution are inherently unequal and contravene human rights approaches. Practitioners were divided on the issue of discretionary approaches to welfare provisions. Some voices advocated for a discretionary approach, because it allows for some flexibility and tailoring to specific needs; others lamented the fragmentation of services inherent in discretionary funding schemes, and the entailed difficulties in meeting everyone's needs. The caution we raise with respect to discretionary approaches to resource distribution is rooted in concerns relating to discretionary, and often arbitrary, decision-making processes. Discretionary resource distribution approaches are a fitting example of governing 'at a distance', and fragmentation of the system raises concerns about gaps in oversight and accountability.

Valuation discourses: constructing 'worthiness'

An important element of achieving social justice is interrupting or countering disempowering and disenfranchising discourses. Our analysis in the previous sections shows how practitioners go to great lengths to advocate for their clients with the aim of meeting their needs and securing successful outcomes for SR violations. In this section, we show that even though practitioners may actively oppose and challenge dominant negative discourses, at times these discourses, or rather the dynamics that underlie them, are unwittingly reproduced. Moreover, the data show how rights holders themselves reproduce negative dominant discourse in efforts to create legitimacy for themselves. We illustrate this through a few examples, first showing how practitioners position themselves in relation to particular discourses. This positionality can be conveyed in the analytical concept of 'stance'.[52] Stance taking is instrumental in the drawing of social boundaries, a component integral to processes of differentiation and categorization. A closer evaluation of the stances taken up by the practitioners is valuable in terms of understanding the knowledge they draw on in their daily work and progressing SR for the clients they serve.

In the previous chapter on the adjudication journey, we spoke with Eva in Wales regarding access to information and advice, and she relayed that during the COVID-19 pandemic, many people were forced to seek help who might not have needed assistance previously. She described that people would not necessarily know how to access help if they were not already linked in with agencies or service providers. We repeat the excerpt in part here:

---

[52] Alexandra Jaffe, *Stance: Sociolinguistic Perspectives* (Oxford: Oxford University Press, 2009), p 3.

> I think a lot of people just don't know where to turn ... I think services often struggle to be there when people need them because people typically get to a place of crisis, so they're living in vulnerable circumstances and they're dealing day to day with extreme multiple extremely stressful life events that are pushing them to that point where they are at risk of destitution. And if they're not engaged with agencies, and we're seeing this a lot in the pandemic, *these aren't people who are problems you know [laughs] to society*. So, they don't have a social worker, they might not be working or getting any help from mental health service providers and so on. You have to be quite ill to meet the threshold to be allowed to even get support from those teams so lots of people just aren't on the radar. (Wales, Eva, Development Manager, NGO to combat child poverty, emphasis added)

Eva clearly aligns herself with the position that the people she is referring to are *not* 'problems' to society. What is implicit is that her comment sits in dialogical relation to other discourses that *do* characterize certain people as problems to society. This is by no means a critique of Eva, a dedicated advocate; the example merely makes visible how our words often signal other discourses. Here it makes salient the interdiscursive connections to broader circulating discourses, in this case valuation discourse, which creates opposing categories with people who are characterized as problems at one end of the spectrum and those who are not at the other end. We share this example as a note of caution, because in her efforts to oppose the valuation discourse, Eva in fact reproduces the binary distinctions that fuel the constant drive for legitimation to prove one's worthiness. Rights claiming, we argue, can help reshape the narrative and empower rights holders.

The following example from Rose is more explicit about her engagement with the valuation discourse of 'worthiness', in which she acknowledges circulating discourses and takes an unequivocal opposing stance, refusing to participate in the hierarchization of people:

> I'm lucky in that everybody I work with in my team – it's a small team – but everybody is very dedicated and very committed to the ethos of our team, which is to do all we can to maximize people's income and to do that in a sort of nonjudgemental way. I think that what sometimes creeps in from management above us is *that they do actually want us to be more judgemental*. People don't always use the term, but *what they're getting at is there's a sort of deserving and an undeserving poor* and so sometimes what they want us to do is to do more work with pensioners that they see as deserving, because there's

quite a paternalistic view of poorer pensioners. It's not that I don't think poorer pensioners need advice, I definitely think they do and I think they miss out on benefits as much as anyone else, but there's … heroin addicts with mental health problems that I was talking about earlier, they miss out on benefits a lot, but in the views of some people they're not as deserving, whereas I do my job because I think *it's crucial that people aren't judgemental* and that people approach work like that and *think this is somebody in need. I'm not gonna put them in a pecking order of whether I thought they brought some of this on themselves or not.* And invariably, I think once people start going down that road, I think so many of the people I deal with, when you ask them about their upbringing, their family, so many have been in care or been abused as children or have very difficult family circumstances … it's not surprising sometimes that people then have ended up with addictions or living on the street or alcohol or whatever … they're all in a bit of a circle or a pattern, if you like. And so, for me, that's why I think it's so important to be able to offer services to those that present themselves, rather than deciding that actually this group of people is maybe more fashionable to help … so that to me is changing some of the perceptions of the people above and certainly those who make decisions about funding, etc etc. (Wales, Rose, Welfare rights advisor, local county, emphasis added)

Rose's example shows how the valuation discourses can sometimes be very visible in the steering from upper management – for instance, reproducing categories of worthiness that differentiate between poor pensioners and poor heroin addicts. One cannot challenge the valuation discourse by articulating convincing arguments that the heroin addict or person seeking asylum is worthy of help. The only way to subvert the prevalent valuation discourse is to not engage in the processes of categorization it calls for, and instead adopt a human rights-based discourse.

Our final example shows how the prevalence of the valuation discourse results in rights holders internalizing the valuation discourse themselves. We asked Miles whether he thought rights holders recognized their challenges in accessing their social security rights as rights violations. He responded that claimants' ideas of fairness or unfairness were more related to not having their needs met, in terms of immediate material interest, but that the notion of fairness was generally not cast in terms of rights or justice. We then asked whether a rights-based conversation would help people access their rights or whether there might be other ways of talking about it that would make it more accessible for people to feel that they have a right to access. Miles responded:

> Very often ... the claimant will feel a sense of injustice, of unfairness, but also ... you get claimants who feel undeserving and then the way in which they articulate their sense of justice is by distinguishing themselves from what they see as the general undeserving case. *So they totally accept that entitlement to social rights aren't rights, that's how they think about it, they think it's a privilege.* Like, you deserve this if you're good and then they try to distinguish themselves into that group ... I mean that's very divisive amongst claimants. So when you get a claimant go, 'yeah I know most people are faking this but I'm not, I'm genuine. If it wasn't for all the fakers they would have believed me right'. So *their entire way in which they see their case is like through hostility to other claimants* and I mean this is really interesting for a welfare rights advisor who sees a hundred of these people who *all* think that their case is the fair one but everyone else's is bad. I mean it's quite often I'll have to explain to someone, a person who doesn't make that transition, who just doesn't feel worthy at all, I have to explain 'well look, what the law says is if you meet those conditions you get it and you *do* meet those conditions, it's just they haven't believed you. Do you not think this is true about yourself? Yes, it is true, well, there you're entitled'. And you get people who are incredibly grateful for being assisted in a case and you have to say 'all I did was assist you to show that you meet the conditions, you haven't got anything special from me other than satisfaction of your legal rights' and I think people often appreciate that but they don't move to thinking that way in general. (England, Miles, Welfare rights advisor, NGO to combat child poverty, emphasis added)

Miles describes how many rights holders interpret entitlement to SR not as rights but privileges, meaning that they feel the need to distinguish themselves as someone who deserves the entitlement. This, in turn, takes the shape of differentiating oneself from others who are 'less worthy', creating divisions among claimants. The account described by Miles resonates with Sukhwant Dhaliwal and Kirsten Forkert's research[53] in which they also observed a tendency of recent migrants and people from established ethnic minorities to make a distinction between deserving and undeserving or good and bad migrants/citizens in a bid for recognition and legitimacy. Rather than disrupting the divisive narrative of the valuation discourse, Miles' account of the benefit claimants creating divisions between the deserving and undeserving, reproduces negative discourse. We asked Miles

---

[53] Sukhwant Dhaliwal and Kirsten Forkert, 'Deserving and Undeserving Migrants' (2015) 61 *Soundings: An Interdisciplinary Journal*, pp 49–61.

why he thought that claimants have such a negative image of themselves and accessing services:

> That's how services, these services, are presented in the media ... that's the dominant way in which these things are discussed. There's two ways of dealing with it when you're actually one of those people: you can either accept the dominant way and then make yourself an exception ... which is an easier thing to do than reject the entire way in which it's discussed and I think for a lot of people the first route is easier. You have to disagree with less, but rather than disagreeing with the whole way in which something is in general discussed you're saying 'oh yeah, yeah, that's all correct, it's just I'm different', it's an easier option than saying 'actually benefit claimants are humans, maybe they should be treated like humans'. (England, Miles, Welfare rights advisor, NGO to combat child poverty)

Miles points to dominant discourses in the media as one of the drivers of benefit claimants' perceptions of themselves and others. The internalization of the valuation discourse may also serve as an example of governmentality and its capacity for power to influence the self and shape human conduct.[54] The power of producing particular 'representations of the world', or discourses, resides not in the words themselves, but in the perceived legitimacy of the person, government or other entity uttering them. Bourdieu's notion of 'symbolic violence' and Gramsci's concept of 'cultural hegemony'[55] are also relevant in expressing the ideological-hegemonic aspect of power that operates covertly below the surface. In their work they aimed to explain how and why subordinate groups accept as legitimate the power of the dominant.

Susan Gal explains: 'The capacity of language to denote, to represent the world, is not considered transparent and innocent ... but is fundamentally implicated in relations of domination ... Control of the representation of reality is not only a source of social power but therefore also a likely locus of conflict and struggle.'[56] We shared these examples to draw attention to the power of discourse and the ways in which it can be used to perpetuate and (re)produce inequalities, but can also be harnessed to counter dominant disempowering discourses.

---

[54] Michel Foucault, *Dits et Écrits IV* (Paris: Gallimard, 1994), p 237.
[55] Pierre Bourdieu and Loïc J. D. Wacquant, *An invitation to reflexive sociology* (Cambridge: Polity Press, 1992); Antonio Gramsci, *Selections from Political Writings (1921–1926); with Additional Texts by Other Italian Communist Leaders* (London: Lawrence & Wishart, 1978).
[56] Susan Gal, 'Language and Political Economy' (1989) 18 *Annual Review of Anthropology*, pp 345–367, p 348.

Complexity and fragmentation

In our data, elements of fragmentation include different constitutional arrangements under devolution and, to a lesser extent, Brexit.[57] Challenges related to devolution include intersections between reserved and devolved law, including limited decision making power (see the Welsh case study in Chapter 3), as well as different case law and legislation between jurisdictions and related tensions and conflicts. Fragmentation of the framework governing SR also comes to the fore through the outsourcing of social services and housing, automation/digitization and discretionary funding schemes. One of the enduring elements of power is complexity and fragmentation.

Miles notes that social welfare systems are 'tremendously complicated … a feature of all social welfare systems everywhere'.. He goes on to explain: 'they're designed to cater for poverty in its diverse forms and to manage poverty in its diverse forms and therefore they need to be complicated to alleviate poverty just enough, in just the right way, and just the right places'. The competing pressures within the state, he believes, are to cut costs on the one hand, but have a complex system on the other, and they do not fit. The way he sees it, the government tries to simplify the running of this complex bureaucratic system by removing expertise from their decision makers. He says that 'if you get like lowest grade of civil servant, largely computerize their job and then present them with a complex system, it doesn't work' and does not produce the intended results. We asked him how to mitigate this problem and he replied that 'they [the government] could spend more on administration, like *significantly* more' (England, Miles, Miles, Welfare rights advisor, NGO to combat child poverty).

This complexity, and its management, is one of the overarching themes across the data, which is constituted in manifold policies and procedures, difficult and lengthy application processes, frequent changes to rules and regulations, obscurity, poor visibility of available services and programmes, complicated and lengthy complaints procedures, and a lack of cognisance of the interrelationship of SR and people's needs.

We briefly highlighted the complexity of Universal Credit, which came to the fore during the COVID-19 pandemic when the government promoted Universal Credit as a resource, but failed to make it clear that there are

---

[57] The impact of Brexit did not feature prominently in the data, but was raised in the context of direct impacts on EU and other foreign nationals (Julie), as well as in relation to loss of funding, such as EU structural funds (Sam). For a detailed overview of the various risks to economic and SR protections in the UK due to Brexit, see Katie Boyle, *Economic and Social Rights Law: Incorporation, Justiciability and Principles of Adjudication* (Abingdon: Routledge, 2020); and Tobias Lock, 'Human Rights Law in the UK after Brexit' (2017) vol. Nov Supp (Brexit Special Issue), pp 117–134.

significant differences with legacy benefits, such as tax credits, which resulted in people applying who were not eligible, thereby losing existing benefits or becoming worse off.

The complex and fragmented governance system for realizing and upholding SR in the UK warrants that access to information, advice and advocacy, as well as legal representation is made readily available. Our conversations with practitioners already highlighted the shortage of lawyers across jurisdictions to address SR violations. This was noted not only by legal practitioners, but also by welfare rights advisors, as the burden is acutely felt by those on the frontlines of providing support.

In addition to a shortage in legal expertise, Julie discusses how she believes the justice system is not designed in a manner that is well-aligned with people's needs and daily realities:

> From my perspective, you know, law is for the people and our courts are for creating accountability and addressing and fixing problems that happen. And your procedures, your processes, should probably be ones that are fitted around what we know about how people are, so their level of literacy, the barriers they face, the time that they have off work to do things, you know, how much it might cost to start a case, how much it costs to continue a case, if you are needing them to show up for 20 hours over the course of a year. Our justice system is not designed like that and I see very little that is written about redesigning it in that way. The discussions we have about our justice system are about saving money. They're about efficiency, they're about people ... this government dangerously talks about people wasting time in the justice system and they're looking to reduce the volume of cases. It's seen as an infrastructure cost and the value of justice is not taken into account. (Scotland, Julie, Solicitor specializing in asylum/immigration, NGO for legal services)

Our justice system is, simply put, not fit for purpose. Julie's insight on this is reflected in the literature. McGarvey, for example, highlights that:

> appeals processes, while giving the outward appearance of being inclusive and democratic, often act as filtering mechanisms which deter disadvantaged people in areas like ... welfare... [Appeal processes] are often arduous, time-consuming, stressful and costly. It therefore follows that those who possess the resources to fully engage with such processes stand a chance of greater success than those who do not – this is an example of a structural class barrier.[58]

---

[58] Darren McGarvey, *The Social Distance between Us: How Remote Politics Wrecked Britain* (London: Penguin, 2023).

Complexity is structural injustice.

Julie's comments reflect her awareness of the prevalence and ubiquity of ideological rhetoric in line with neoliberal ways of governing, which direct primary attention to the values of cost saving and efficiency. We are indeed fighting an uphill battle if the perception of government is that 'people are wasting time in the justice system' rather than seeing the courts as a mechanism of accountability for ensuring SR compliance. Julie and her organization adopt a human rights-based approach in their work, and she questions how such an approach to justice and accountability can be implemented:

> If we succeed in incorporating economic and SR in Scotland ... and there are remedies, then slowly, over time, human rights lawyers like me and [name of another practitioner] will chip away, will use that as a tool [laughs] to chip away, but it will always be using the stick. It will always be defended by governments, so they will have to defend those cases and the gains will be limited. The right way round is the other way, is to re-evaluate what we do, but it's Byzantine and anyone who has been through the justice system or has a friend who's been through the justice system, will be astonished and surprised at how inaccessible it is. (Scotland, Julie, Solicitor specializing in asylum/immigration, NGO for legal services)

Julie highlights an important point – also raised by other practitioners – that merely garnering legal status for SR is not enough without a) adequate accountability structures, and b) changing the conversation. One of the prevailing insights from our work is that reclaiming the narrative for SR is essential in terms of effecting enduring change to how SR are perceived and understood, and thereby create pathways for securing effective remedies when violations occur.

Conclusions

We approached the data with a critical discursive lens to locate moments of conflict and contestation that expose competing tensions. These tensions were evident in intersecting discourses, as well as in the deployment of different tools and mechanisms that intersected with law and policy. The data also showed how reproduction of the valuation discourse undermined practitioners' efforts in promoting SR and resulted in rights holders themselves internalizing valuation discourses in an effort to create legitimacy and distinction for themselves.

The project team set out to investigate empirically how SR are realized in practice, and how legal frameworks across UK jurisdictions protect SR and facilitate access to an effective remedy when rights violations occur. SR violations significantly impact on human wellbeing and the enjoyment of a decent life with dignity. SR form part of the international human rights framework, including the right to housing, the right to food and fuel, and the right to social security. Under international frameworks, the UK has an obligation to protect these rights in the domestic context.[59] These international obligations require the UK to provide access to an effective remedy when SR violations occur, including access to a legal remedy in court if necessary.[60]

Interwoven with legal analysis, this book presents our empirical findings from data collected through individual semi-structured interviews with a variety of legal and nonlegal practitioners across the four UK jurisdictions. We adopted a combined legal and discourse analytic approach to better understand conceptions of justice and address gaps in the current legal framework. A critical discourse lens highlighted how barriers to social justice are socially and discursively produced and, more importantly, how understanding these dynamics can inform practice and chart ways forward to create legitimacy for SR in the UK.

In our analysis, we have shown how competing logics and discourses were made visible in local struggles and tensions relating to conceptions of entitlement, welfare, poverty and justice. The processing and sorting of information and people through various strategies of valuation creates hierarchies that are organized according to the perceived worthiness of individuals, further marginalizing those who already struggle to access and participate in the 'system'. In this sense, we see competing rationalities in relation to the notion of 'entitlements', framed on the one hand as (scarce) resources or commodities that must be carefully managed and rationed by the state and being made available to some according to discretion, and, on the other hand, as social/human rights that are universal and entitle all human beings to the basic *right* to an adequate standard of living, which includes food, housing, health, social security, education and employment.

The increased outsourcing of public services raised significant concerns relating to gaps in accountability, often resulting in contraventions of human rights. This was made salient in the *Ali* case concerning the recontextualization of section 6 HRA. Technological tools such as medical

---

[59] The UK ratified the International Covenant on Economic, Social and Cultural Rights in 1976.
[60] UN Committee on Economic, Social and Cultural Rights (CESCR), *General Comment No. 9: The domestic application of the Covenant*, E/C.12/1998/24, 3 December 1998; International Commission of Jurists, 'The Maastricht Guidelines on Violations of Economic, Social and Cultural Rights, Maastricht, January 22–26, 1997' (1998) 20 *Human Rights Quarterly*, pp 691–704.

assessments, automation, digitization and the use of algorithms facilitated access barriers that caused rights holders to experience social injustice. These mechanisms also illustrated negative impacts of arbitrary and discretionary decision making, as well as evidence of poorly reasoned policies. In addition, challenges relating to housing made it clear that prejudicial practices, combined with poor oversight and accountability mechanisms, impeded access to justice for the right to adequate housing. The various mechanisms and tools highlighted in our analysis are embedded within a complex, fragmented and multilayered system of governance.

Reclaiming the narrative

Across all dimensions of the analysis, one enduring and resonating element has been the silencing of voices. This points to the inequality embedded in a system that structurally, and often intentionally, undermines the voices of its people. Our analysis examined how the systematic categorization and filtering of information and people is facilitated by various mechanisms[61] that have a disproportionately negative impact on certain groups of people, including women, children, lone parents, minority ethnic groups, persons seeking asylum and persons with disabilities (including mental health issues and learning disabilities). These processes intersect with wider discursive currents relating to immigration, austerity, Brexit, sectarianism and COVID-19 to name but a few, often resulting in the (re)production of stigma, prejudice and exclusion. These discursive factors are, as Zinaida Miller[62] cautions, not to be treated as separate from our enquiry, but as closely entangled with how laws and policy provide the contours of the SR protection frameworks across the UK and the access to justice journey.

These dynamics are enmeshed with how SR are provided and the goals and procedures of the UK welfare system, based in law and policy.[63] Fragmentation of the system and governing 'at a distance' complicates embedding adequate mechanisms for consistent and appropriate oversight and accountability, but is of the utmost importance for upholding SR. Concerted efforts must be directed to reclaiming the narrative for SR: a) as legal rights in and of themselves; and b) in ways that mobilize counterdiscourses that subvert the dominant valuation discourse along the axis of deserving and nondeserving.

As Karen Zivi reminds us, change may not always be immediately visible, but incremental change will challenge the dominant narrative. She urges

---

[61] Shohamy (n 1).
[62] Zinaida Miller, 'Effects of Invisibility: In Search of the "Economic" in Transitional Justice' (2008) 2 *International Journal of Transitional Justice*, pp 266–291.
[63] Ibid, at 274.

us to think of 'both rights and democracy as ongoing, always unfinished projects, rather than as stable objects or specific procedures'.[64] In that sense, the performative practice of rights claiming helps to provide the contours of democracy:

> Though rights claiming may not end social and political practices that many find objectionable, though it may not guarantee protection against grievous harm or ensure the desired degree of freedom from external forces, and though it may challenge majoritarian decision making, it is, nonetheless, a practice through which we come to be democratic citizens. Rights claiming, understood as a performative practice of persuasion, provides an opportunity for individuals and groups to form and share ways of seeing the world; to shed light on and reimagine ways of thinking, being, and doing; and to take an active role in the political life of a community.[65]

Rights claiming is a strategy of 'giving voice'; an attempt to make visible and disrupt dominant mechanisms of power and privilege that serve to marginalize. It is clear from the data that not having a voice is not a question of skill or ability; it is a question of power. Our analysis clearly shows that remaining silent is often the product of being silenced, not having a platform on which one's voice is heard or taken into consideration. Practitioners relayed story after story of people getting worn down by a system that often provides no legitimate ways to make one's voice heard (for instance, the inability to challenge errors in medical assessment reports). Blommaert reminds us that in bureaucratic practice, centring institutions play an important gatekeeping function by regulating access to contextualizing spaces and having the power to assign people particular bureaucratic identities, such as 'an asylum seeker', 'an urgent case for social welfare' or a 'criminal'.[66] These ascribed social identity categories are not necessarily negotiable and, as the data on asylum seekers have shown, certain labels and identities are infused with dominant racialized and gendered perspectives that delegitimate particular voices.

However, it is essential that rights claiming goes hand in hand with addressing the complex structures and processes that produce suffering and entrench existing power relations. Advocacy and raising legal consciousness are meaningless without efforts to address the structural inequalities

---

[64] Karen Zivi, *Making Rights Claims: A Practice of Democratic Citizenship* (Oxford: Oxford University Press, 2012), p 115.
[65] Ibid.
[66] Blommaert (n 32), p 206.

that give rise to silencing certain voices. As our analysis has illustrated, disempowering discourses are also closely linked to mechanisms that perpetuate discriminating practices. Accountability for those practices depend, in part, on the legal framework and proper legal mechanisms to create accountability for SR compliance. Indeed, an overarching theme that runs throughout our data, analysis and in each chapter of the book is the added value of legally enforceable social rights. Their absence from practice means that social rights violations are not examined or interrogated within our existing system and therefore go unaddressed. The fact that lawyers have to try and shoehorn social rights cases in under discrimination claims or arguments around irrationality is exactly why SR should be recognized in law. At the very least, embedding SR as legal rights would facilitate an interrogation of the relevant evidence.

We relayed earlier that as a research team, we adopt the stance that rights claiming and giving voice is best facilitated by efforts to integrate oppressed and marginalized voices into dominant discourse, as well as making visible the policy mechanisms and practices that perpetuate an unequal system.[67] Discursive currents mobilized ideological conceptions of human rights, as well as discourses of valuation and categorization. The data also showed how the reproduction of the valuation discourse can undermine practitioners' efforts in promoting SR and result in rights holders themselves internalizing and reproducing valuation discourses in order to create legitimacy and distinction for themselves. The practitioners' (unconscious) reproduction of binary categories of worthiness and unworthiness potentially undermines the work they undertake to empower rights holders. We raise awareness of this to avoid unwittingly participating in practices of 'othering', essentializing or categorizing that reproduce dominant valuation discourses. The only way to subvert dominant valuation discourses centred on notions of (un)worthiness is to base entitlements in rights, not contrasting categories of worth.

In terms of facilitating agency,[68] we reimagine the relationship between rights holders and practitioners in which everyone recognizes the performative, interdependent and contextually bound nature of voice. In other words, practitioners can and, as the data show, *do* encourage the agentive powers of the individual rights holder by providing a context or environment in which the person feels they have something to say and the

---

[67] Simone Plöger and Elisabeth Barakos, 'Researching Linguistic Transitions of Newly-Arrived Students in Germany: Insights from Institutional Ethnography and Reflexive Grounded Theory' (2021) 16(2) *Ethnography and Education*, pp 402–419, p 414.

[68] Christine Ashby, 'Whose "Voice" Is It Anyway?: Giving Voice and Qualitative Research Involving Individuals That Type to Communicate' (2011) 31(4) *Disability Studies Quarterly*.

listener possesses the skills to 'hear' them.[69] In order to disrupt the inherent inequalities and the silencing of voices in the access to justice journey, practitioners may value discourse training that enables them to best empower individuals who have been marginalized within the UK welfare system to access their SR.

Reshaping the narrative for SR is also an attempt to reconstruct the frames, in an effort to democratize the processes by which frameworks of justice are drawn and revised. If access to justice for SR is to be realized in the UK, attending to both structural injustice as well as a keen understanding of social and discursive barriers is necessary. The ways in which SR have historically been made invisible has to be overcome by reclaiming the narrative for SR, by recognizing and addressing the tools and mechanisms that block the access to justice journey, and by embedding SR as legal rights in the UK. This will provide pathways to justice for SR that include not only 'access' but also meaningful ways of participating in frameworks that can lead to social justice and effective remedies.

Transformative movements challenge injustice not only by making salient areas that warrant change or improvement, but also by challenging the very assumptions on which dominant frames are based. They push the conversation towards more democratic arenas to entertain arguments about the frame. At the UK level, the frame for the protection of SR is monopolized by outdated conceptions that assume SR are nonjusticiable, cannot legitimately be enforced by the court, contravene parliamentary supremacy and are aspirational in nature. Transformative movements thus challenge the metapolitical activity of frame setting,[70] calling for institutionalized parity of participation to include additional voices in deliberations and decisions that construct notions of 'who' is entitled to justice.

As was made clear in our analysis, the UK Home Office's 'hostile environment' policy, at a national level, is instrumental in the construction of 'who' is entitled to justice, which specifically excludes those seeking asylum in the UK. This dominant discourse, and the concomitant conception of who has a right to claim rights in the UK, has a direct impact on the frameworks that protect and govern SR provisions. We see similar problems on framing in relation to the social security regime where the frame is incentivization to work, efficiency and cost-cutting; however, on the ground, laws, policies and their implementation routinely marginalize women, children and those with disabilities in contravention of their SR (as accepted by the court).

---

[69] Zach Rossetti et al, ' "I Like Others to Not Try to Fix Me'': Recognizing and Supporting the Agency of Individuals with Developmental Disabilities' (2008) 46(5) *Intellectual and Developmental Disabilities*, pp 364–375.

[70] Fraser (n 13), p 26.

Current processes and procedures also alienate other groups of rights holders, such as those suffering from mental ill-health, by means of inadequate medical assessment instruments and procedures. Although the devolved jurisdictions are on a trajectory to enhance human rights and access to justice, the intersections between reserved and devolved law limit participation in conversations about the frame setting for SR due to their complexity.

Recommendations

SR are legal rights, but, as our analysis shows, are often not recognized as such in the UK. As part of its international human rights obligations, the UK is required to provide access to an effective remedy if there is a failure to meet these obligations The lack of legal recognition in the UK causes significant challenges for accessing justice for violations of SR. It is clear that SR narratives must be reshaped on multiple scales to facilitate transformative change and the redistribution of power. The evidence for legally embedded SR is compelling. At the very least, as discussed earlier, without recourse to SR as a matter of law, practitioners have to tie themselves in knots making legal arguments to try and secure SR for their clients. This gap in and of itself represents the case for the added value of embedding a normative framework for SR. It would mean that the relevant evidence and law would be open to scrutiny in cases involving SR violations.

We therefore conclude with number of recommendations which, if implemented by the relevant decision makers, could begin to address the accountability gaps that restrict effective SR adjudication in the UK, facilitating a rights-based approach and broadening the scope of 'who' is entitled to justice.

Greater emphasis should be placed on practitioners and rights holders reclaiming narratives around SR as legal rights to enable new discourses to emerge that are focused on redistributing power. Reclaiming the narrative is about transformative and incremental change over time by reclaiming the power and voice to challenge a system laden with structural injustice that is not functioning in a way that upholds SR. All remedies should be exhausted – political, legislative and judicial. Parliament and government should scrutinize legislation and policy in order to understand the impact on SR. And when there are blindspots, inertia or violations of SR, the court should not abdicate its role in scrutinizing (non)compliance. Ideally, in a multi-institutional setting, all those exercising state power, including the regulatory and administrative spheres, should be guided by SR standards as part of an everyday accountability framework. It would be helpful to develop (discourse) training and education programmes on reframing narratives that marginalize and develop empowering narratives that SR are legal rights.

Devolution of areas of economic and social policy has created divergence on SR provision and compliance. Processes of progressive human rights protection, including economic, social, cultural and environmental rights in Scotland and Wales may mean that England and NI fall behind SR protections and access to justice mechanisms available in other parts of the UK. Devolved jurisdictions should promote the use of devolved powers to challenge narratives that marginalize or reproduce SR violations and act as both an anchor and a vehicle to encourage progress elsewhere.

Legal incorporation of international human rights law can enhance accountability for violations of SR. There are different processes of incorporation occurring across each part of the UK. At the national level, examples of civil society and political counterdiscourses are emerging claiming SR as legal rights. This provides an opportunity for evidence-led research to continue to inform national discussions. As part of the recommendations relating to discourse and narrative, we further recommend that civil society organizations, practitioners, rights holders and other stakeholders who are engaged in SR campaigns use the language of SR to make these claims. The objective is to ensure that evidence on SR compliance can be interrogated and scrutinized according to SR normative standards – rather than people and practitioners trying to find solutions under the rubric of something else.

Privatization and outsourcing of decision making (where the state delegates the decision-making process to a private body) creates an accountability gap for SR violations that needs to be addressed (for example, it is very difficult to challenge unlawful decisions by privatized benefit medical assessments). The outsourcing of services creates an accountability gap for SR violations that has to be addressed. Both the state and the private service provider should be accountable for human rights violations.

Digitization of decision making creates an accountability gap for SR violations where algorithms are not designed to account for SR compliance (either deliberately or inadvertently overlooked as part of the planning process). Algorithms should be adopted using inclusive rather than exclusionary frameworks.

We encourage a reconceptualization of access to justice as an area of study and practice that moves beyond an understanding that is primarily concerned with equal access to legal processes to a definition that includes effective substantive remedies as a result of those processes. While removing barriers that impede access to legal processes is of fundamental importance to access to justice, the discipline should also engage with the normative framework and the outcomes of these processes in terms of adequacy and efficacy. This is a significant gap in both the literature and practice. We use normative SR standards and the concept of effective remedies derived from international human rights law to bridge this gap, including the use of structural orders to respond to systemic violations.

People face multiple obstacles on the route to access justice. Each of these needs to be addressed to ensure accountability for violations of SR.

Accessibility should be determined by the diversity of needs of those with the least access rather than accessibility of the majority (bearing in mind that there is no homogeneous group, but may be many different groups requiring different access needs). For example, online information may be accessible for most people, but not those without any access to the internet. More research is needed to address the specific needs of different specified groups in accessing justice including children, ethnic minorities, and people with physical and mental disabilities, among others.

Legal consciousness presents as a significant gap in enabling access to justice. There need to be awareness-raising campaigns in the public sphere identifying SR as legal rights and providing people with information and education on their rights and how to claim them, including highlighting where there are gaps in provision – that is, informing the public discourse if legal avenues are available and also, when they are not, if SR protections fall short.

The justice system should provide the resources needed to access justice for SR, including:

a) Access to first-tier advice in a place that is accessible. Funding and support for first-tier advice across all SR, ideally co-located in physical premises where rights holders already engage (such as GPs, food banks, CAB, schools, places of work and libraries).
b) Recognize the psychological and emotional burden, including fear of retribution, required to pursue a case and address the individual burden, enabling and promoting collective complaints and collective remedies wherever possible.
c) Provide people with advocacy services to ensure they are able to meaningfully participate in their case.
d) Provide access to legal aid. Fund legal aid for violations of SR through properly funded legal aid schemes and salaried expert lawyers in social welfare law.
e) Provide access to legal representation. Ensure lawyers specialize in SR areas of law and are located across jurisdictions, including in rural areas. Enhance law curriculums in law schools to ensure adequate training in SR. The justice system cannot rely on partial funding – lawyers should be paid for the time spent on the case. Consider expanding salaried law centres that do not rely on case-by-case applications for funding. Change the objective of the funding – funding should not be solely dependent on a realistic prospect of financial gain, but a realistic prospect of SR compliance.
f) Facilitate collaboration between different sectors of advice (street-level/first tier/lawyer/barrister) – a joined-up approach to support rights holders in participating and navigating the complexity of avenues.

g) Recognize and respond to clustered injustice – legal issues cannot be siloed into standalone problems. SR violations are often clustered and the violation of one right can impact on the protection and enjoyment of another, creating a snowball effect. The justice system needs to adapt to recognize and respond to clustered injustice.
h) Recognize and respond to the different needs of different groups. The preceding steps are not a 'one-size-fits-all' approach and more research is needed to respond to the collective needs of specified groups.

Alternative routes to justice including internal complaints and appeals should not unduly delay access to a remedy for a violation of a SR (for example, mandatory reconsideration under the DWP system is not working in practice). Decisions at the tribunal level and other administrative accountability mechanisms must be fed back into decision-making processes (a feedback loop) to improve these processes and prevent ongoing and systemic unlawful decision making. The administrative and regulatory sphere should be recalibrated to embed SR scrutiny as part of the remit of ombudsmen, complaints mechanisms, regulators and inspectorates. Each of these routes to a remedy should be assessed according to whether genuine effective remedies are possible. Ideally the remedy providers should work more closely together to understand and address complexity in the system when multiple routes to remedy coexist simultaneously, including exploring opportunities for referral between providers to enhance routes to justice. Each of these alternative routes to justice could adapt to recognize issues such as clustered injustice and systemic problems, as well as learn from lessons regarding effective remedies and structural responses.

We encourage exploring routes to justice (via parliamentary committees, direct to the government or the responsible minister , or engaging directly with civil servants) while recognizing that these routes do not sufficiently ensure accountability when things go wrong, meaning other accountability mechanisms are essential and courts should be available as means of last resort. Legal routes to remedy should be configured to adjudicate SR issues. Courts are often reluctant to engage in matters of economic and social policy; however, by failing to engage with the content of rights and the means of enforcing them, the court risks abdicating its role as an accountability mechanism.

We recommend an enhanced understanding of what constitutes an 'effective remedy' for a violation of a SR. Effective remedies should be accessible, timely and affordable, and should lead to effective outcomes. To the extent possible, remedies should also ensure nonrepetition. At the moment, even those applicants who are 'successful' in reaching a legal remedy do not necessarily receive an effective one (meaning the violation goes unaddressed or is inadequately addressed).

We recommend enhancing public interest litigation and collective complaints/remedies that help address a SR violation for all those who are experiencing it rather than focusing on individual relief for one individual case (including responding to the specific needs of different groups). In cases where the nature and extent of the collective remedy are unclear, we encourage the development of remedies in collaboration with the litigants and coordinate branches of government.

Overall, what we have sought to do here is to reframe the justice journey for those who experience violations of SR. In so doing, we hope to make social injustice visible in a way that challenges dominant discourses and provides practitioners with the tools to address systemic structural injustice. We dedicate the book to the three individuals who bore the brunt of seeking justice in a system unfit for purpose. It is with them in mind that we urge others to explore the social justice gap in the UK, drawing on novel, interdisciplinary and disruptive methods for social change. Future research, we hope, will deploy interdisciplinary and critical theoretical lenses that seek to create new routes forward to deliver effective remedies for violations of social rights and counter discourses that marginalize.

Index

References to figures appear in *italic* type; those in **bold** type refer to tables. References to footnotes show both the page number and the note number (20n82).

A

Abigail (evictions caseworker, Scotland) **87**, 96, 100, 150, 159, 193–194, 195–196
access
  principles of adjudication **18**
  technological tools as barriers 219–220
  thematic analysis **37**
  to contextual spaces 39
  to effective remedies 51–52, 162–163
accessibility
  diversity of needs 226
  effective remedies 162–163
  right to adequate housing 58
  right to food 54
  right to fuel 74
  right to social security 63–64
access to justice 2–4, 153–158
  barriers 3, 153, 225–226
  complexity 150–152
  defining 29–30
  effective remedies 159–160, 162
  as an 'empty signifier' 27
  fear of retribution 150
  gap for SR 11
  iterative process 168
  legal consciousness 226
  narrow and broad understandings 142
  resources 226–227
  see also social rights violations (SR violations)
'Access to justice for social rights' study 43
access to social justice 4–5, 27–32
accountability 11, **37**, 199, 222
accountability gaps 155, 195–198, 225
adequacy
  AAAQ framework 46
  effective remedies 158–161
  food 54–55
  social security 63
adjudication principles 17–18, **18**

administrative justice 5–8
advice deserts 145–146
affordability
  effective remedies 163
  right to adequate housing 58
  right to fuel 73–74
  right to social security 63
agency 41, 222–223
aggregate of remedies 15
algorithms 205–208, 220, 225
Ali v Serco Ltd 86
  accountability gaps 195, 219–220
  appeal 90–91
  appellant as 'failed asylum seeker' 189–190
  companies' human rights responsibilities 196
  company regulation 96–97
  HRA 1998 s. 6 88–96, 198
  'hybrid public authorities' 93–95
  living conditions of asylum seekers 100
  reserved and devolved powers 99
  see also lock-change evictions; Scotland
allocation of resources 46–47, 219
All-Party Parliamentary Group for Terminal Illness 131
Alston, Philip 77, 110
alternative routes to justice 11–12, 227
American Convention on Human Rights
  Additional Protocol Article 11(1) 67
  Article 13 161
  Article 41 161
ancestral lands 178
Anderson, Bridget 190
Andrea (welfare benefits advisor, England) **101**, 102, 103, 110, 204–205
anti-democratic critiques 14–15
apologies for wrongdoings 165, 167–168
'appeal rights exhausted asylum seekers' 97, 189–190

229

appeals
  accessibility 162
  decisions overturned 169–174
  delays 164
  mental health problems 203
  structural class barrier 217
arbitrary decision making 204–205
Armstrong, Kellie 133–134
Ashby, Christine 40
Aspen cards 193, 208
Associated Provincial Picture Houses Ltd v Wednesbury Corporation 154
asylum seekers
  closely monitored 193
  dehumanizing policies 140
  housing 92, 195–196
  inhumane treatment 96–97
  living conditions 100
  marginalization 190
  processes and procedures 190–191
  support 167
  see also failed asylum seekers; immigration; lock-change evictions; refugees
audits 201–202
austerity 7, 10–11, 26, 187
automation 84, 110, 205, 216, 219, 220
  see also digitization
availability
  right to adequate housing 57
  right to food 53–54
  right to fuel 74
  right to social security 63
availability, accessibility, acceptability and *quality* (AAAQ framework) 46, 57
awareness of rights 142–144

B

'banks' (charities) 139–140
Barakos, Elisabeth 36–37
bedroom tax 10n37
Belfast 62
Belgium 58–59n72, 75, 76
benefit cap policy 100–102, 104–105, 167, 210
benefits
  claimants' perceptions 215
  and the costs of living 56
  miscalculations 102
Biklen, Sari 40
Black and Asian minority ethnic communities 61, 137
Blommaert, Jan 32, 40, 197–198, 221
Boardman, Brenda 78, 81
Bogdan, Robert 40
'bogus refugees' 192
Bourdieu, Pierre 20n82, 215
Boyle, Katie 9, 99
Brexit 112–113, 216
Broniowski v Poland 178

Brown, Wendy 25
Buck, Trevor 6
Bulgaria 180
bureaucracy 23
bureaucratic justice 5–6

C

Canada 177, 179, 181, 183
Capita plc 201
Cappelletti, Mauro 2, 8, 29
Carole (consultant and activist, Scotland) **87**, 143, 149, 175–176
Case of Molina-Theissen v Guatemala 179
Case of the Xákmok Kásek Indigenous Community v Paraguay 178
case studies 86, 187
cash payments 127–128, 207–210
CESCR *see* United Nations Committee on Economic, Social and Cultural Rights (CESCR)
challenging rights' violations 139, 143, 153–154
Chaoulli v Quebec 181
Child Poverty Action Group (CPAG) 106–107
children
  challenging decisions 122
  cost-of-living crisis 26
  disadvantaged 117
  food poverty 126–128
  food security 56
children's rights 113, 126–128
Chloe (volunteer, NI) **129**, 143, 148–150, 152, 163
Chorzów Factory 160n25
Citizens Advice Bureau (CAB) 187
citizenship 20–21, 190
City of Johannesburg Metropolitan Municipality v Blue Moonlight Properties 39 (Pty) Ltd 184–185
civil and political rights (CP rights) 12–13, 42, 71
claimants' negative self-image 215
Claire (solicitor, England) **101**, 104–105, 110, 144–145, 157–158, 167
class actions 175
clustered injustice 3–4, 24, 227
collective complaints/remedies 228
collective justice 175–176
Colombia 69, 177, 183–184
Committee on Fuel Poverty 78
compensation 164–165
complexity of decisions 154–155
complexity of social welfare 216–218
compliance **37**, 154
contextualization 39
Convention on the Elimination of Discrimination Against Women (CEDAW) 67–68, 179

INDEX

cost-of-living crisis 26
Cost of the School Day project 127
countermajoritarian adjudication 17, **18**, **37**
Court of Appeal 108–109
courts 16, 140–141, 152–153
COVID-19 pandemic 7, 10–11, **37**, 125–127, 187–188, 211–212, 216–217
Cox, Lorraine 128–136
  death 136
  PIP benefits 86, 128–132
  six-month rule campaign 131
  terminal illness 128–130, 134, 135
  timescales and delays 163–164
Cox, Re Application for Judicial Review 86, 128, 131, 133–134, 167
critical approaches to discourse 13–14, 33, 36, 219
critical sociolinguistics 33
crowdfunding 126
cultural adequacy 57
'cultural hegemony' (Gramsci) 215
culture of responsibility 165

D

Daniel Blake phenomenon 10
Darnham J 106
David (researcher, Wales) **112**, 117, 122–123
deductive approaches 36
degenerative illnesses 130, 131
dehumanizing policies 140
deliberation
  principles of adjudication **18**
  thematic analysis **37**
deliberative democracy 13–14, 19, 20
Denning, Lord 195
Department for Communities and DWP v Lorraine Cox 132–134, 167
Department for Environment, Food & Rural Affairs (DEFRA) 55
Department for Work and Pensions (DWP) 101, 102–103, 105–106, 110, 118, 167, 206–208
De Schutter, Olivier 76
devolution 10, 99, 111–112, 216, 224–225
Dhaliwal, Sukhwant 214
dialogic forms of judicial remedies 52, 176, 184
digitization 205, 220, 225
  see also automation
Dillon [2024] NIKB 191
diminution of rights 191
disabilities 116–117
discourse analysis 23, 38
discourses 20–26, 38–40, 215
  see also language
discourses of valuation and categorization 222
discourses of worthiness 26, 198, 209, 211–215

discretionary approaches 210–211
discretionary decision making 200, 204–205
discrimination 132, 222
discursive approaches 36–38
disempowering discourses 222
domestic law 12, 155–158
domestic remedies 51
dominant narratives and discourses 33
dominant valuation discourses 222
Dorrian, Lady 90
Doucet-Boudreau v Nova Scotia 183
Doyle, Margaret 7–8
'due regard' approaches 114, 122
Duncan Smith, Iain 210
duty
  of nonregression 50–51
  to ensure nondiscrimination 47–48
  to gather and deploy maximum available resources 46–47
  to provide a minimum core 48–50
  to respect, protect and fulfil 45–46
  to 'take steps' 44–45

E

economic and social policies 153
economic and social rights 8–9
economic, social and cultural rights (ESC rights) 42–50, 67, 71, 84
  Article 2 ECHR 72
  civil and political rights 12–13
  'dialogic' forms of remedies 52
  government spending 46
  minimum core obligation 48–50
  progressive realization 43–44
  taking steps 44–45
  using MAR 45–47, 75
'economization of democracy' (Brown) 25
Edgewood Independent School District v Kirby 182
effective allocation of resources 46
effective remedies 5, 31, 160–168, 227
  access to 51–52, 162–163
  adequacy 158–159
  affordability 163
  collective remedies 167
  defining 29–30
  effectiveness 158–159, 164–168
  legal right to 160–161
  thematic analysis **37**
  timeliness 163–164
  UDHR Article 8 161
  see also social rights violations (SR violations)
effective rights-based housing strategies 58
efficient allocation of resources 46
Ekhuthuleni Overnight/Decant Shelter House Rules 184–185
electricity 67–68, 71
Emergency Fuel Payment Scheme 83

emotional resources 148–149
Employment and Support Allowance (ESA) 201, 204–205
empty signifier analogy 27, 28, 29
Energy Action Scotland 82
energy efficiency 77–81
Energy Performance Certificates 79
energy poverty 68
enforcement **37**, 166
England 100–111
  case studies 86
  case study participants **101**
  differences in law with Wales 113–115
  fuel poverty 78–80
  homelessness 61
  poverty 10
  Race Disparity Audit 61
  tensions with Wales 115–116
  see also Pantellerisco judgments
English Housing Survey data 79
entextualization 38
entitlements 214, 219
entitlement to justice 223
epistemic communities 28
Equal Education and Others v Minister of Basic Education 182–183
equality and nondiscrimination 96, 187
'equality of arms' issue 147–148
equitable allocation of resources 46
Erica (solicitor, Scotland) **87**, 93–96, 162–163, 165, 166, 173–174, 197
Esther (housing activist, NI) 114n46, **129**, 136, 152, 158–159, 164
European Committee on Social Rights 66
European Convention on Human Rights (ECHR) 9, 71, 145, 155
  Article 1 of Protocol 1 131, 157–158, 178
  Article 2 72, 191
  Article 3 91
  Article 8 72, 91, 131, 157–158, 180
  Article 14 131, 132, 157–158
  Article 25 161
  Article 63.1 161
European Court of Human Rights 178
European Social Charter 66, 73
European Union Victim's Directive 191
European Union (Withdrawal) Act 2018, section 7A 191
Eva (development manager, Wales) **112**, 118, 121, 127–128, 144, 152, 165–166, 208–212
evictions 91, 92, 138–139, 147, 198–199
  see also homelessness; housing; lock-change evictions
exhausting appeal rights 97, 189–190

F

failed asylum seekers 97–98, 189–195
  see also asylum seekers; lock-change evictions

fairness **18, 37**, 213
fear of retribution 150
feedback loops 5, 168–169, 227
financial resources *see* legal costs
Finland 58–59n72
First Minister's Advisory Group on Human Rights Leadership (Scotland) 99
First-tier Immigration Tribunals 103, 169, 172–174, **173**, *174*, 192
first-tier social security appeals 169–172, *170*, *171*
First-tier Social Security Tribunals 169
food 52–57
Food and Agriculture Organization (FAO) 54
food banks 55–56, 140
'food deserts' 56
food insecurity 57
food poverty 120, 127–128, 208–209
Forkert, Kirsten 214
Foucault, Michel 22, 26, 38, 188, 194
fragmentation 23, 118–119, 140, 189, 216, 220
framing 20
Fraser, Nancy 19–20
Freya (solicitor, Scotland) **87**, 95, 96, 97, 138–139, 145–146, 147, 148, 150
fuel poverty 77–84

G

Gal, Susan 215
Garnham J 108
Garth, Bryant 2, 8, 29
'giving voice' 40–41, 221, 222
Glasgow 92, 187, 189, 208
governmentality (Foucault) 25–26, 188, 215
government noncompliance 182
government spending 46
Gramsci, Antonio 215
Greece 75
group proceedings 175
Gulland, Jackie 7
Gypsy and Traveller people 60–61

H

habitability 57
harassment and illegal evictions 198–199
  see also evictions
Hargey, Deirdre 133
Hargreaves, Helen 106–107
heating 73–74
hegemonic exercises of power 8
Hesselman, Marlies 70
hierarchies of power and privilege 40
HMRC 105–106
Hodges, Chris 8
homelessness 59–60, 61, 195–196
  see also evictions
Home Office 191, 192–194, 223

hostels 201
'hostile environment' policy (Home Office) 191, 192–195, 223
housing
  appropriate locations 58
  and asylum seekers 195–196
  and the Home Office 194
  legal rights 62
  private rentals 60, 137–139
  Wales 124
  see also evictions
Housing Ombudsman Service (HOS) 12
housing standards 12, 62, 137–139
human rights 5–6, 8, 71, 85, 95–99, 145, 225
Human Rights Act 1998 (HRA) 9, 155, 197
  s.6 88–89, 92, 93–95, 197–198, 219
human rights-based approaches 96, 196, 208
Human Rights Committee (HRC) 71, 161, 179
hunger 55
hybrid public authorities 88–89, 91, 94
hybrid remedies 51–52, 176
Hymes, Dell 21

I

(ideal social) justice 28
ideologies 21
IDG v Spain (CESCR) 179–180
Illegal Migration Act 2023 191, 192
immigration 172–174, 189–195
  see also asylum seekers
Immigration and Asylum Act 1999, s 4(11) 193
incapacity critique 15
incompatible legislation 191–192
Independent Review of Administrative Law 7
indeterminacy critique 15–16
India 180
indivisibility of rights 85
inequalities 21, 33, 39
inhumane treatment 96–97
injustice 29
Inter-American Court of Human Rights 178, 179
interdiscursivity 38–39
interinstitutional confrontation 52
International Covenant on Civil and Political Rights (ICCPR) 22
  Article 2(3) 161
International Covenant on Economic, Social and Cultural Rights (ICESCR) 22, 30, 42–43
  Article 2(1) 43–45
  Article 2(2) 47–48
  Article 9 62, 67, 105
  Article 11 52, 57, 67, 105

international human rights law
  'algorithmic accountability' 206
  effective remedies 5
  growth of remedies 175
  indivisibility of rights 42, 85
  legal recognition 9, 155–158, 224, 225
  minimum core obligation (MCO) 48–49
  remedies for violations 30–31
International Law Commission 160n25
international treaties 42–43
interrelationship of rights 119–120
intertextuality 38–39
interviews 4, 14, 36, 86–87, 219
'in-work' poverty 66–67

J

Jane (welfare rights advisor, England) **101**, 151
Job Seeker's Allowance 118
Jonas (solicitor, Scotland) **87**, 88, 91, 97–99, 167
Joseph and Others v City of Johannesburg 69–70
Josie (NGO Chief Executive, NI) **129**, 136–139, 143, 148, 166, 174–175, 198–200
judicial review 7, 15
Julie (solicitor, Scotland) **87**, 88, 97, 99, 190, 192, 217–218
Just Fair (NGO) 60, 66–67
justice 27, 29, 32
justice systems 217–218

K

Kamilla (welfare rights advisor, NI) 129–130, **129**, 134, 135, 158
Kelly (solicitor, Scotland) **87**, 162–163
Kentucky 181–182
Kenya 177
Kim (programme manager, Wales) 112, **112**, 117–118, 120, 122, 123–124, 125, 127, 143
Kirkham, Richard 6, 7
Klinck, Dennis 195
knowledge of rights 142–144, 226

L

Landau, David 185
landlords 198–199
language
  capitalism and social inequality 33
  discourses 21, 33
  discursive approaches 38
  ingredient of power processes 32
  interdiscursivity 39
  and training programmes 33
  see also discourses
legal advice and representation 146–148
legal aid 124–126, 144–145
Legal Aid, Sentencing and Punishment of Offenders Act 2012 (LASPO) 125, 145

'legal capability' 144
legal consciousness 123–124, 142–144, 226
legal costs 126, 144–146
libraries 116, 205
Liebenberg, Sandra 50–51
life expectancy 10–11
Limburg Principles 44
linguistic ideologies 197–198
linguistic inequality 21
Lipsky, Michael 24
local authorities 208–210
lock-change evictions 87–88, 92, 93, 97, 100, 189
  see also *Ali v Serco Ltd*; asylum seekers; evictions; failed asylum seekers
Lofquist, Lars 70
lone parents 137
Low Income High Costs (LIHC) 79–80
Low Income Low Energy Efficiency (LILEE) 79–80
low incomes 137
LW v Sodexo Ltd 91

M

Maastricht Guidelines 44, 160
managing expectations 29
Mantouvalou, Virginia 23
marginalization 16, 33–34
Matthew (solicitor, Wales) **112**, 113, 115–116, 125–126, 147, 152, 166, 205
maximum available resources (MAR) 46–47, 76
McGarvey, Darren 217
McGregor, Lorna 206
Mears Group 92
media 215
medical assessments 201–205, 219–220
medical evidence 204
mental health 116–117, 201, 203–205
Michelman, Frank 16
Middlemiss, Lucie 79
migrants 190, 214
  see also asylum seekers; refugees
Miles (welfare rights advisor, England) **101**, 146–147, 168, 206–207, 213–215, 216
Miller, David 27
Miller, Peter 202
Miller, Zinaida 220
minimum core obligation (MCO) 48–50, 76
minority groups 61, 117
Morgan LCJ 133
motor neurone disease 128, 130, 131
Mullen, Tom 29
Murray, Daragh 206

N

National Energy Action 83
National Food Strategy (DEFRA) 55
national housing strategies 58

Nationality and Borders Act 2022 191
natural resources 76
'negative move-ons' 194
Nencheva and Others v Bulgaria 71–72
neoliberalism
  automation and digitization 205
  entitlements 208
  governmentality 202, 218
  logics and practices 24–25
  rationalities 25–26
Netherlands 58–59n72, 72
Ng, Vivian 206
'no DSS' approaches 139, 199
'no-fault evictions' 198–199
  see also evictions
noncompliance 182
nondiscrimination 47–48, 96, 187
nonregression 50–51
nonrepetition of rights violation 51
no recourse to public funds (NRPF) 117–118, 193
Northern Ireland Assembly 132
Northern Ireland Human Rights Commission 192
Northern Ireland (NI) 128–139
  case studies 86
  case study participants **129**
  Department for Communities 130–131, 132, 202
  fuel poverty 78, 83–84
  House Condition Survey 83
  implementation of change 114n46
  landlord licensing scheme 199
  legal advice and representation 148
  legal aid 145
  post-Brexit devolved framework 191–192
  poverty 10
  privatized housing 198–201
  right to adequate housing 61, 136–139
Northern Ireland (NI), legislation
  Northern Ireland Troubles (Legacy and Reconciliation) Act 2023 191
  Northern Ireland (Welfare Reform) Act 2015 131
  Social Security (Terminal Illness) Act (Northern Ireland) 2022 133, 135
  Universal Credit Regulations (Northern Ireland) 2016 128
  Welfare Reform (Northern Ireland) Order 2015 128
Northern Ireland Public Services Ombudsman (NIPSO) 202
North Gauteng High Court, Pretoria 183
Nuffield Foundation 43
Nussberger, Angelika 185

O

O'Brien, Nick 7–8
OHCHR 53, 54–55

INDEX

Oliver (solicitor, NI) **129**, 131, 132, 201–202
online application processes 205
online information 226
'othering' 222
outsourcing public services 94–95, 195–198, 203, 219–220, 225
  see also privatization
Own Initiative Follow up (NIPSO) 202

P

Pantellerisco judgments
  algorithmic capping of benefits 86, 206–208
  calculations of hours and wages 105–106
  challenges for irrationality 154
  Court of Appeal 106, 109–110, 207
  effective collective remedies 167
  initial decision 140–141
  judicial review 100–103, 104
Pantellerisco, Sharon 100–111
Paraguay 178
parliamentary scrutiny 108–109, 141, 206
participation
  principles of adjudication **18**
  thematic analysis **37**
participatory parity 19
pay cycles 107
Pennycook, Alistair 22
people as problems to society 212
People's Union for Civil Liberties v Union of India and Others Writ Petition 180
Permanent Court of International Justice (PCIJ) 160n25
Personal Independence Payment (PIP) 134
  appeals 24, 169, 171–172, **171**, **172**, *172*, *173*
  medical assessments 201
  terminal illness 86, 128–132
Poland 58–59n72, 178
policy mechanisms 188
'the politics of framing' (Fraser) 20
poor decision making 169–172
Portugal 58–59n72
'positive move-ons' 194
'(potential) refugees' 189–190
poverty 10–11, 26, 112, 117–118, 216
power relations 39, 221–222
principles of adjudication 17–18, **18**
private companies 88–89, 96, 201–202
private health insurance 181
private rental sector 60, 137–139, 198–201
  see also housing
privatization 94, 195, 203, 225
  see also outsourcing public services
progressive realization 43–52, 64, 75, 76
pro-hegemonic critiques 15, 17, 184
psychiatric disorders 204
  see also mental health
public and administrative law 8–9

public authorities 93–95
public interest litigation 175, 228
public sector equality duty 98–99

Q

qualitative data 4, 29, 35
Quebec, Canada 181

R

Race Disparity Audit 61
racialization 33–34
Rashford, Marcus 127
R (DA and Others) v SSWP 104
'RealTime Information' employers 105
reasonableness test 154
recognition 19–20, 119–120
redistributing power 224
Reed, Lord 16
reflexivity 35, 40
refugees 115, 117–118, 190
  see also asylum seekers
regressive rights discourse 9
remaining silent 221
remedial **18**
reparations 160n25, 161
representation 19–20
resilience 135, 159
resource distribution 208–211
resources 46–47, 219
restitution 51
rights-based conversations 213
rights claiming 20, 221–222
rights holders and practitioners 222–223
Rights of Children and Young Persons (Wales) Measure 2011 113
The Right to Adequate Food (OHCHR) 53, 54–55
right to adequate housing 57–62, 73, 135–139
right to an adequate standard of living 67, 72–73
right to an effective remedy 27–32, 160–161
right to electricity 68n105, 69, 71
right to energy 68–69
right to food 52–57, 126–128
right to free school meals 126–128
right to fuel 67–84
  affordability 73
  heating 73–74
  identifying 70–72
  meaning and content 72–74
  natural resources 76
  and progressive realization 75–76
  and the UK 77–84
right to social security 62–67
Roach, Kent 31, 32
Rodriguez v San Antonio School Board 181–182
Roland (King's Counsel, England) **101**, 103–104, 146, 153, 155

Rolnik, Raquel 59
R (on the Application of AAA and Others) v Secretary of State for the Home Department 191
R (on the Application of Cornerstone (North East) Adoption and Fostering Service Ltd) v Office for Standards in Education, Children's Services and Skills 90, 91
Rose, Nikolas 186, 188, 202
Rose (welfare rights advisor, Wales) **112**, 124–125, 164, 167–168, 203–204, 212–213
routes to justice 227
Rowan (welfare rights advisor, NI) **129**, 130–131, 134–135, 167
R (Pantellerisco and Others) v SSWP see Pantellerisco judgments
R (SC) v SSWP 16, 109
Rwanda 191
R (Williams) v Caerphilly County Borough Council 115

S

Saeedi 88, 91–92, 98
Safety of Rwanda (Asylum and Immigration) Act 2024 191
Sam (policy developer, Wales) 112–113, **112**, 114–115, 117, 118–119, 120–122, 125, 151
schools 116
Scotland 87–100
  case study 86, 208
  case study participants **87**
  First Minister's Advisory Group on Human Rights Leadership 99
  food banks/food charity 56
  fuel poverty 78, 80–82
  Fuel Poverty (Targets, Definition and Strategy) (Scotland) Act 81
  hostile immigration environment 62
  housing and immigration 189–195
  legal advice and representation 148
  legal aid 145–146
  minimum core obligation (MCO) 50
  National Human Rights Institution (NHRI) 66
  poverty 10
  social housing 60
  see also Ali v Serco Ltd
Scottish House Condition Survey 81–82
Scottish Parliament Equalities Committee 61
Secretary of State for Work and Pensions (SSWP) 101, 106, 108
security of tenure 58
the 'self' and 'worthiness' of individuals 26
self-reflexive stances 35
Serco Ltd 87, 90, 93–95, 99, 196
Seth (researcher, Wales) **112**, 113–114, 116, 117, 118, 119
Shelter (charity) 126

Shelton, Dinah 29, 31, 32, 159
Shohamy, Elana 186, 188
'significant decisions' 206
'significant influence' 206
silencing of voices 40, 220
siloed approaches 119–120
siloed issues 139, 149
social actors 21
social and political ideologies 197–198
Social Care Act 2008, s145 89
social control 210
social determinants of health 10–11
social differentiation 21
social housing 12, 59–60, 136–137
social inequalities 21, 33
social justice 3, 7, 27–28
social rights (SR) 1–2
  and access to social justice 29
  accountability gap 5–13
  adjudication 14–17, 184
  discrimination claims 222
  enforcement 10, 22–23
  international human rights framework 219
  intersectionality 24
  legal frameworks in UK 218–219
  as legal rights 14, 222, 224
  legal vacuum 105
  as nonjusticiable 8, 223
  reclaiming the narrative 220–221
  reshaping the narrative 223
  scrutiny 227
social rights violations (SR violations) 4
  aggregate of appropriate remedies 15, 31
  domestic remedies 51
  hybrid remedies 51–52
  impact on human wellbeing 219
  lack of enforcement 10, 13
  remedies 30–32, 176
  stigmatizing and marginalizing people 144
  systemic 149, 174–175
  see also access to justice; effective remedies
social security
  and child support cases **170**
  and the costs of living 56–57
  incentivizing work 223
  Wales 118
social security tribunal data 169, **170**, *170*
social welfare 145, 216
sociolinguistic research 33–35
South Africa 50–51, 177
  Blue Moonlight 184–185
  National School Nutrition Programme (NSNP) 183
  right to energy/electricity 69–70
Spain 58–59n72
special educational needs 123
specialist legal advice 147
stance taking 211
starvation deaths 180

INDEX

'street level bureaucracy' (Lipsky) 24–25, 28
structural approaches to economic, social and cultural rights 185
structural inequalities 7, 192, 221–222
structural justice 28
structural orders 177, 178, 180, 184–185
structural remedies 177–184
  declarations and retention of jurisdiction 182–183
  domestic adjudication 180
  state of unconstitutionality 183–184
  supranational level 178–180
  suspended declarations 181–182
subjective decision making 200, 205
Submission to UN CESCR (Just Fair) 60
substantive standards 166
suspended declarations 181–182
sustainability 54, 56, 74, 76
Sustainable Development Goals
  Goal 2 54
  Goal 7 74
Sweden 58–59n72
Switzerland 58–59n72
'symbolic violence' (Bourdieu) 215
systematic categorization of people 220
systemic injustices 23, 174–176
systemic issues 177, 180
systemic remedies 179

T

tax credits 65, 103, 217
technological tools 219–220
temporary accommodation 60
terminal illness 167
  12-month rule 133–134, 135
  access to benefits 128–129
  defining 130–134
test-and-learn approaches 109, 110–111, 207–208
test-and-sist approaches 99
Texas 181–182
text and context 38
thematic analysis 36, **37**
theory of structural injustice (Young) 19
third sector 187–188
Thompson, Brian 6
three-dimensional theory of justice (Fraser) 19–20
TH v Chapter of Worcester Cathedral 90, 91
timeliness 163–164
Tobias (barrister, England) **101**, 105–108, 141, 154–155, 206
Toussaint v Canada 179
training programmes 33
transformative movements 223
tribunal data 169–174
trust and distrusting people 117, 204, 210
Tushnet, Mark 16
twin-track supranational remedies 179

U

ubi ius ibi remedium principle 159–160
Ukraine 58–59n72
Underhill LJ 109, 207
Unger, Johann 36–37
United Kingdom (UK)
  ESC rights 42, 84
  fuel poverty 73, 77–78, 81
  Gypsy, Roma and Traveller communities 61
  minimum core obligation (MCO) 50
  ratifying ICESCR 42
  right to adequate housing 58–62, 73
  right to food 55–57
  right to food strategy 55
  right to fuel 75, 77–84
  right to social security 64–67
  SR enforcement 9
  SR justice gap 5
  SR not recognized in law 12, 155–158, 224–225
United Nations (UN)
  General Comments 48
  Guiding Principles 161
  human rights monitoring bodies 156
  minimum core obligation (MCO) 48–50
United Nations Committee on Economic, Social and Cultural Rights (CESCR) 60
  adequate housing 59
  fuel poverty 68
  General Comment No. 3 44
  General Comment No. 4 54, 57, 58, 73
  General Comment No. 7 57, 73
  General Comment No. 12 52–53
  General Comment No. 15 70
  General Comment No. 19 62–63
  and ICESCR 30
  IDG v Spain 179–180
  observations on Belgium 75, 76
  regressive measures 50
  reports on the UK 56, 64–66, 77
  right to food 52–53
  right to fuel 68
  right to social security 64
  SR violations 157
United Nations Committee on the Rights of the Child (UNCRC) 56, 61, 68, 75, 113, 156–157
United Nations Special Rapporteur for Extreme Poverty 56–57, 61, 68
United Nations Special Rapporteur on contemporary forms of racism, racial discrimination, xenophobia and related intolerance 61
United Nations Special Rapporteur on the Right to Food 53, 57, 68
United Nations Special Rapporteur on the Right to Housing 58, 59
United States (US) 177

Universal Credit 66, 101, 118, 128–129, 216–217
Universal Credit Regulations (Northern Ireland) 2016 128
Universal Declaration of Human Rights (UDHR) 22
  Article 8 161

V

valuation discourses 195, 209–210, 211–215
voice 40–41

W

Wales 111–128
  case study participants **112**
  children's rights 126–128
  complexity of justice system 151
  devolution 112–115, 122–123
  engaging with government 120–121
  food banks and food security 56
  food poverty 120, 126–128
  fragmentation of services 118–120
  free school meals 126–128
  fuel poverty 78, 82–83
  Gypsy and Traveller people 61
  housing rights 124
  human rights-based approaches 122
  knowledge of rights and remedies 123–124
  legal funding 124–126
  legal routes to remedies 122
  local authorities 118, 120
  marginalization 116–117
  right to food 126–128, 208
  social security 118
  special educational needs 123
  tensions with England 115–116

United Nations Human Rights Council (UNHRC) 56–57, 77
Wales, legislation
  Children (Abolition of Defence of Reasonable Punishment) (Wales) Act 2020 114
  Renting Homes (Wales) Act 2016 113–114
  Rights of Children and Young Persons (Wales) Measure 2011 113
  Well-being of Future Generations Act 2015 115–116
Walter Rader report 130, 133
Wednesbury reasonableness test 154
welfare-related legislation 141
welfare rights advisors 202
welfare 'safety net' 26
Welsh Refugee Council 122
Western Isles 82
Windsor Framework 191
  Article 2 191, 192
Winter Fuel Payments 78
Woolard, Kathryn 40
'worthiness' and the 'self' 26

X

Xákmok Kásek Indigenous Community (Paraguay) 178

Y

YL v Birmingham City Council 88–90, 91
Yordanova and Others v Bulgaria 180
Young, Iris Marion 19
Young, Kathrine 16

Z

Zivi, Karen 20–21, 92, 220–221

www.ingramcontent.com/pod-product-compliance
Lightning Source LLC
Chambersburg PA
CBHW051536020426
42333CB00016B/1958